PERFORMING

Some modern performances of Shakespeare are faithful reproductions of the past, and others are determined to counter or rewrite it. *Performing Nostalgia* is an account of contemporary productions of Shakespeare in the context of an almost obsessive interest in the past, whether that fascination leads to a recreation or destruction of it. In this trenchant work Susan Bennett examines the authority of the past in modern cultural experience and the parameters for the reproduction of the plays.

Bennett, who is both academic and theatre practitioner, addresses these issues from the viewpoints of both literary theory and theatre studies. She shifts Shakespeare out of straightforward performance studies in order to address new questions about his plays and to consider them in the context of current theoretical debates on historiography, post-colonialism and canonicity. *Performing Nostalgia* is an invigorating study which crosses the divide between performance and theory, and is enlightening, challenging and eye-opening reading for students and scholars alike.

Susan Bennett is Associate Professor of English at the University of Calgary. She is the author of *Theatre Audiences: A Theory of Production and Reception* (Routledge, 1990).

PERFORMING NOSTALGIA

Shifting Shakespeare and the contemporary past

Susan Bennett

London and New York

First published 1996
by Routledge
11 New Fetter Lane, London EC4P 4EE

Simultaneously published in the USA and Canada
by Routledge
29 West 35th Street, New York, NY 10001

© 1996 Susan Bennett
Typeset in Bembo by Florencetype Ltd, Stoodleigh, Devon

Printed and bound in Great Britain by
Biddles Ltd, Guildford and King's Lynn

British Library Cataloguing in Publication Data
A catalogue record for this book is available from the British Library

Library of Congress Cataloguing in Publication Data
Bennett, Susan
Performing Nostalgia: Shifting Shakespeare and the Contemporary
Past / Susan Bennett.
p. cm.
Includes bibliographical references and index.
1. Shakespeare, William, 1564–1616 – Stage history – 1950–
2. Shakespeare, William, 1564–1616. King Lear. 3. Shakespeare,
William, 1564–1616. Tempest. 4. Theater – History – 20th century.
5. Historicism. 6. Nostalgia. I. Title.
PR3100.B38 1996
792.9'5 – dc20 95–8574

ISBN 0–415–07325–1 (hbk)
ISBN 0–415–07326–X (pbk)

CONTENTS

For Sophie Catherine Stella

ACKNOWLEDGEMENTS

Many people have done much for me in the course of my writing this book. They've asked the questions that really matter; provided both formal and informal support at crucial stages; uncovered wonderful examples of renovated texts and shared their own research willingly; and, above all, offered the kinds of friendship and fun without which I would have been lost. Sincere thanks to Alexandria Patience, Tracy Davis, Kathleen Foreman, Eric Savoy, Linda Hutcheon, Reid Gilbert, Ellen Donkin, Eleanor Ty, Barbara Drennan, Catherine Graham, Heather Jones, Ric Knowles, Susan Stone-Blackburn, Tony Brennan, Denis Salter, Kelly Pitman, Mary Klaver, Yaw Asante, Dorothy Chansky, and my '680' graduate class on 'writing the Renaissance.' And I would like to thank those at Routledge, and especially Talia Rodgers and Tricia Dever, who have supported this project and who have indulged me with some elasticity of deadline. Sarah-Jane Woolley and Lisa Williams offered much assistance at the editing stage. I am grateful, too, to Routledge's readers for their incisive and helpful assessments of my work. Thanks also go to Robin Zlatin at New Line Cinema for her help in obtaining permission to reproduce the wonderfully queer nostalgia of Jarman's film as a cover to this book. And especial thanks go to the practitioners and administrators who told me about their companies' productions of the past and who packed up all kinds of treasures in large brown envelopes so I could keep thinking about how classic texts were (re)produced in/for the present.

Many of the ideas in this book have had the benefit of some sort of previous public performance at conference and campus venues across Canada, and in the USA and Australia. I have much appreciated those audiences and the very many thought-provoking and inspiring questions they asked. I'm particularly grateful to the

ACKNOWLEDGEMENTS

University of Calgary Faculty of Humanities Colloquium (and especially Pam McCallum) for an early opportunity to rehearse. I would also like to thank the Social Sciences and Humanities Research Council of Canada for a grant in support of the latter stages of my research and writing, and the Calgary Institute for the Humanities for the award of a Fellowship during which final revisions were made to this text.

Some other people deserve special mention and extra-special thanks for their roles. Cindy Murrell never failed to answer my e-mail and made finding obscure reviews a breeze. With what seemed like the wave of a magic wand, Adrienne Kertzer found me more time to work on a first draft of this book. She met my last-minute request for a new teaching schedule with an efficiency and willingness I hardly deserved. Time and time again Susan Rudy Dorscht knew when I needed to go to the Famous Restaurant and be cheered up. Our conversations both there and elsewhere sustained and nourished me. Peggy Phelan's conviction that I could finish this book gave me the confidence and energy to do just that. I am grateful always for all she has done. In all available media (and with some outrageous long-distance phone bills we used to try and pretend we didn't have) Maria DiCenzo has always been my most willing and astute listener/reader. I have relied upon that and upon her many many times. I am also more than indebted to Jeanne Perreault for great walks and greater questions; I have learned much from trying to answer at least some of them. More than this, she deserves huge thanks for braving a response to the opening pages of this book late on a windswept Friday afternoon and for everything else before and since. And in this study of the past in the present, it is apt that long-overdue thanks go to Andy Lloyd Jones who once bought me the birthday present I asked for, even though she could not imagine why I wanted it, and to Janet Pollon who, more than twenty years ago, put Shakespeare and transgression in the same classroom and whose teaching remains an inspiration.

Finally, and once again, I write my thanks and love to those remarkable people who have put up with this for far too long. Sophie has been cheerfully content to bond with my laptop as well as with me. She has also provided the happiest evidence that disobedience is, indeed, more interesting to study. Barnaby and Toby pretend they remember times before the laptop moved in with us. Thankfully their nostalgia is consistently dissident; amazingly, their support is unconditional.

1

NEW WAYS TO PLAY
OLD TEXTS

Discourses of the Past

The past is only a figure of the desire of the present.

(Lucia Folena 1989: 221)

This is the true Shakespearian wood – but it is not the wood of
Shakespeare's time, which did not know itself to be Shakespearian,
and therefore felt no need to keep up appearances. No. The wood
we have just described is that of nineteenth-century nostalgia,
which disinfected the wood, cleansing it of the grave, hideous and
elemental beings with which the superstition of an earlier age had
filled it. . . . However, as it turns out, the Victorians did not leave
the woods in quite the state they might have wished to find them.

(Angela Carter 1986: 69)

If the past is a foreign country, nostalgia has made it 'the foreign
country with the healthiest tourist trade of all.'

(David Lowenthal 1985: 4)

INTRODUCTION

That global industry of remarkable energy and profit – Shakespeare
– provides perhaps the very best symptom of a present-day
epidemic, the past. This book takes up the (dis)articulation of
the past through the cultural apparati that produce Shakespeare
(the man, his plays, his times) in order to locate some of the issues
involved in and explored by contemporary performance. Many of
the performances constituting this discussion fall explicitly under
the categorization usefully invoked by Jonathan Dollimore, 'creative
vandalism.'[1] They take up a deliberately antagonistic relationship
to their source text(s) as well as to the operations under which

1

that source is generally produced and/or received. What happens, then, is that both the gaps and the excesses of the Shakespeare corpus become the foundation for a performance of the present. While those gaps and excesses are always inherent, even in a 'straight' production/reading of a Shakespeare play, it is when they become the text that their inclination to disrupt the notion of the linearity of progress is made manifest. And this is a trajectory which Michel de Certeau, more broadly, locates for the writing of history:

> [W]hatever this new understanding of the past holds to be irrelevant – shards created by the selection of materials, remainders left aside by an explication – comes back, despite everything, on the edges of discourse or in its rifts and crannies: 'resistances,' 'survivals,' or delays discreetly perturb the pretty order of a line of 'progress' or a system of interpretation. These are the lapses in the syntax constructed by the law of a place. Therein they symbolize a return of the repressed, that is, a return of what, at a given moment, has *become* unthinkable in order for a new identity to *become* thinkable
>
> (de Certeau 1988: 4)

It is the inevitable and symbiotic relationship between the writing of the past and the performance of the present that (in)forms the subject of this book.

The chapters that follow involve a negotiation between the unthinkable and the thinkable through the mechanism of the apparently very well known. They concern themselves with the effects of proliferation on performances of textual truth and history; with active representations of transgression, dissidence and desire which enact a longing for at least micropolitical change; and with surveillance of the errant and disobedient bodies which persist in their urge to be seen. I do not mean the readings, the questions raised here, to be specific only to the dissemination of Shakespeare, merely to suggest that it is in 'Shakespeare' that they are most acutely and vividly posed.

But, as a preliminary manoeuvre, it is useful to log and account for the obsessiveness with which the past has its selves performed in the contemporary moment. Don Wayne has argued that '[t]here has been a noticeable lag between our ability to recognize the role of power in the plays and poems of Shakespeare and his contemporaries, and our ability to articulate the forms that power takes in our own historical moment' (1987: 58). And, viewed from the perspective of literary and/or theatre studies, this is arguably so. With another lens, however, the role of power in contemporary cultures is frankly less obscure. If academic criticism has been slow to examine contemporary (play)texts which read the operations of power in their own historical moments, the texts themselves display an obsessive interest in the past as a figure for the desires of the present. In other (non-literary) disciplines, both the apparent stability *and* the very real anxieties of the dominant Western cultural body are revealed by the insulation of that same body through the dissemination of 'protective and narcissistic illusions' of a common past (Robins 1991: 44). Often what is perceived as 'lost' is reasserted by its cultural representation. The strategy of this particular text is to examine the performance of the past in different agencies of public meaning and to question how particular vested interests project their desires for the present (and, indeed, the future) through a multiplicity of representations of past texts as well as through the attempt to trespass into already-(over)coded traditions.

Yet why is it, to recycle David Lowenthal's words which appear at the opening of this chapter, that there is, engaged with and in the past, such a healthy – or even potent – tourist trade? How has it happened that these global consumers have been persuaded to travel to and through the past? Is this epidemic production/consumption of historical texts necessarily only 'evidence of a process of economic and cultural decline: a systematic substitution of replica for reality, simulation for experience, enactment for lived history' (Holderness 1992a: 248)?

The once monolithic History of great men and major events has, as we know, in recent years been dispersed into a multiplicity of histories which compete with greater and lesser success in representing the past and which do so in the awareness of what Louis Montrose calls 'the textuality of history':

> we can have no access to a full and authentic past, a lived material existence, unmediated by the surviving textual traces of the society in question – traces whose survival we cannot assume to be merely contingent but must rather presume to be at least partially consequent upon complex and subtle social processes of preservation and effacement; and ... those textual traces are themselves subject to subsequent textual mediations when they are construed as the

3

'documents' upon which historians ground their own texts, called 'histories'.

(1989: 20)

If such a self-consciousness about historiographic writing has reshaped not only the methods but the kinds of histories that are written (and I share Montrose's caution that 'History,' like the 'Power' Don Wayne invokes, is 'in constant danger of hypostatization' [Montrose 1989:20]), this has not, however, prevented a determined attempt to preserve a single vision of History, of a past which forms a continuous trajectory into the present and through into the future. The representation of a seamless past has, not surprisingly, been an important strategy in the politically regressive governments of the New Right (most obviously in the United Kingdom and America). From Margaret Thatcher, Britons heard:

> First, we are more than a one-generation society. As Edmund Burke put it, people who never look backward to their ancestors will not look forward to posterity. We are interested in keeping the best of the past, because we believe in *continuity*. . . . Second, we are *conserving* the best of the past.
>
> (cited in Kaye 1991: 95)

Ronald Reagan made much the same point in his 1981 commencement address:

> My hope today is that in the years to come and come it [sic] shall – when it's your turn to explain to another generation the meaning of the past and thereby hold out to them the promise of their future, that you'll recall the truths and traditions that define our civilization and make up our national heritage. And now, they're yours to protect and pass on.
>
> (cited in Kaye 1991: 97)

While the well-documented rhetoric of these two national leaders provides an undisguised affirmation of the power of a traditional history, what is more interesting is translation of that rhetoric into a popular demand for the past. Almost incognizant of the crisis of 'History' being played out in the academy, the Western world has, in the last decade or so, disseminated a powerful notion of duty to the past, the possession of which through cultural property in the form of commodity fetishism is used to shore up and maintain the status quo. And this duty to the past is, necessarily, not

4

to any authentic representation of earlier events or values, but is instead situated through a nostalgia for that authenticity which is not retrievable. As Lowenthal describes, '[a] perpetual staple of nostalgic yearning is the search for a simple and stable past as a refuge from the turbulent and chaotic present' (1989: 21).

The age of so-called postmodernity in which we live has been described as 'a kind of macro-nostalgia' (Chase and Shaw 1989a: 15) where consumers vie for a diverse but eclectic range of commodities with which to anchor their experience and desires. In its most restricted forms, nostalgia performs as the representation of the past's 'imagined and mythical qualities' so as to effect some corrective to the present (Walvin 1987: 162). The taste or appetite for nostalgia, in such readings, gets used as the requisite evidence that 'we find ourselves living to a great extent in a cultural and emotional vacuum' (Rubens 1981: 150). This simplified notion of the effect/effectiveness of nostalgia relies on its function as a marker of both what we lack and what we desire; expressed another way, nostalgia is constituted as a longing for certain qualities and attributes in lived experience that we have apparently lost, at the same time as it indicates our inability to produce parallel qualities and attributes which would satisfy the particularities of lived experience in the present. In fact, in all of its manifestations, nostalgia is, in its praxis, conservative (in at least two senses – its political alignment and its motive to keep things intact and unchanged): it leans on an imagined and imaginary past which is more and better than the present and for which the carrier of the nostalgia, in a defective and diminished present, in some way or other longs. This dynamic of the good past/bad present is, as Fred Davis points out, nostalgia's 'distinctive rhetorical signature' (1979: 16). Moreover, collective nostalgia can promote a feeling of community which works to downplay or (even if only temporarily) disregard divisive positionalities (class, race, gender and so on); when nostalgia is produced and experienced collectively, then, it can promote a false and likely dangerous sense of 'we' (Davis 1979: 112). Yet the attractions of such a performance cannot be easily ignored in the contemporary moment. The attractions reside especially in the rigor of displacing individual pasts (realized in part through a more private nostalgia) into a collective nostalgia which is often highly and powerfully regulatory. The optic of nostalgia insists, with all inherent dangers, upon a stable referent (Doane and Hodges 1987: 8).

In such a context, it is useful to recall that nostalgia comes with a particular history as diagnostic category. The term was first designated at the end of the seventeenth century to account for physical symptoms registered as a result of the psychic experience of homesickness.[2] Davis suggests that nostalgia has, in this century, been demedicalized (1979: 4), but it is perhaps yet necessary to retain something of the sense of its root in a physical condition. The invention of a Swiss doctor, nostalgia came into being first through its anchoring in language (by naming as a disease something that is more than mere homesickness) and subsequently through the description of a cure for the bodies so afflicted. For, after all, nostalgia retains its currency as an affliction – it is what apparently occupies an empty space that a more productive cultural and emotional life is supposed to satisfy. As Susan Stewart has named it, 'nostalgia is the desire for desire' (1984: 23). Stewart's argument is an important one in staging the ideological foundations of nostalgia; she asserts:

> the past it [nostalgia] seeks has never existed except as narrative, and hence, always absent, that past continually threatens to reproduce itself as a felt lack. Hostile to history and its invisible origins, and yet longing for an impossibly pure content of lived experience at a place of origin, nostalgia wears a distinctly utopian face.
>
> (1984: 23)

Lowenthal makes a related point in his corrective to British and American theorists who imagine nostalgia to be rampant only in their own cultures and times. Noting that '[y]earning for a lost stage of being is part of the fabric of modern life the world over,'[3] he insists that '[t]he view of nostalgia as a self-serving, chauvinist, right-wing version of the past foisted by the privileged and propertied likewise neglects half the facts. The left no less than the right espouses nostalgia' (1989: 27).[4] This almost universal utopianism would indeed seem to be characteristic, and the pervasiveness of nostalgia across time, gender, class, race (among others) gestures at its own inherent resistance to the dominant paradigms of History that Stewart has referred to. Where it might be that '[n]ostalgia for a lost authenticity is a paralyzing structure of historical reflection,' its function as a conduit for the 'authentic and inauthentic experience' of any particular social group or individual means that its symptoms, its practice and, indeed, any attempts to effect a cure remain close to a writing of H/history that assumes the possibility of retrieval of an authentic past (Frow 1991: 135, 136). Thus, when Janice Doane and Devon Hodges set up their important and timely investigation of nostalgia and sexual difference, as a means of accounting for a backlash economy that would curtail the practices of contemporary feminism, they unfortunately retain a rather monolithic use of nostalgia which ignores the subtleties of its different, but no less prevalent, uses across gender as well as (other) forms of discourse.[5]

Nonetheless, nostalgia at its most virulent has been the property of the Right in the Western world and, in a British context at least, it is conspicuous how often Shakespeare performs the role which links the psychic experience of nostalgia to the possibility of reviving an authentic, naturally better, and material past. And this nostalgic production is not limited to the recent past; after the First World War, Stephen Graham suggested:

> In England and Scotland also, it is noticeable that the war has given us a truer perspective and cleared away the Lilliputian obstructions of modern life. We see Shakespeare great and wonderful again, and our mockers of Shakespeare shrink to figures like those men made of matches that used to appear on Bryant & May's match-boxes.
>
> (cited in Wright 1985: 24)

Cautionary words indeed – but which, despite Graham's intentions, evidence that there is no greater 'truth' in the postwar perspective, only a particular battle for a so-called authentic representation of the past as the present. While it is 'true that we "make up" history, we do not have full and arbitrary latitude to make it up as we please' (Abu-Lughod 1989: 126).

Nostalgia might best be considered as the inflicted territory where claims for authenticity (and this a displacement of the articulation of power) are staged. The shifted Shakespearean texts of this book, then, are all profoundly and essentially nostalgic. They situate a desire for desire and it is the very terms under which and for whom such desire is spoken, embodied and subsequently read that I would insist obliges our more careful attention. If there can be fostered a much more elastic and pervasive comprehension of nostalgia, it is perhaps also possible to liberate that felt lack. This might enable re-memberings which don't, by virtue of the categorization, conjure up a regressively conservative and singular History.

So how do 'we,' both collectively and individually, remember the past? What is the connection between those brute events that once did take place at some or other present moment, the making-up of narratives designated as their history, and a desire for desire that is nostalgia? In an essay seeking to charge public historians with the more responsible exercise of memory, Michael H. Frisch concludes that we must take on 'the sources and consequences of our active ignore-ance' (1986: 17). He continues: 'We need projects that involve people in exploring what it means to remember, and what to do with memories to make them active and alive, as opposed to mere objects of collection' (1986: 17). This is a task with which this book has obvious connection and considerable sympathy. But it is also important to recognize the mechanics of memory, to account for why '[s]ome versions of the past persist more successfully than do others and [why] different agencies of memory operate to different effect' (Schudson 1992: 65). The answer lies in the social fabric of remembering.

Michael Schudson's fascinating account of how Americans have remembered Watergate describes an architectonics of memory primarily engaged as social practice. In its most systematized form, memory is conveyed through institutions such as the law and public offices of record or in 'collectively created monuments and markers: books, holidays, statues, souvenirs' (Schudson 1992: 51). But the archive on which memory draws is always more than the sum of its texts: 'between tradition and oblivion, it reveals the rules of a practice that enables statements both to survive and to undergo regular modification. It is *the general system of the formation and transformation of statements*' (Foucault 1972: 130, emphasis in the original). So even where memory seems to be exercised as individual cognition, it relies, always, on a connectedness to the social: '[T]he act of remembering is . . . occasioned by social situations, prompted by cultural artifacts and social cues that remind, employed for social purposes, even enacted by cooperative activity' (Schudson 1992: 52). One significant effect of the predominance of the social in the construction of memory is that memory, like nostalgia, might resemble only superficially the past which it is said to represent. Memory is the (social) production of images and 'our images of the past commonly serve to legitimate a present social order' (Connerton 1989: 3). In other words, what is available to remember often results from those cues that are disseminated through public agencies: 'images of the past and recollected knowledge of the past are conveyed and sustained by (more or less ritual) performances' (Connerton 1989: 40).

If the social is accountable for the construct of memory, then, according to Paul Connerton, it is commemorative ceremonies which provide its facility. He argues that 'if considerable precautions are to be taken to assure the identity of a culture's symbolic material, it will be advisable to direct those precautions to ensuring the identity of its ritual' (1989: 57). Such an assertion is crucial to this project and its discussion of the verbal and gestural repetitions which activate and enable remembering:

> We preserve versions of the past by representing it to ourselves in words and images. Commemorative ceremonies are pre-eminent instances of this. They keep the past in mind by a depictive representation of past events. They are re-enactments of the past, its return in a representational guise which normally includes a simulacrum of the scene or situation recaptured. . . . In habitual memory the past is, as it were, sedimented in the body.
>
> (Connerton 1989: 72)

Thus how we construct and engage memories cannot be seen as an individualized act but, instead, something prepared by the dissemination of a collective history and lodged in the physical selves of its subjects. This, however, is not a transparent and unimaginative strategy:

> [I]t is not simply a matter of producing and marketing presentations and representations of history which celebrate capitalism and the 'leadership' of the powers that be (though that is definitely very much a part of it), but, beyond that, of articulating and cultivating renditions of the past and its relation to the present *and* the future which are perceived by the subaltern and lower classes as reflecting and expressing not solely the experiences, concerns and aspirations of the dominant class, but those of 'the people,' 'the nation,' as a whole.
>
> (Kaye 1991: 69)

And opportunities to exploit publicly acknowledged and sanctioned (so-called) popular memory have not been squandered. Yet while memory is relentlessly social and prone to the manipulation of a rhetoric conveyed by dominant cultural practice, it is, too, always liable to alteration: 'memory derives its interventionary force from its very capacity to be altered – unmoored, mobile, lacking any fixed position' (de Certeau 1984: 86). As a contested but inevitable relation to the past and its articulated grammars, memory (like nostalgia) must be recognized for its mobility and for the generative potential of re-membering; it is, as de Certeau puts it, 'a sense of the other' (1984: 87). This is the kind of project that Gus Van Sant takes on in his re-membering of Shakespeare's Henry plays as a texture for *My Own Private Idaho* (1991), a film accurately described as 'ransacking references from Western culture's collective memory' (Francke 1992: 55). Van Sant's nostalgia is, of course, profoundly and determinedly queer, a fracturing of History which generates contrary (oppositional and perverse) ways of seeing.

Keeping in mind such possibilities for nostalgia and memory (which this text explores through performances that, like Van Sant's film, stage a trespass into the myth of a single and factitive History), it is the case, however, that memory and nostalgia can couple to enforce a particularly potent regulatory practice, that of tradition. It is not only that there has been an overwhelming drive to preserve and conserve the various (sometimes, seemingly, any) markers of tradition, but that this process of effecting and ensuring moral continuity has been effectively managed as consumer product. This, as Lowenthal notes, is far from a simple process: 'Viewing the past as wholly ideal, the traditionalist seeks refuge in mystical connection with his [sic] great and ennobling heritage, but is partially absorbed in and subconsciously attracted to the new influences he affects to despise' (1985: 71).[6] The complexity of this process, not always limited to or by the 'traditionalist,' is evident in this book's next chapter, an account of the refuge presumed in a myriad of connections to Shakespeare's *King Lear*. Its nostalgia, proliferated excessively as it has been in the (over)production of *King Lear*, suggests the instability of both past and present, the tendency toward and the potential in (as de Certeau would have it) history's capacity to be unmoored.

In a fascinating account of the French Government's inauguration of Heritage Year (1979–1980), Philippe Hoyau accounts for the inflection of government policies towards a plurality of representation anchoring 'an imaginary object, the Past' (1988: 30). He points to the potential in 'adjusting ethnological and historical research to the "ideological" imperatives of the day, and particularly of *rationalizing nostalgia by providing it with "real" content*' (1988: 31; my emphasis). By bringing into focus more local ethnohistories and giving value to previously neglected 'minor' objects, the French Government policy sought a more popular experience of tradition, all the time that it ensured the trajectory of tradition in what has to be termed its most 'traditional' sense. Such strategies are not uncommon.

In a British (or, more accurately, English) context, Simon Barker has outlined the pervasive representation of the sixteenth and seventeenth centuries as a history of the present. He draws attention to the neutralizing effects of a revived history in which there is some particular appeal to popular participation (1984: 15–16). One of his subject examples, the recovery and rehabilitation of the *Mary Rose* (the flagship of Henry VIII's fleet, which unfortunately sank in Portsmouth Harbour before any participation in the 1543–1551 Anglo-French war), provides an explicit performance of investing nostalgia with 'the real.' Despite the historical fact that the *Mary Rose* did not participate in any war, its raising took place immediately after the Falklands Victory Parade, and was watched in Britain by a television audience of millions. Barker reads not only the television commentary surrounding the event but also the numerous texts that were produced to record and celebrate the recovery: 'most of the texts which narrate the raising (or rescue?) of the ship, which might colloquially be described as "coffee table" volumes, invite a sense of historical continuum which, in ideological purpose, is quite as powerful as the Falklands Parade itself' (1984: 17).[7] Patrick Wright's reading of the *Mary Rose* rehabilitation involves a particularly theatrical metaphor, calling the ship the 'background scenery for late melodramas in the continuing repertoire of Imperialism' (1985: 191). My own attention to a more literal performance of nostalgia takes as its focal point this background scenery and, in particular, those moments where the tenets of an ongoing imperialist project come under scrutiny and/or dissent.

While Barker sees performances such as raising the *Mary Rose* (re)constructing History as palliative (1984: 21), Wright takes the critique even further:

> There need accordingly be no essential discontinuity between past and present as long as the ceremonies of re-enactment are carried out and respected. As an essence that is embodied in such ceremonies the nation is immutable – either it finds its witness in the present or it is lost and betrayed.
>
> (1985: 178)

What is so effective in the paradigm of the *Mary Rose* is the thoroughness of its insistence on inclusivity (in support of a very exclusive cause): '[w]ith the "minor heritage" rescued from oblivion, and with popular tradition now released from its subservience to "Tradition" and recognized as being positively in the public interest, everybody can be enlisted in the cause' (Hoyau 1988: 33). Moreover, Barker's argument offers careful connection between the dramatic staging of history (as in the case of the *Mary Rose*) and the dissemination of the same seamless narrative by way of the study of literature. And, of course, tradition embraces the canon. And at the heart of the literary canon is always Shakespeare.

There is at this conjuncture the dilemma around whether there are, in fact, new ways to play old texts. Theatre is, anyway, generally and rightly regarded as a conservative art form, and the devotion to Shakespeare a manifestation of that inherent conservatism. Yet the plethora of 'vandalized' Shakespeares suggest that their producers, at least, fantasize the possibility of the new. By performing (including writing) a text which in some or other way makes reference to an already existing (thereby value-laden) text, the production and reception of the 'new' text necessarily become bound to the tradition that encompasses and promotes the old. In short, is containment an inevitable effect of re articulating the past? Or can a new text, by way of dislocating and contradicting the authority of tradition, produce a 'transgressive knowledge'[8] which would disarticulate the terms under which tradition gains its authority? And what bodies have the capacity to re-member that which is already sedimented in them? To attest to the contingent and fractured performance of 'tradition,' there is a need to locate a canon of the 'past' and to position against it those texts apparently claiming for themselves the possibility of the 'new.' Or are we, to cite Holderness's question,

> content to dismiss the millions who patronize "the heritage"
> as helplessly manipulated subjects of the culture industry, one-
> dimensional replicants tastelessly consuming the commodified
> products of a reified society, to be redeemed from cultural
> degeneracy only by the critical potency of high culture?
>
> (1992a: 261).

It seems less than sensible to dismiss the complex interactions between the multiplicity of performances marketed at an equally diverse demography of consumption. And, equally, the nostalgic performance of the past requires much more than a cultural dupe to produce its conservative effects.

Michael Bristol has noted that tradition is generally, and mistakenly, thought of as a process of transmission and that '[t]he idea of a social action . . . seems to be easily confused with the notion of actual cultural goods that have been or ought to be transmitted' (1990: 40). His point helps us to remember that notions of 'tradition,' and especially in their assuming the performance of continuity, are always and necessarily a masking of the potential for tradition's own disarticulation of itself:

> If I hand something over or hand something down to you, there will be a moment at which I must let go of it. It is in this moment that the possibility of a cultural abyss or rupture opens up. Since that possibility is always present within what we call tradition, we can never understand this cultural phenomenon as a process of undisputed succession.
>
> (Bristol 1990: 40)

It is thus necessary, as well, to comprehend in a more complicated and interrogatory way the operations of that canon of the past, that which is sold as the tangible and present object of cultural tradition. How is it that the mask is upheld and the possibilities for abyss or, at the least, rupture remain, for the most part, obscured?

Howard Felperin suggests that the canon (meaning here, quite specifically, the literary canon, but his assertion works just as well with an extended reading of the term) 'is all we finally have to define ourselves' (1990: xiii). While I would claim the need to resist such a notion, his plea for a thorough understanding of the continuing cultural negotiation on which the canon depends is, I believe, an important one. Felperin himself engages with only one area of such negotiation – 'Shakespeare' and contemporary critical theory – but it would undoubtedly be useful to extend the field of cultural negotiation to consider the power of texts 'read' and 'performed' outside specifically academic contexts. In some of these other sites, it might be possible to witness strategies of performing the past which demand of their actors as well as their reading/viewing publics an engagement which denies the inevitability of containment. So when Felperin argues that 'self-consciously political critique of the canon is shown to collaborate unwittingly in its perpetuation and consolidation' (1990: xiii), he may well be right – except that this is not the only point to be made. There are other itineraries for exploring new/old texts embedded in the past. When some of these other perspectives are brought into view, the particular trajectory of institutionally supported critical practice (in which, of course, both his and my own texts participate) can be seen as only one – if a particularly powerful – type of cultural tourism. Certainly, the articulation of 'Shakespeare' functions, as Peter Erickson has suggested, as 'the last line of defense in the protection of a cultural ideal' (1991: 4) and it is thus not at all surprising that this site is an overdetermined and overinvested real estate on which the various obsessions, fetishizations and dislocations of the past can be staged.

But performances of past tradition take many shapes. Perhaps the most literal example comes in the production of historical re-enactments. Some of these are passive re-enactments like Anne Hathaway's cottage and the *Mary Rose* (actively recovered, then rendered a passive marker of the past as present). Their function is, as Holderness indicates, as '[p]ure, unimpeded images of an idealised historical past. . . . An idealised 'English' past, picturesque and untroubled, is thus embodied and incorporated into commodities for sale to national and international markets, the transaction simultaneously satisfying both cultural and commercial demands' (1988a: 6). Many re-enactments are even more dependent on a conviction of authenticity than the restoration of the *Mary Rose* or the romantic claims of Hathaway's cottage, and can be thought of, according to Lowenthal, as 'a *sine qua non* of popular participation in history':

> Some re-enactors simply seek to entertain, some to convince themselves or others of the reality of the past, some to heighten history's revelatory significance, some for a sense of purpose or excitement lacking in the present. Live actors repeat what was supposedly done in the past, and restored or replica houses are staffed with 'replica people' or 'human artifacts.' Like restorers, re-enactors start with known elements and fill in the gaps with the typical, the probable, or the invented.
>
> (Lowenthal 1985: 295)

A striking feature of an industry which makes the past its business, re-enactments occur all over the world to encourage local and visiting populations to participate in that past. While most studies – and this is an area in desperate need of some theorization as well as a much more complicated scholarship[9] – assume some coincidence of locality and audience, the economic and other drives of such productions seem to be far more complicated. One example at least – of the Los Angeles-based Past Times with Good Company who perform lifestyle re-enactments in English country houses[10] – suggests the cross-cultural, if not global, imperatives of such performances. What emerges in the re-enactment is a powerful demonstration of the currency of the past in an embodied form. These, of course, are only explicit versions of those ritual re-enactments which are best recognized as the traditions which underpin the social organization of culture practice and, as Richard Handler and Jocelyn Linnekin suggest, 'tradition is a model of the past and is inseparable from the interpretation of tradition in the present' (1984: 276). Or, in other words, tradition is 'a category of thought, not a residue of the past' (Schudson 1992: 54).

Re-enactments of History are perhaps the most literal, if not always the most spectacular, examples of what Patrick Wright refers to as a trafficking in history.[11] While Foucault has persuasively accounted for history 'as inertia and weight, as a slow accumulation of the past, a silent sedimentation of things said' (1972: 141), it is also true that what has been accumulated has also been appraised for its currency (both cultural and economic) and that the silent sedimentation has been encouraged to (re)discover both voice and body.[12] The past, in the present, has become a powerful trading economy on a global scale. Or, as Hewison puts it in a discussion of the repositioning of the museum in a heritage-saturated society, everything – irrespective of its own history of authority – becomes just another commodity in a 'vast cultural marketplace' (1991: 173).

If trading in the past seems particular, if not peculiar, to the Western world and to various expressions of national identity within the grouping of tradition, it might also be remembered that contemporary marketing strategies reveal that the 'leisure worlds of heritage culture' (Corner and Harvey 1991a: 11) are a global phenomenon. The preceptive illustration is advertising giant Saatchi and Saatchi's assertion that 'there are more social differences between midtown Manhattan and the Bronx than between Manhattan and the 7th Arrondissement of Paris' (cited in Robins 1991: 27). The result of this schematic of market segmentation is 'the increasing importance of targeting consumers on the basis of demography and habits rather than on the basis of geographical proximity; marketing strategies are "consumer-driven" instead of "geography-driven"' (Robins 1991: 27). In this regard, Kevin Robins notes:

> [G]lobal standardization in the cultural industries reflects, of course, the drive to achieve ever greater economies of scale. More precisely, it is about achieving both scale and scope economies by targeting the shared habits and tastes of particular market segments at the global level, rather than by marketing, on the basis of geographical proximity, to different national audiences. The global cultural industries are increasingly driven to recover their escalating costs over the maximum market base, over pan-regional and world markets.
>
> (1991: 29)

It is precisely this marketing logic which makes the performance canon of Shakespeare's plays so contemporary: they are, without doubt, sellable to theatre audiences everywhere. One happy example of this comes in Michael Pennington's story of how 'in this chilly Age of Feasibility, . . . a new Charity, the English Shakespeare Company, came about' (Bogdanov and Pennington 1990: 3). He recounts how he and Michael Bogdanov went to the Arts Council of Great Britain 'with plans to do a production with two actors on a single set with a modest budget, and were immediately sent away with an open brief to think big – £100,000 big – epic, and Shakespearian' (1990: 3).[13] It is a similar economy of scale that fuels Kenneth Branagh's Renaissance Theatre Company world tours of their Shakespeare (re)productions.[14]

None of this has anything to do with the retrieval of an authentic history; it is much more Patrick Wright's evocative description of the 'moonlight impression of pastness' (1985: 69). He asserts that at the moment history is made abstract, the political tensions which must necessarily inform it are purged: the residual product is a 'unifying spectacle, the settling of all disputes' (1985: 69). A manifestation of this 'unifying spectacle' is tradition; the past, like any other text, is overdetermined by the social institutions for whom it has some use and the reader's relationship with that text is necessarily mediated (see de Certeau 1984: 171). Tradition is a repository for memory (Lowenthal 1985: 209) and an *agent provocateur* for nostalgia.

The past, then, operates by way of a shifting vector of nostalgia, memory, and tradition. The cumulative effect of its historical narratives is recognized as cultural heritage. But this still almost underestimates the intensity with which the past continues to speak. In his important study *Culture and Imperialism*, Edward Said reminds us that '[m]ore important than the past itself . . . is its bearing upon cultural attitudes in the present' (1993: 17). The rest of this chapter is concerned with particular manifestations of such a bearing: how in the contemporary moment the past prevails upon both performance and criticism.[15] After all, heritage, even if it materializes in an apparently monolithic form (such as 'Shakespeare'), 'can be inflected in a variety of different political directions' (Corner and Harvey 1991a: 14).

OPENING ON STAGE

It is then, but it is also now.
(Notes on the setting for David Allen's *Cheapside* (1985))

Brecht in *Coriolanus*, Edward Bond in *Lear* (1971), Arnold Wesker in *The Merchant* (1976), Tom Stoppard in *Rosencrantz and Guildenstern Are Dead* (1966) and Charles Marowitz in a series of adaptations have appropriated aspects of the plays for a different politics (not always a progressive politics). Even here, it is possible that the new play will still, by its self-conscious irreverence, point back towards Shakespeare as the profound and inclusive originator in whose margins we can doodle only parasitic follies.
(Alan Sinfield 1985c: 179)

During the summer of 1992 a 'hot' theatre ticket in London was the Royal National Theatre's production of *A Midsummer Night's Dream*. This Shakespeare play was directed for the RNT by Québécois writer/composer/director/designer/actor/collaborator Robert Lepage. The British press, however, were almost uniformly caustic in their responses:

Alas for high hopes! I ended my review of Robert Lepage's *The Dragons' Trilogy* by saying one looked forward to seeing what this French-Canadian illusionist would make of *A Midsummer Night's Dream* at the Olivier. The result turns out to be the most perverse, leaden, humourless and vilely spoken production of this magical play I have ever seen.
(Michael Billington in the *Guardian*)

17

My timing was always a little off.

When the show-off Canadian Robert Lepage was engaged by the National Theatre to direct *A Midsummer Night's Dream*, I thought of fleeing the country. But I got my dates mixed and was back in London for this event.

(Kenneth Hurren in the *Mail on Sunday*).

Robert Lepage's leadenly paced, unfunny *Midsummer Night's Dream* . . . just opened in the Olivier.

It's a show that will appeal principally to mud-wrestling fanatics or to chronic sufferers from *nostalgie de la boue*.[16]

(Paul Taylor in the *Independent*)[17]

In Canada's *Globe and Mail*, however, Lepage's production is heralded as 'one that looks to be as much a touchstone for the 1990s as Peter Brook's legendary 1970 Royal Shakespeare Company staging with trapezes and acrobats was for its time' (Wolf 1992: A10). On the one hand, it is not surprising to find Canada's national newspaper running a review which champions the success of one of the country's prodigies,[18] especially when he is contextualized as export to the former colonizer. On the other, this more enthusiastic review marks the apparent difference between actual ticket-buying audiences and the very specific viewing public of London media critics who apparently have altogether different criteria for doing Shakespeare 'properly.'

Peter Brook's radical and innovatory productions of Shakespeare's texts were also in the summer of 1992 still very much in the spotlight. As the *Globe and Mail* review reminds us, it is now more than twenty years since Brook's *Dream* brought in a new, more physical performance style for Shakespeare (and theatre, in general) to the mainstream stage and, in the intervening period, Brook has emerged as one of the mostly highly regarded voices on both Shakespeare and theatre.[19] At the First Drama and Education World Congress in Portugal (Porto, 20–25 July 1992), the French delegation's contribution to scholarly exchange involved a screening of video documentation of Peter Brook discussing his adaptation and direction of Shakespearean plays.[20] He presented his ideas in French. In this instance, it seems, both Shakespeare and Brook-on-Shakespeare have been appropriated as French cultural export, a striking example of Shakespeare's impressive international currency. A little later in the year, in New York, sell-out crowds watched another French cultural export, although not, this time,

Shakespeare. This new/old text was the Théâtre du Soleil's *Les Atrides*.

Director Ariane Mnouchkine brought to North America a four-part, nine hour version of Aeschylus's trilogy prefaced by the later Euripides play, *Iphigenia in Aulis*. These Greek classical texts were performed in French, but at the Park Slope Armory in Brooklyn, which squeezed almost 1,000 people into every show, the audience needed neither classical Greek nor modern French since a headset providing simultaneous translation into English was readily available for a nominal extra charge. None of these performances (either Brook's or the more literal ones) rely on any kind of textual purity but instead on the power of, and desire for, the re/presentation. Indeed, the playwright's words are evidently vulnerable to 'translation' into any market-driven language and not necessarily even to be spoken by actors or at least not necessarily to be spoken 'well.'[21] What appears to be the common selling device is an innovatory approach to the classical text and the performance of that innovation within the limits of tradition. As reviewer Michael Coveney put it in a (positive) review of the Compagnia de Collettivo of Parma's 1983 production of Shakespeare for the London International Festival of Theatre, 'Once you translate Shakespeare into any language, the shock of a new idiom and rhythm allows for almost any further liberty [the Collettivo had Prince Hal on a motorbike]. The point only remains as to how responsibly and creatively that shock is exploited' (cited in Armistead 1994: 163).[22]

In any case, each of these contemporary versions of the past is in some way an event of the year and each in some way relies completely on a collective sense of the authority of that past to which their subject texts belong and which their reproductions transgress. This is not to say that any or all of these reproductions rely on an uncomplicated or naive sense of tradition. Ariane Mnouchkine has a long and well-earned reputation for innovative and spectacular production techniques.[23] Robert Lepage – in Québec and Canada at least – has attracted wildly enthusiastic media and popular attention for his part in Théâtre Repère's collaborative and visionary creations.[24]

Perhaps itself a kind of dissident or deviant nostalgia, Lepage's process for this Royal National Theatre production of *A Midsummer Night's Dream* marks an attempt to disavow the fetish of Shakespeare's text. Lepage only introduced the text 'at the end' of the rehearsal period. First workshopped in December for an August opening, the company 'worked with people's dreams, and recurrences and drawings, so people had the impression they were playing; they were actually having fun. At the end, we read *A Midsummer Night's Dream*' (Lepage, cited in Wolf 1992: A10). And if the British press showed a little wariness, if not hostility, to a tampering with the Bard at the hands of someone from the 'colonies' (and French-speaking Québec at that), then Americans were just as suspicious of imported French-identified culture. In his review of *Les Atrides* for *Village Voice*, Michael Feingold writes:

> [T]here was every reason to suspect the arrival of another Eurotrash phony, another empty experience dressed up in elaborate audience discomfitures and pseudoexotic stage trimmings, of the kind a certain sycophant-internationalist segment of the press has so often urged on us in the dismal recent past. I was ready to be bored.
>
> I wasn't, of course. Mnouchkine's choice of material should have told me that her inconveniences to the audience were a way of preparing them for a bigger experience than usual. And that is what we got.
>
> (1992: 107)

For Feingold, it was choice of material that both permitted and made engaging the strategies of interpretation which the director put in place.

What all these reworkings of the classical texts of theatrical tradition illustrate is a contemporary obsession with staging old texts to explore the possibilities of performance in the present, to explore the present itself. They belong to what Roger Bromley has called a 'genre of remembering' (1988: 5). They rely on willing audiences who recognize and are nostalgic for the classical text but who are attracted to the event for its innovation with and renovation of that text. That events such as Lepage's *Midsummer Night's Dream*, Mnouchkine's *Les Atrides* and Brook's analysis of his own Shakespearean interventions are seen to represent the cutting edge of high art performance in the early 1990s – and this assertion is given some weight by the quantity of attention given to Brook, Lepage, and Mnouchkine in the popular and scholarly presses – further suggests the fetishization of the old text as a new one. Under what conditions is the past is re-presented for spectators in both global and local viewing economies? And what do we make of that past when we 'see' it?

Fredric Jameson has suggested that 'at the very moment in which we complain of the eclipse of historicity, we also universally diagnose contemporary culture as irredeemably historicist, in the bad sense of an omnipresent and indiscriminate appetite for dead styles and fashions, indeed for all the styles and fashions of a dead past' (1989b: 526) and performance is, of course, a particularly conspicuous site for such obsessions with 'a dead past.' What binds the material discussed in this book is the past, a reference point (apparently available to both readers and viewers) which enables the reception of a contemporary performance to be undertaken through recognition (if not always knowledge) of a particular historical antecedent. It would be possible, I realize, to choose almost any moment or moments from the historical past, from the very recent to the most distant, and to locate performance texts which recreate those histories in and for the present. But the performances which attach to the signifier Shakespeare add up to the most intensive and most obvious reuse of the past since Shakespeare's plays form, as Terence Hawkes has recently stated, one of the central agencies through which culture generates meaning: 'That is what they do, that is how they work, and that is what they are for. Shakespeare doesn't mean: *we* mean *by* Shakespeare' (1992: 3).[25] Or more wittily (or more insolently) put, Shakespeare stands as 'the ultimate Dead White Male: the pinnacle of an oppressive, canonical hierarchy and an ally of conservative elitism, patriarchal sovereignty, and colonial imperialism' (advertisement for 'Multicultural Shakespeare,' the 1992 theme for the Annual Shakespeare Institute at the City University of New York). Such a designation signals his function at both ends of a continuum of quotation: he can be both the 'seamless cloak of univocal authoritativeness for citers to hide behind' and the claim for attention to representation 'as garment . . . [which] invites judgement of its cut' (Rosler 1983: 194).[26]

If these reasons make the selection of Shakespeare perhaps an obvious one, it is true too that other historical periods, either through scripts already identified as primarily dramatic or through other literary/non-literary texts, are regularly performed in the present and that many, perhaps all, of these 'pasts in the present' deserve careful critical attention. As my Mnouchkine example implies, the originating texts of dramatic production continue to be a particularly sought-after antecedent both for contemporized production and for more radical rewritings. More broadly, the repertoire of the Greek drama – as exemplified in Mnouchkine's recent work – has attracted practitioners concerned with testing and redefining the possibilities of performance. Marianne McDonald's *Ancient Sun, Modern Light: Greek Drama on the Modern Stage* provides an interesting account of some contemporary adaptations, although the antipathy of at least one reviewer to the book's being 'too eclectic in its methodology' (Wiles 1992: 394) suggests the more general critical resistance to straying too far from those originating texts. Somewhat differently, my own criticism would be that McDonald does not take her exploration nearly far enough, eschewing the many, albeit more marginalized, uses of Greek drama in the present for a few of the more highly regarded names of the theatrical avant-garde (Peter Sellars, Suzuki Tadashi, Thomas Murphy, and others). She might well have engaged, for example, with the prolific rewritings of Greek myths (the plots of her subject texts) which have, for obvious reasons, been popular with feminist dramatists.[27]

As McDonald's text ably illustrates, the strategies and effects of adaptation are fascinating objects of study but the motivations, as well as the wider cultural effects, of representing the past in these ways need to be better understood. It is not enough to acknowledge that a text can be and is rewritten, we must also explore how such rewritings function within the constructs that are culture. Furthermore, it might be thought crucial to examine in whose voice a text is performed and with what relation to a mainstream culture that is (as Robins has argued) increasingly practised on a global–local nexus (1991: 33–36). While McDonald's text undoubtedly fulfils a useful function in the detailed documentation of these productions, it is necessary, too, to engage with the multiplicity of performances that are invented around a certain text. In this way it is possible, perhaps, to learn more about the limits of performance and about the writing of histories. Moreover, for these reasons, it seems apposite here to take on the most highly regarded of pasts, the Renaissance, as constructed through the texts of, and surrounding, William Shakespeare.

The citation of the past through some or other connection to Shakespeare is also, for my text, a usefully inclusive strategy. It has facilitated a project I have long thought necessary: a book on contemporary cultural production which does not limit itself to particular generic constraints. My emphasis, deliberately so, is cultural production which might be attached to the genre(s) of theatre/drama in its broadest configuration. The range of writings on the contemporary manifestations of theatre/drama are all too often contained by overly restrictive scope: surveys by nationality, author, period or interest.[28] Texts on contemporary theatre/drama, whether survey or single-author based, almost always carry, implicitly or explicitly, the agenda of who will make the/a canon, whose plays will be produced and/or taught one hundred years from now. Moreover, a prerequisite of such a claim is the publication of a printed playtext, something that will generally only happen if the play itself has seen one or preferably two professional productions. Michael Vanden Heuvel is absolutely right when arguing for a new 'dialogics of theater' that

> critics and academics responsible for forming the almost exclusively 'literary' dramatic canon have consistently come down squarely on the side of the written word. Unless there is a dramatic text to analyze, it is thought, there is no theatrical event to consider.
>
> (1991: 17)

Instead of a process of mediation which seeks to exclude more than include, to predecide the 'best' of the moment, it should be more important to undertake a complex approach to reading and entertaining not only the multiplicity of theatres and dramas which exist in this historical moment (irrespective of whether these are widely available as published artefacts) but also their relationships to other agencies of public meaning. Here, then, the quotation of the past has been a useful linking thread since the problem, I suspect, would be to find a text which didn't suggest an antecedent. This is, of course, the poststructuralist argument of 'iterability,' that no text can be made sense of unless it is both a quoter of other texts and itself capable of quotation.[29] We might also remember Judith Butler's caution that '[t]he citing of the dominant norm does not [necessarily] displace that norm; rather it becomes the means by which that dominant norm is most painfully reiterated as the very desire and the performance of those it subjects' (1993: 133) – a caution which might inflect significantly the project of 'radical' Shakespeare.

The iterability of Shakespeare's texts has certainly been explored before. As Gary Taylor demonstrated, the business of 'reinventing'

Shakespeare is a long-standing and inevitable one (1990). Each generation of theatre producers and of critics has invented an apparatus which is Shakespeare and the present moment is, of course, no exception. What is interesting about contemporary reinventions is their part in the historicist impulse that Jameson speaks of, as well as in the general field of dramatic production – how the past competes with so-called original works. Ruby Cohn's *Modern Shakespearean Offshoots* (1976) and her chapter 'Shakespeare Left and Righted' in her more recent *Retreats from Realism* (1991) are exemplary in their readings of contemporary British drama which has taken some relation to a Shakespearean antecedent. Cohn's useful description of the range of British dramas which have more or less overt connections to Shakespeare indicates, as she puts it, that 'one way of escaping contemporary realism is, paradoxically, to treat Shakespeare as our contemporary' (1991: 49). Michael Scott's *Shakespeare and the Modern Dramatist* has explored similar connections, focusing on how 'modern dramatists from different ontological positions have attempted to defamiliarise Shakespeare' (1989: 136). My return to this territory is provoked by a sense of the need for both a more theoretically informed account of the function of the past (Cohn herself admits in the introduction to *Retreats from Realism* her generational separation from more overtly theoretical practice) and a more inclusive repertoire – not simply British revisions, nor simply the drama that appears on the main stages of the English-speaking world.[30]

This is not to suggest that the reinvention of the past is the same in all the geographies considered here – far from it. Instead it is an attempt to take into account both the rather homogeneous global trading economy for the Bard in mainstream theatrical practice and the definitely heterogeneous practices of Shakespeares constructed for particular local economies. But although I have attempted to include examples of all kinds of performances of the past, this is not an attempt toward the encyclopedic. I am all too aware that there are many more examples available even when the historical past is narrowed to Shakespeare and his immediate surroundings.[31] I have tried only to bring together a collection of performances that might not otherwise be considered as a group; in some cases that might not be considered at all. In short, these are the performances that have interested me.[32] I hope this collage will engage with readers' own performances of the past and that their interaction will further explore the notions and effects of the nostalgia that wills them to appear.

SHAKESPEARE, AGENT OF POWER

> Probably more than any other figure in western culture, Shake-speare has been used to secure assumptions about texts, history, ideology, and criticism. . . . He functions, in many quarters, as a kind of cultural Esperanto.
>
> (Jean E. Howard and Marion O'Connor 1987: 4)

> There is no new stuff. This is a traditional act. No politics, no arseing around. They know what they're going to get, give it to them. Now, the codpiece gag.
>
> (Thomas in Stephen Jeffreys' *The Clink*, 1990: 4)

Lepage's *A Midsummer's Night's Dream* and Mnouchkine's *Les Atrides* betoken the substantial demand for resuscitated remnants of the textual archive and these well-funded and well-attended spectacles illustrate, in performance terms, the arguments surrounding history that this chapter has already noted. They can also function as signs of contemporary social organization: 'Our society has become a recited society, in three senses: it is defined by *stories* . . . , by *citations* of stories, and by the interminable *recitation* of stories' (de Certeau 1984, 186 – emphasis in original). Yet interminable (and, it might be argued, often dissonant) recitations can produce effects that escape the discipline implied in the recitation. If 'we' are bound to cite and recite, then 'we' might well explore this as a generative practice. In the context of Shakespeare, aside from recitation as performance, there is, of course, the parallel and equally intense industry of recitation produced in the form of scholarship.

If it is now something of a commonplace to argue that the Humanities are 'in crisis' (a topic ably surveyed by Patrick Brantlinger in the opening chapter of his *Crusoe's Footprints*), one of the symptoms of that crisis is recognized in the proliferation of academic discourses, in the range of readings now claiming currency in the classroom and elsewhere. And within that most proliferative discipline in the Humanities, literary criticism, nowhere is the expansion more evident – or more contested – than in the field of Shakespeare studies. When Brantlinger wryly comments on 'the intellectual free-for-all of the Modern Language

Association's thousand-and-one sessions (through which a King Shahriyar could not stay awake – but perhaps there is safety in both numbers and turmoil)' (1990: 14), he fails to point out that some of the thousand-and-one sessions attract (and, equally, demand) more of an audience than others. And that some of the sessions produce for themselves an audience far larger than the original room of their performance could accommodate. Ivo Kamps's collection *Shakespeare Left and Right* has as its foundation four papers 'initially presented at a Special Session of the Modern Language Association on "The Role of Ideology in the Criticism and Metacriticism of Shakespeare" held in Washington, D.C. in 1989' (1991: ix). The contest, as Kamps calls it, stems from the proliferation of radical interpretation by the Left which has the following effect on the Right (I reproduce the categories Left and Right as they are used in the title and text of Kamps's book):

> [T]oday there is a feeling of deep apprehension among many
> of them [the Right] that the Left will soon control English
> departments, the curriculum, and the professional journals
> and university presses – an apprehension manifesting itself in
> the call to rescue the traditional canon of Western Civilization
> from being dislodged from anthologies and course syllabi by
> the literatures of women, minorities, and ideologues.
>
> (1991: 2)

In short, in the decade or so since 1980, the practice of academic criticism on Shakespeare and other Renaissance playwrights has irrevocably changed. If this assertion – or Kamps's – needs any elaboration at all, a cursory glance at the Folger Shakespeare Library journal *Shakespeare Quarterly* tells all. In the 1980 volume, articles published include 'The Structure of *King Lear*,' 'Shakespeare's *The Tempest*: The Wise Man as Hero,' 'Logic versus the Slovenly World in Shakespearean Comedy' and 'Thematic Contraries and the Dramaturgy of *Henry V*.'[33] More recently (Fall 1991), the journal carries the following: '"Knock me here soundly": Comic Misprision and Class Consciousness in Shakespeare,' '"Documents in Madness": Reading Madness and Gender in Shakespeare's Tragedies and Early Modern Culture' and 'Where are the Mothers in Shakespeare? Options for Gender Representation in the English Renaissance.'[34] These later titles reveal the interests of Cultural Materialist, feminist, and New Historicist criticism, which, if only emergent in 1980, dominated Shakespeare studies in the early 1990s.

26

And, as Gary Taylor points out in his cultural history of Shakespeare and the Shakespeare industry, the critical technologies and vocabularies are now drawn (for the first time) from writers who are not recognized or accredited as Renaissance specialists – from Derrida, Lacan, Barthes, Foucault, Williams, Hall (they, of course, represent another symptom of the crisis in the Humanities which J.G. Merquior names as 'theorrhea').[35] Yet, as Taylor makes his readers aware, all too aware, critical paradigms cannot be avoided: they are a product of the historical moment and critics are bound to use them to tell stories about themselves (1989: 362–364). So, like it or not, in the academic production of the Renaissance, the stories that now get told by way of readings of Shakespeare's and others' texts are different stories from those that were told in 1980.

And, in this championing of new ways to play old texts, the byword of the day (or perhaps that is of the last decade) is radical. It is the ineluctable fact of Shakespearean criticism, on either the Left or the Right, that the grounds of his foundational importance within institutional choreographies be established. Jean Howard and Marion O'Connor's conjuring up of Shakespeare as 'a kind of cultural Esperanto' makes precisely that point. If this seems undisguised within a British tradition, as Margot Heinemann contends in her fine essay 'How Brecht read Shakespeare' – 'Shakespeare is *there*, deeply embedded in the culture, the language, the media and the educational system of Britain' (1985: 204)[36] – it must be remembered yet that he also has a global there-ness, particularly in the English-speaking world. Michael Bristol has reminded us that it is a precise effect of humanist scholarship which purports Shakespeare's universality, his ability to represent 'the generic human condition, the ability to transcend the parochial aspects of historically specific culture that supposedly accounts for Shakespeare's international reputation' (1990: 23). He further remarks that '[o]ne of the more conspicuous indications of Shakespeare's special importance in the politics of literary culture within late capitalist North America is the very large quantity of critical scholarship and commentary that continues to accumulate around his works' (1990: 28). In the radicalizing of the Shakespeare project, New Historicist (characterized by Walter Cohen as describing 'historical difference' although not explaining 'historical change' [1987: 32][37]) and Cultural Materialist (the best of which is described by Hawkes as offering 'powerful examples of the un-settling purchase this newly historicized and politicized British criticism can obtain on the Elizabethan past and the post-Thatcher present' [1992: 151]) criticisms have been primarily instrumental in effecting the paradigm shifts noted already.

Excellent summaries of the differences between these by-now dominant modes of criticism are available in Cohen's 'Political Criticism of Shakespeare' (1987) and Wayne's 'Power, Politics, and the Shakespearean Text' (1987) and I don't want to replicate their surveys here. Nonetheless, it is important to flag a particular effect of these critical practices. Their axial connection is one that disregards the traditional strategy 'to treat Shakespeare's work as *poetry*, his medium as language, to forget all the rest' (Kavanagh 1985: 147). And when James Kavanagh declares 'if there is one thing we can say about Shakespearean theatre, it is that it was not intentionally implicated in what we now call "the literary"' (1985: 147), he marks that line between these methodologies as one that traverses the socio-ideological performance of the source texts. And as this body of criticism has taken account of that performance (in the broadest sense – on the stage, but also its imbrication in social practices), the positionalities of gender, class, race, and sexuality have re-entered the arena in ways that traditional humanist interpretation and collective nostalgia would seek to inhibit. Part of this energy concerns itself with Elizabethan dramatic practice, but another part insists on attending to those dramatic practices which vitalize contemporary stages.

Once again, there is a determined attention paid to the British theatre (as in the case of Alan Sinfield's 'Royal Shakespeare: theatre and the making of ideology' (1985c), a useful reminder of Shakespeare's ongoing currency as an agent of royal power), but other national examples abound and almost always indicate the thoroughness of imperial 'education.' Martin Orkin, for instance, draws attention to this particular function:

> In South Africa, as often elsewhere in colonial and post-colonial worlds, Shakespeare has been primarily appropriated by most amongst the English-speaking educated members of the ruling classes as a means of evidencing their affiliations with the imperial and colonial centres. Possession and knowledge of Shakespeare texts becomes evidence of empowerment. . . . Shakespeare has . . . become for members of the educated ruling classes one signifier of 'civilisation', astoundingly that is, it should never be forgotten, in South

Africa one signifier for white apartheid 'civilisation'. The web
of such a use of Shakespeare spins not only through institutions of education, the media, establishment theatre, public
cultural bodies, but even into the thinking of some of the
country's large conglomerates of capital.

(1991: 235)

In such a 'web,' an understanding of the performance conditions
(on the stage, in the classroom) emerges as the contested territory
in which contemporary experiences and manifestations of power
can be tested and consolidated:

Shakespeare after all is construed within this [New Right]
cultural milieu as a privileged embodiment of Western values
and as a fundamental element in the substantive curriculum
of Western Culture. On this view, correct interpretation of
the plays is a matter of national interest.

(Bristol 1991: 32)

For the 'radical' team, there has to be some cultural purchase
in deconstructing the mechanisms for and of power that are both
produced by and with this particular body of texts. Dollimore
concludes his own assessment of 'Shakespeare, cultural materialism
and the new historicism' with:

the need to disclose the effectiveness and complexity of the
ideological process of containment. . . . [T]he very desire to
disclose that process is itself oppositional and motivated by
the knowledge that, formidable though it be, it is a process
which is historically contingent and partial.

(1985: 15)

Others, like Bristol, take a more equivocal stance:

[I]nstitutions are actually peopled by social agents who
themselves may have agendas that differ substantially from
those initially mandated. The release of those potentialities
would presumably be the over-arching interest of a critically
motivated research program. Those interests cannot, however, be actualized by a novel re-staging of the counter-
normative script, nor simply by saying forbidden things about
Shakespeare.

(1990: 61)

This, of course, has not stopped a great many academics and theatre practitioners from attempting to do just that.

In Stephen Jeffreys's play *The Clink* (1990), set in London at the end of the reign of Elizabeth I, much of the action results from a contradictory understanding of the generic limits of comedy. Thomas (as the quotation given at the opening of this section indicates) asserts the necessity of continuity: there can be 'no new stuff.' On the other hand, his brother Lucius (the other half of their double act) claims a new performance style, one that wins him a rich and important patron. But Lucius's transgression of the 'rules' of comic practice stalls as it is seized for quite different political objectives: he becomes no more than a device by which England's European competitors can feel the full weight of royal contempt. With these stakes, Lucius's fate is far from funny: despatched to the stocks on the frozen River Thames where, if the river remains frozen, he will die from hypothermia or where, if the river melts, he will drown. Such a double-edged sword Lucius describes as a 'Jacobean punishment. It's more intellectual than what we're used to' (Jeffreys 1990: 84). And, in the reunion, on the frozen river, between the two brothers, the limits of comedy are marked:

THOMAS: So. Did it go down well, the new comedy?
LUCIUS: They liked it, yes. They liked it a lot, only. . . .
THOMAS: It annoyed someone.
LUCIUS: Yes. Yes, it did. Being funny . . . carries certain responsibilities.
THOMAS: I wouldn't know.
LUCIUS: What?
THOMAS: Three days without you. Doing the act. I realised I'm not funny.

(1990: 83, ellipses in the original)

To transgress the constitutive practices of the genre is to invoke punishment by law; to mime without slippage or deviation those same practices is to fail to institute the category at all. When the brothers perform together, they effect a symbiosis of transgression and regulation which assures the efficacy of the law. When that performance is ruptured and revealed in its separate elements, then the obligatory limits and failures are marked. The tradition of comedy relies on an excess of its own practices which it can then recover for its own constitution. [38] To some extent, this is a performance which a criticism of recycling, reappropriating, revisioning and rereading Shakespeare takes as its object.

Much of the scholarly discussion of appropriation and reappropriation is, obviously, concerned with how the jewel in the crown of the English(-speaking) literary/dramatic canon has been appropriated for culturally and historically specific social processes. Most of those processes reinforce category designations and distinctions; some attempt to elucidate the conditions which both demand and elaborate those same designations and distinctions. And, given the leftist/ish impetus of recent Shakespearean scholarship already described in this chapter, there has been an intensity of academic production proposing and examining conditions under which reappropriations against the normatives of dominant cultural practices (might) take place.

Two particular subcategories of this genre of criticism are of especial interest. One is the recycling of Shakespeare to examine notions of history; the other is the movement of Shakespearean criticism into the field of cultural studies. In thinking about history, I want first to consider an example in performance, Ariane Mnouchkine's version of *Richard II* (1981), described by Dennis Kennedy as orientalist Shakespeare, which 'achieved its success through enormous cultural dislocation' (1993a: 296). Mnouchkine ironically chose to work on Shakespeare because of his timelessness, because his plays represented a kind of neutral textual landscape. Kennedy rightly marks the dangers of an intercultural theatrical methodology which detaches texts from their originating enunciative terms and conditions:[39]

> Certainly Mnouchkine managed to estrange Shakespeare for her audiences, to point out the wondrous otherness of the fables. There was no danger that a comfortable Anglocentricity would overtake the responses to these productions. Nonetheless, her insistent imposition of superbly foreign modes on the history plays tended to detach them from *any* political and historical meanings, Elizabethan or contemporary. *Richard II* was a dangerously political play in Shakespeare's time because it acts out the deposition of a king, an action not many monarchs like to see represented on the public stage. . . . But Mnouchkine was concerned with style and substituted a powerful aesthetic experience for a social one.
>
> (1993a: 296–297)

What her production of *Richard II* in an aesthetic frame of South Asian theatrical traditions effected, I'd suggest, is the impossibility of a responsible intercultural performance when any grammar of expression is divorced from its historical impetus. But even an objective of aesthetic seduction speaks of History. It speaks of a veiled set of circumstances which give voice and movement, and which make both visible/audible. Kennedy's characterization of audience response to *Richard II* makes this palpable: 'Some spectators . . . noted with melancholy the losses in the right's and intellectual dimensions' (1993b: 287). If Mnouchkine insisted on an ahistorical history play (cited in Kennedy 1993b: 286), then the conference organized by the British section of the International Association of Theatre Critics to test Jan Kott's thesis, *Shakespeare Our Contemporary*, some twenty-five years after its publication in 1961, provided different anchors for historical perspective. While Kott himself rails against a trend to locate Shakespeare 'in no time and in no particular place' (Elsom 1989: 15), Michael Bogdanov picks up the discussion, contending:

> when I walk into a rehearsal with my group in *Henry IV* and *Henry V*, I look for the way in which the political circumstances were handled then, and find inspirational parallels in what is happening now. We governed disgustingly in the fourteenth century and we are still governing disgustingly today.
> (cited in Elsom 1989: 17)

Bogdanov asserts, conservatively, an insistence on the continuity of H/history, at the same time as he marks that process of conservation with its repressed texts.

Thus Bogdanov's insistence that Shakespeare is still, and must be, 'our contemporary' relies on a careful and thorough reading of the history that is staged in the source text. It is, for him, the relation between different representations of historical circumstances which inspires and produces theatre. Graham Holderness's project in *Shakespeare Recycled* (1992) is to identify the primary historiographical nature of Shakespeare's history plays, a task he develops both through readings of the individual plays and of the methodological questions which surround such readings. Furthermore, Holderness (*pace* Anne Barton) draws attention to the very flexibility of the genre of history play, accommodating as it does popular, romantic modes with historiographic inquiry. The history play enables 'varied and possibly antagonistic ideologies to interact'

(Holderness 1992b: 17). Unlike History, the history play can perform the discourses of the past as fantasies, posing characters and events in the realm of 'what if?' This is clearly a productive site for the articulation of the past in/as the present, and Holderness's investigations on theatrical productions of Shakespeare's history plays 'distinguish clearly and sharply between reactionary and progressive reproduction; and between productions designed to preserve intact the Tudor ideology of national unity, and productions which revive the historical conditions of Shakespeare's theatre to make staging history a radical cultural intervention' (1992b: 128–129). The practice of 'complex montage' which Holderness articulates for Shakespeare's history texts (1992b: 227) offers a usable framework for the production of historical materials (and not just Shakespeare) which will take account of the diversities of demographies and geographies. It is a framework which will stage the complexities of social formations, and not simply line them up for their place on the continuum recognized as History. This marks a need to be better able in whatever disparate and diverse communities to engage with a globally disseminated cultural product and to recognize those moments where a viewing economy might be fragmented in its response.

In an account of 'imperial theatre in India' in the nineteenth and twentieth centuries, Christine Mangala Frost complicates a simple opposition of England and India located in dissemination through the agencies of both theatre and education.[40] Her locations of performance histories which contravene such a coding (for example, the casting of Baishnavacharan Auddy in a 1848 Calcutta-based British production of *Othello*) demonstrate not only racial anxiety (which is most certainly present) but also moments of recognition of the political tensions which produced such anxiety. Bringing to bear, as Mangala Frost does, the complexity of production and reception economies on any manifestation of 'theatre history' will dislocate the tenure of all kinds of binaries which work to secure the dominant cultural perspective (Frost 1992). As Holderness does in his re-imagining of the history (plays), she asks new questions of already oft-told tales.

Holderness concludes his text by designating 'a reactionary "Shakespeare," constructed and designed to hold that [bourgeois] culture together. There is also a "free Shakespeare," potentially a force for destabilising that culture and pushing it towards social transformation' (1992b: 232). And it is this latter manifestation of

Shakespeare that impels Marowitz to 'recycle' Shakespeare, which involves claiming him back from the shackles of academic scholarship and production. In a most exaggerated form, Marowitz rails at both scholar and practitioner for a stultifying approach to Shakespeare that he believes characterizes the contemporary moment. His essay entitled 'Jail Scholars! Free Shakespeare!' seemingly provocatively takes on the traditional biases in the field. His determined attack on John Russell Brown (in his capacities as both a university professor and an associate director at the Royal National Theatre) – an account of what Marowitz terms the Brownian fallacy and to which Brown himself is permitted a short and to the point response – marks, however, the same obsessiveness with which this chapter began. Marowitz argues:

> The most repugnant of all scholars' obsessions is trying to recapture the Elizabethan sensibility. Even if it could be done, and I do not believe it can, it would be the most unrewarding act imaginable. Which have been the most exciting productions of Shakespeare in our time? The museum replicas in painfully reconstructed Globe Theatre conditions, or the custom-made works of directors such as Peter Brook, Peter Hall, Terry Hands and Trevor Nunn?
>
> (1991: 58)

Marowitz, of course, is deliberately outrageous,[41] but his criticisms graphically outline the effects of eradicating historical context (or, at least, allowing only a monolithic History in which the plays might appear).

In yet another sortie into revisions of Shakespeare, Holderness locates the power of heritage (or tradition) in the (re)emergence of reconstructions in London of the Globe and Rose Theatres. Resonant with theories already outlined here on the economically driven fetishization of the past, he outlines the motivations of the Globe Theatre reconstruction project, noting that initial difficulties with land-use permits were resolved by an appeal to historical continuity: the site selected for the construction of the replica is located close by the now partially excavated remains of the 'authentic' predecessor (1992a: 251). But the replica Globe, even if it is to be built using authentic materials and methods, is precisely that: a replica, a souvenir of some other age and experience. And there is, as Susan Stewart determines, 'no continuous identity between these objects and their referents' (1984: 145). She adds:

Restoration can be seen as a response to an unsatisfactory set of present conditions. Just as the restoration of buildings . . . has as its basis the restoration of class relationships that might otherwise be in flux, so the restoration of the souvenir is a conservative idealization of the past and the distanced for the purposes of a present ideology.

(1984: 150)

Lying somewhere between a restored building (restoration of a phantom past) and a souvenir (reconstruction of a myth), the Globe Theatre project, despite its own best aims, marks the discontinuities of history. It gives performance to what we do not know, yet are obliged to invent, so as to anchor ourselves in the turbulent experience of the present. These are, perhaps, some of the most compelling performances of nostalgia.

The uncovering and subsequent battle for the protection of the remains of the Rose Theatre surface as an interesting counterpart to the project of the Globe. The Save the Rose Campaign was instituted to permit a full excavation of the site and to halt a planned office development there.[42] Holderness offers this observation: 'The Globe and the Rose were constituted within this discourse into a series of classic binary oppositions: centre and margin, high and low priority, senior and junior partner, Shakespearean and not-really-Shakespearean, mature Shakespearean and early Shakespearean, even male and female' (1992a: 255). What this illustrates is a determined advantage for heritage/tradition over history; of marketability over scholarship (Holderness 1992a: 256), but it also denotes the inability of both sites to recreate the past for, after all, '[t]he nostalgic is enamored of distance, not of the referent itself. Nostalgia cannot be sustained without loss' (Stewart 1984: 145). If it were really possible to experience the original conditions of those theatres in which Shakespeare's plays were performed, it would effectively eradicate 'the desire that is nostalgia's reason for existence' (Stewart 1984: 145). But desiring subjects we are bound to be and the parameters of such desire can be disclosed in contemporary cultural criticism engaged with the shifting citation of Shakespeare.

Two trajectories characterize such investigations. In one, Shakespeare is examined for those physical properties that are recirculated in the contemporary moment as perhaps the transcendental signifier of high culture. In the other, it is the invocation of lines (or bastardized versions) from his plays that are plundered for their capacity to mean in particular ways. Both approaches deserve books of their own. Here, as elsewhere, I want to use a few brief examples to mark the characteristics of such appropriations. Michael Bristol launches his important *Shakespeare's America, America's Shakespeare* (1990) with the exemplar of the Charlie the Tuna advertisement. The purchase in an advertising campaign of a fish purporting to 'do' Shakespeare functions, Bristol suggests, in two different contexts:

> First, he makes it clear that Shakespeare has some kind of normative force within American culture. Doing Shakespeare signifies cultural advancement since it places Charlie on the side of 'good taste' even though it has nothing to do with 'tasting good,' that is, with Charlie's market-worthiness. Second, although Shakespeare has a culturally normative aesthetic value, it would appear that he is also a figure of considerable emancipatory potential, since 'doing Shakespeare' saves Charlie from the fate of the tuna that taste good, that is to be butchered, cooked, and canned.
>
> (1990: 15)

The frequency with which Shakespeare's image and/or lines appear to recommend a particular product or service suggests that his is the signifier beyond all others in an international marketing economy. His face and voice are literally everywhere.

Beyond advertising (invoking a desire for product which will both defer and feed our nostalgic longing), the same traces of 'Shakespeare' can be found adorning functional and non-functional objects. Bryan Loughrey and Graham Holderness provide a clever and important reading of the relation of his marketed/marketing image with those 'authentic' representations of Shakespeare's visage. They comment: 'Shakespeare's face is one of the most insistently reproduced icons in the world. It adorns countless book covers, hotel and restaurant signs, beer mats, tea caddies, confectionery packets, cigarette and playing cards, ceramics, theatre and museum foyers, advertisements, and banknotes' (1991: 186) – later citing, too, my own favorite example of the iconographic flexibility of his image, from the 1960s television version of *Batman* where the entrance 'to the "Batcave" is controlled by a switch concealed within a bust of Shakespeare' (1991: 186). Their elucidation of the derivations of these images is, like Bristol's assessment of Charlie the Tuna, not simply to extend the discussion of Shakespeare into ever more esoteric margins, but to realize the contribution of those material aspects of history which are represented visually and texturally, and not only textually, in social processes of legitimation. Moreover, the list that Loughrey and Holderness cite also establishes the prevalence and currency of Shakespeare as literal souvenir, 'not an object arising out of need or use value; it is an object arising out of the necessarily insatiable demands of nostalgia' (Stewart 1984: 135). Drawing on Shakespeare outside of the theatre but in distinctly theatrical ways, 'the nostalgia of the souvenir plays in the distance between the present and an imagined, prelapsarian experience, experience as it might be "directly lived." The location of authenticity becomes whatever is distant to the present time and space' (Stewart 1984: 139–140). No wonder, then, that 'Shakespeare' has so many contemporary uses.

Alongside its powerful imagination of a regulatory authenticity, there is also the cultural advancement that Bristol spoke of in his Charlie the Tuna example. In a brilliant reading of Shakespearean citation in the Anita Hill/Clarence Thomas hearings, Marjorie Garber addresses 'the voice of Shakespeare ventriloquized, speaking through our nation's lawmakers and those called to testify before them' (1993: 23).[43] Garber asks:

> Why Shakespeare? Well, for one thing Shakespeare is 'safe'; neither too high nor too low. He is not an author whom Lynne Cheney or her colleagues at the National Endowment for the Humanities could have accused of being the property of narrow specialists, but rather the abiding, ventriloquized voice of us all, of disembodied wisdom.
>
> (1993: 28)

Whether in Britain or America or elsewhere, Shakespeare, simply put, has a normative value. These examples – and many studies like them – corroborate this again and again and again. His availability to be enlisted in the regressive discourses of the New Right is without question. What is trickier to establish is the 'considerable emancipatory potential' of that same availability which Bristol identifies and which many of the revisioned texts discussed in this book seek.

Subsequent chapters follow a grammar of performance, taking account of what is legible, what becomes legible, and what is only legible under certain, specific, and often local sets of circumstances.

The narrative relies on the shifting (and sometimes competing) voices of actor, director, reviewer, academic critic; at different moments, each occupies the place of 'truth' but in the end none can claim that as a stable site. In the disarticulation of the past, counter-histories are bound to struggle to find both voice and body. In short, they seek their own radical performance which will shift other perspectives and other truths. As Connerton tells us,

> what is lacking in the life histories of those who belong to subordinate groups is precisely those terms of reference that conduce to and reinforce this sense of a linear trajectory, a sequential narrative shape: above all, in relation to the past, the notion of legitimating origins, and in relation to the future, the sense of an accumulation in power or money or influence.
>
> (1989: 19)

Against such a trajectory in the name of Shakespeare, the radically revised texts that interest me cannot easily fit into the narrative 'home' of academic criticism. How counter-histories might attempt such a shifting performance is the puzzle that this text enacts.

2

PRODUCTION AND PROLIFERATION

Seventeen Lears

'I've reinvented the lines. I've reinvented the plot.
Now it's up to the characters. Or maybe it's the actors.'
(William Shakespeare Junior V in
Jean-Luc Godard's *King Lear*, 1988)

We now live in a world of simulacra: perfect copies of originals
that never existed.
(Robert Hewison 1991: 173)

The woman who would be king.
Ruth Maleczech as LEAR.
(Promotional material for Mabou Mines's *Lear*, 1990)

King Lear is to postmodernism what Hamlet was to Romanticism:
the icon of an age.
(Arthur Holmberg 1988: 12)

PRODUCING SHAKESPEARE'S *LEAR*

To focus now on Shakespeare's particular contribution to the
macro-nostalgia of contemporary culture, I turn to the production
of *King Lear*. The frequency of its staging (a testament to its 'greatness') and at the same time some inherent lapses in the syntax of
its performance mark theatre's propensity, in all of its discourses,
to shift. Nonetheless, while the academy might be obviously reeling
from the effects of the epistemological shift attributed to theory
(or any other of the crisis symptoms) and causing a leftist/ish coup
in English departments, it would seem that the paradigms of
theatrical practice have not been so readily revolutionized. In fact,
it might be argued in the case of the performance of Shakespeare's
texts that they have shifted apparently very little in the last decade.

To describe the tenacious web of nostalgia and tradition that has Shakespeare as performance in its grip, I want to sketch the production methodologies and the reception economies of twelve stagings of *King Lear* undertaken in Britain between 1980 and 1990: two of these productions are made-for-television versions, the remaining ten for mainstream (subsidized or commercial) theatres. Nearly all the major British theatre institutions are represented in this brief history – the Royal National Theatre, the Royal Shakespeare Company, the Renaissance Theatre Company, the Old Vic, the BBC – as are several key 'players' from the postwar British stage – Laurence Olivier, Kenneth Branagh, Jonathan Miller, David Hare.

Let us start with the most recent example in the surveyed period: July 1990, at the Royal National Theatre in London, a production directed by Deborah Warner with Brian Cox in the title role. This combination of director and lead performer might, at first glance, promise a performance more than capable of a new articulation of a dramatic text so overcoded with classic status. Cox is most probably considered as a good repertory actor, albeit not an obvious 'star' name, and he is playing his first King Lear. Warner might easily be marked as challenging tradition by virtue of her biological coding; and she is not only a woman directing Shakespeare but one doing it at a particularly prestigious theatre.[1] While the combination of Cox and Warner certainly suggests some potential for an innovative and perhaps radical reading of this canonical text, and while the textual criticism being produced by faculties in English departments and elsewhere would insist on this, the conditions of performance suggest something rather less new:

> Our first sight of the old man in this new production of *King Lear* is not encouraging. Brian Cox's Lear races on at high speed in a wheelchair, his daughters whooping at his side and the entire party wearing paper hats. My heart sank. At least, I thought to myself, we won't have the dreaded plastic noses that the Royal Shakespeare Company have done to death in recent years. But, drearily enough, a red plastic nose is planted on Lear and even on the dead Cordelia.
>
> (Edwards 1990: 952)

This new production is then already a re-production; it's the 1982–3 Royal Shakespeare Company *King Lear* directed by Adrian Noble, which, by critical account, made the Fool, played by Anthony

Sher, the centre of the play. Sher comments: 'We began with the red nose and . . . it was so immediately successful. There is something very liberating about wearing a red nose, both externally and internally' (cited in Leggatt 1991: 75).[2] If a red nose liberates Lear's fool – and apparently perhaps Lear and Cordelia too – it seems possible to imagine that a woman directing this canonical 'masterpiece' might also liberate Shakespeare's text.

The 1990 *King Lear*, it should be noted, was Warner's second of the decade. The first she had directed in 1985 for her own Kick Theatre Company in a production that originated at the geographically, if no longer politically, fringe Edinburgh Festival. Reviewers of the Kick production were quick to note Warner as *the* emergent director in the mid-1980s, more often interviewed on British television than the directors in the employ of the Royal Shakespeare Company. Mary Harron writes of Warner's first *King Lear*: 'more productions like this and the walls of the RSC will come tumbling down' (1985: 1169). Theatre review hyperbole notwithstanding, it is possible to recuperate Warner's extensive media attention and critical success at the fringe with Shakespeare's play as the decisive contribution towards her getting a major offer from a major theatre in a major city. Her apparently radical *King Lear* for Kick Theatre employed the doubling of the Fool and Cordelia, and it is a suggestive pairing which is seen in its critical reception to reveal the subtleties of Warner's interpretive and directorial skills. But, like the red nose, it's been done before. In 1982 for the Orange Tree Theatre (a long flourishing pub theatre in south-west London), Sam Walters directed a no-frills, workmanlike *King Lear* which, according to its reviews, indulged in a little academic pedantry by doubling Cordelia and the Fool.[3] Radical or even innovative readings, then, are neither the sole nor unique possessions of director, actor, spectator, or critic; they are instead constructed (or not) within the matrix of material conditions by which they are staged and received. And it is this matrix, despite the imagination of nostalgia and tradition, which ensures a potentiality of shifting. Not that such shifts will necessarily occur.

To return to the 1982–3 Royal Shakespeare Company *King Lear* (the one which, as far as I can uncover, was the first mainstream red nose *King Lear* of the decade), this particular staging uncovers yet more difficulties in trying to provide a new interpretation of this so-heavily coded play. For the critics of Adrian Noble's production – and it is one that is generally well received – it calls to

PRODUCTION AND PROLIFERATION

mind (among others) Brecht, Beckett, Bergman, and Kozintsev. Moreover, it is cited by several mainstream critics as the best since Peter Brook's 1962 version, the one production of *King Lear* that has legendary status in the second half of the twentieth century.[4] Other *King Lears*, while not the 'best' since Brook, likewise cannot escape containment within a set of other, usually contemporary, benchmarks: David Hare's direction of Anthony Hopkins for the National Theatre in 1986 achieves the Beckettian Lear once envisaged by Jan Kott; Jonathan Miller's direction of Eric Porter at the Old Vic in 1989 is Kurosawa-style; Andrew Robertson at the Young Vic provides a nineteenth-century Chekovian *King Lear*. And, on television (Granada 1983), Michael Elliott directs Lord Olivier in the lead role as a Victorian – one can 'almost imagine Granville Barker giving notes,' suggests Alexander Leggatt (1991: 128) – and, of course, Olivier's portrayal is inevitably read against his own earlier interpretation, something Olivier actively encouraged in his repetition of the entrance sequence of Lear 'chatting' with Cordelia.[5]

While the possibility of doing anything new with the *King Lear* text is so obviously fraught, perhaps the answer then is to do nothing at all, as in the 1989 Royal Shakespeare Company production directed by the company's Head of Voice, Cicely Berry. This production is praised for its timelessness, for its wise decision to do the best we can with Shakespeare, to let the text speak for itself with no other distractions (Hoyle 1989: 1249). After all those red noses, I take the point. Berry's tactic resonates with the approach that Kristin Linklater (another voice specialist) has articulated:

> If the plays are spoken and performed, not academically studied, and if the sounds of the words and the rhythms of the language are felt, Shakespeare's voice will call to the voices of eloquence that live in everyone. ... It comes from the soul of the English language, and once the soul of the language has been discovered by the speaker, the soul and voice of that speaker is liberated to tell her or his own story.
>
> (1992: 195)

Linklater's passionate argument for the liberation of Shakespeare 'from the shackles of a narrow Anglo-Saxon tradition into the wide universal arena where his archetypal works find new life' (1992: 202) attests to the stultifying rigor of most actor training – part of which insists that there is a monolithic Shakespearean voice, a single methodology for doing it right.[6] It is against the same traditional, programmatic assumption that Michael Pennington imagines the English Shakespeare Company: 'If this company of ours gets going . . . it will be the best bloody verse-speaking outfit in the country. . . . The seat of speech is also the seat of desire, which includes the desire to share meaning' (Bogdanov and Pennington 1990: 19). Production of the Shakespearean voice is somewhat tangential to the concerns of this chapter, except that the proliferation of voice, taken quite literally as the articulation of the words of Shakespeare's plays, points significantly to the complicity of training methodologies in a singular and prescriptive preservation of the past. As Richard Paul Knowles has noted in a fascinating account of the discursive context of Canada's Stratford Festival,

> the Cicely Berry/Kristen Linklater/Patsy Rodenburg schools of voice training, the Alexander technique and other physical and movement methods . . . reinforce the psychophysical and linear conceptions of character, motivation, and action which are already culturally privileged and deeply inscribed in theatrical discourse.

> (1994: 215)

But, to return to Berry's *King Lear*, perhaps the distraction here is that this production does not take place on the Royal Shakespeare Company's main stage. Instead it was produced in their studio space, and it is more than a little ironic that when *King Lear* is given over to a voice specialist to really let the text speak for itself, it is despatched to a stage which is generally a venue for alternative or new plays/productions.

The 1981 production at the Young Vic, directed by Frank Dunlop, also played *King Lear* textually 'straight,' although (according to one reviewer) this was tediously mediated by the semiotic of dress – military field-grey uniforms which 'put us unnecessarily in mind of totalitarian regimes' (Atkins 1981: 533). And if this critic, Harold Atkins, didn't like the costumes, then he didn't think much of textual reverence either. He writes: 'School seniors preparing for their A-levels comprised most of the audience at the Young Vic for *King Lear* on Saturday night and the run-of-the-mill production will doubtless be of value to them as Shakespeare brought to the stage' (1981: 533). While such a statement speaks volumes about the reviewer's own expectations and

43

assumptions (not the least of which is his firm belief that young[er] audiences are cultural dupes who might acquire some small improvement from the embodiment of a liberal humanist educa- tion – albeit one that is run-of-the-mill to a sophisticated and superior spectator like himself), does his assessment also suggest that Frank Dunlop is an unimaginative director or that *King Lear* can be just a run-of-the-mill text? Or does it simply reveal – and simultaneously disapprove of – the company's marketing strategy? The financially troubled Young Vic clearly could do a lot worse than a textually faithful, A-level examination Shakespearean tragedy in order to guarantee large block bookings, high percentage capac- ities, and some resulting profit. And perhaps further evidence of this comes from the production's restaging the following year under the direction of Andrew Robertson. This *King Lear* too had uniformly negative reviews, but obviously good seat sales. Such productions, of course, exemplify the ongoing force of traditional academic criticism and its maintenance in many theatrical inter- pretations.

But for the consummate 'let the actor speak the text' produc- tion, there is Kenneth Branagh's 1990 production for his own Renaissance Theatre Company.[7] Opening an eight-month world tour in Los Angeles and closing eventually in London, this production showcased Branagh's philosophy for producing Shakespeare's plays. He declares that his company was formed to foreground

> the imagination and energy of the actors involved, [it would be] a company which placed the actors in a central position. . . . It would be a practical realignment of the collaborative process between writer, actor and director that would step up the contribution of the performer.
>
> (cited in Marowitz 1991: 60)

With this process, each actor must take responsibility for the creation of her/his role and for Jim Hiley, the *King Lear* of these enunciative conditions

> confirmed my suspicions that the Renaissance [Theatre Company] aesthetic itself could not be more paradoxical. Here is a company . . . founded to allow Shakespeare a fresh start, freeing the Bard from the whims of those state- subsidised directorial autocrats who in fact launched Branagh's

career. But does this actor honestly think that his brand of anaesthetised, non-interpretive Shakespeare does anyone any favours?

(1990: 1,070)

Certainly not according to the notorious constructor of Shakespeare collages, Charles Marowitz. He writes:

> Neither Mr. Branagh or Mr. Briers [the actor playing the lead role] had anything to tell us about *King Lear* other than that it was a great play easily mangled by actors' self-indulgence and trivialised by a repertory mentality that views it only as a series of comic or tragic vignettes. . . . Ironically, despite the abhorrence the company had for 'conceptions,' it was the *jumble* of conceptions which produced such disagreeable results. In attempting to demonstrate one proposition, the work had merely reconfirmed another.

(1991: 65)

A similar problem befell Jonathan Miller's 1982 production for the BBC television Shakespeare marathon. While here the interpretation is clear – *King Lear* is a tale of family life[8] – the proposition it attempts to demonstrate, that great plays can make great television, merely reconfirms another: that different media require very different techniques. Indeed, Miller himself makes this point:

> In the television productions of Shakespeare for which I was responsible I am embarrassed to admit that the most successful were those in which the scenery was more real and more pictorial than the nineteenth-century stage versions I have reacted violently against when directing in the theatre.

(1986: 65)

And if Miller expressed his dissatisfaction with this production, it's worth noting that, like the other *King Lears* discussed so far, this *King Lear* was hardly an original. As Susan Willis explains in her account of the BBC Shakespeare plays, Miller tried to reuse the *King Lear* that he had made for the BBC's 'Play of the Month' series in 1975:

> [T]hey [the BBC] insisted a new one had to be produced. Still fascinated and drawn to the play in 1982, Miller essentially remounted his 1975 production and its interpretation,

45

using more of the text but the same leading actors for Lear and the Fool, the same costume and design concepts, even some of the same blocking and characterization.

(1991: 127)

Twelve mainstream productions in less than ten years testify to some of that mainstream's assumptions about Shakespeare and the significance of his plays. First of all, it is clear that *King Lear* is, at this particular historical moment, an (if not *the*) example of a great play (the same is true in the substitution of the category 'tragedy,' this category standing as the most privileged example of its supra-category 'drama') and that it should (even if it does not always) make great theatre. It is equally clear that this first assertion can be proven in one of two ways: by producing a traditional approach, staying 'true' to the text, or by producing a radical approach which rearticulates the play's original discursive formation. But does this really work? Authenticity, we know, is impossible: we cannot *reproduce* (since we do not *know*) the original conditions of Shakespeare's stage or text and all performances, by virtue of the genre itself, are necessarily different. And, in the case of radical interpretation, this seems at best dubiously radical since theatre critics, and not only that specific viewing community, are always able to align a particular revision with one which has gone before. Neither is the currency of radical any guarantee of an oppositional or dissident impulse. Isobel Armstrong's blistering attack on David Hare's *King Lear* (Royal National Theatre, 1986) makes this point well and deservedly:

> Did so-called 'radical' Shakespeare productions achieve 'contestable values' by releasing 'the oppressed' into language or making power relations visible through it? . . . Masquerading as radical, it [Hare's production] was culturism at its very worst. There were no 'contestable' values in an incoherent reading: 'Family, religion, politics, madness, sex. . . . Take your pick' (programme notes). The logical end of culturism is consumerist Shakespeare. But if a production is to disclose 'contestable' ideology, taking your pick is just what you cannot do.
>
> (1989: 7)[9]

It is hardly a surprise, then, that John Field, a teacher and director of Shakespeare at Westminster School, when asked by *The Indepen-*

dent newspaper what he would wish for Shakespeare's birthday commemoration in 1991, suggested 'a ban on productions of *King Lear* for three years' ('Best Wishes, Bill' 1991: 17). That Field was ignored in fact only makes the sentiment more intense: in a piece published in the *Observer* the following year, actor Simon Treves lists as number four in his ten commandments for Shakespearean production, 'No, repeat no, productions of *King Lear* for at least 10 years. This yawnsome tract is possibly the most over-rated play of all time.' It's also striking that commandment number nine is quite simply: 'No red noses.'[10]

But these twelve productions of *King Lear* are only a partial picture of the reinvented Shakespeare of the 1980s. While they are, of course, powerful evidence of what Michael Bristol terms the 'something [which] certainly exists that compels the attention both of an attentive theatre-going audience and a large community of professional scholars and researchers' (1990: 19),[11] they are also reminders, as Bristol puts it, that obscured by this 'something' is the fact that

> the actual modes of human creativity that first generated the theatrical script of . . . *King Lear* . . . were in all likelihood collaborative and improvisatory . . . [and] were not the institutionally recognizable forms of individualized literary/artistic production . . . taken to be natural under present conditions.
>
> (1990: 18)

If authenticity and/or originality are impossible with the recognized theatrical script, those fetishized traces of the initial collaboration and improvisation now known as *King Lear*, it might be more productive to turn critical attention to some contemporary improvisation with and around those same textual traces. In this way we might better understand, as John Frow indicates, that 'the opposition of an authentic to an inauthentic gaze work[s] to repress an understanding of the investments (both financial and moral) that the circulation of cultural capital makes possible' (1991: 149). A multiplicity of competing Lears foregrounds precisely that understanding which a hegemonic authenticity works to negate.

PROLIFERATING LEAR(S)

'I saw a vision on my vision machine
I saw a vision but what did it mean?
They burned the sea and they burned the air
And I was drowning in my own despair
Till I tore that vision from the vision machine
And I played a different vision that I never had seen.'
(Lord Thomas, *King Real and the Hoodlums*,
in Lowe 1985: 23)

King Lear is no longer merely one part of the residual property attached to the name William Shakespeare. It has, like other Shakespeare(an) remains, become a visible and thus significant site for the contestation of cultural power. Producing *King Lear* might well be said to be, in the end, all about access and control: *King Lear* is (about) power. But King Lear and *King Lear* have proliferated into numerous reinventions, all of whom/which occupy a tense yet sometimes generative relation to their Ur-text. It is this relation posed as question – whether production can exceed the containing impulses of the apparatus of its source, whether some of these proliferations unmoor *King Lear*'s relation to/as power – that requires elaboration here.

The most famous reinvention of this and maybe any Shakespeare play is, undoubtedly, Edward Bond's 1971 *Lear*, and Bond's text fortunately falls into my survey of the 1980s since it was rewritten and revived for production by the Royal Shakespeare Company in 1982 (Stratford) and 1983 (London). Moreover this re-reproduced *Lear* played on consecutive nights to the Adrian Noble *King Lear* (the 'original' red nose) and how the critics read this double-bill is particularly revealing. For the most part, Bond's *Lear* is not a context for reviews of Shakespeare's play. Only one reviewer refers to it and labels the tandem arrangements (clearly pejoratively) 'schoolmasterly' (Cushman 1983: 422).[12] Elsewhere it garners a mention in the book-length survey of *King Lear* in performance (a text which covers eight 'landmark' productions between 1940 and 1983) where author Alexander Leggatt notes some visual echoes between *Lear* and *King Lear* and quotes Noble's intention to use the pairing to 'bring out the political dimension in Shakespeare's play' (1991: 70). On the other hand, reviews of Bond's play abound with comparisons, almost always negative, with Shakespeare's source text. A few examples demonstrate their mood:

Shakespeare's Lear makes a spiritual journey, Bond's a social
and political one.

(Nightingale 1983: 391)

Unlike Shakespeare, Bond has a tendency to preach . . . [a]nd
his play lacks the richness and compassion of the Shakespeare
original.

(Spencer 1983: 391)

There is no point in comparing it to Shakespeare, since Mr.
Bond's point isn't dramatic. It is moral. There is a message.
There is inevitably little or no attempt at characterisation, at
human relationships or at exploring anything.

(Shorter 1983: 390)

Equally, there might seem to be no point in telling the second
reviewer (Charles Spencer) about the multiple texts that make up
the Shakespeare 'original.' The power of Shakespeare's place in
contemporary culture – whether located in the sphere of academic
criticism or in theatrical practice – is in this instance at least starkly
apparent. As Ruby Cohn puts it, 'Unshavian . . . Bond does not
debate with the Bard. On the contrary, he is often in Shakespeare's
debt' (1991: 69).

Nonetheless Bond's *Lear* is one of those texts that contends for
the credit and designation of modern classic. It is an often-taught
play in courses on postwar dramatic literature; it almost always
appears in critical surveys of the same; and, moreover, it appears
on the stages of the Royal Shakespeare Company. Rosalind Carne
notes: 'Edward Bond's savage anatomy of power politics, with its
terrifying violence and huge cast . . . in Barry Kyle's masterly
production has convinced me at last that it is is a truly great play'
(1983: 392), and, indeed, in the terms with which she goes on to
praise Bond's work, she might be describing Shakespeare's own
King Lear. Her discourse includes references to depth of feeling,
cruel suffering, quasi-religious moments in the final act, and so
on. As with the twelve mainstream productions of *King Lear*
described above, Bond's *Lear* tests what a reader/spectator will allow
to happen to Shakespeare as an interpretive act, but it is as carefully and easily contained within the frame of a mainstream cultural
concept identified as theatre. This is, again, Alan Sinfield's caution
about doodling parasitic follies in the margins of that all-powerful
apparatus known as Shakespeare (1985c: 179). Yet one description,

by Carole Woddis in *City Limits*, points both to this and to a possible way out. She describes Bond's *Lear* as a 'modern master-piece (the emphasis is definitely on master, women assume either child-bearing or harpie proportions)' (1983: 392). This, I think, both names *Lear*'s overarching canonical status and hints at some subversive potential in releasing the play's women characters from the accretion of their historical representation. More generally, this might be asked as the following string of questions: What happens when the apparatus of the canon is challenged for its gaps and omissions? What happens when that apparatus is elucidated in a way that exposes its assumptions and the privileges that accrue to them? What happens when the conditions of production and reception materially change?

The trajectory for the roles for women in *King Lear* take two contemporary writers into the creation of prequels to Shakespeare's play: the 1987 *Lear's Daughters* by the Women's Theatre Group,[13] and the 1989 *Seven Lears*, a premiere production by the Wrestling School of Howard Barker's text. Barker introduces his text with this note:

> Shakespeare's *King Lear* is a family tragedy with a significant absence. The Mother is denied existence in *King Lear*. She is barely quoted even in the depths of rage or pity. She was therefore expunged from memory. This extinction can only be interpreted as repression. She was therefore the subject of an unjust hatred. This hatred was shared by Lear and all his daughters. This hatred, while unjust, may have been necessary.
>
> (1990: Introduction page, unnumbered)

If the idea of family tragedy is certainly not new (namely Jonathan Miller's 1975 and 1982 productions), the title to Barker's play appears as a promising strategy to proliferate the tragic hero, to destabilize a traditional focalization on a single and exemplary male character. But, alas, his *Seven Lears* in fact represent the seven ages of the one man. Neither is Barker concerned to re-member the Mother; he wants only, but slightly differently, to insist on her discipline and punishment. The prequel Lear is, like so many Barker plays, a violent and uncompromising (and ultimately misogynist) text, the bleakness of which is not difficult to tie to the Beckett and Bergman to which contemporary productions of Shakespeare's *King Lear* have been compared. Despite the playwright's declared aims and an alternative locus of production, *Seven Lears* relies precisely on its connection with the Ur-text it claims to challenge. More accurately, Barker's play might be read as adopting a Shakespearean antecedent as an intriguing and absolutely marketable device for what Cohn calls 'Barker's preferred theme of a quest for goodness in a world lacking ethical guides' (1991: 68).

In any event, *Seven Lears* transferred from the Wrestling School's home base of Sheffield to London's Royal Court Theatre, an appropriate destination since, of all London's major producing venues, the Court alone did not stage *King Lear* in the 1980s. 'Doing' *King Lear* (or *Lear*, for the Royal Court staged the premiere in 1971) or *Seven Lears* at the Court, the longtime home of literary drama, testifies to the fact that

> the project of reconstructing, reproducing, and disseminating the authority of Shakespeare remains strongly positioned within the politics of literary culture . . . [and t]his is evident in the continued absolutizing of Shakespeare's cultural and spiritual authority in many of the new discourses, irrespective of the ideological content assigned to that authority.
>
> (Bristol 1990: 27)

However strongly positioned, there are, I would argue, some proliferations which, at least in the moment of their performance, exceed and fracture the authority that they, in effect, address.

In the Women's Theatre Group's *Lear's Daughters*, there is perhaps the first 'new way' in this survey of the 1980s to play Shakespeare's text. It is a prequel which suggests different concerns and which explores them so as both to mark and to challenge the authority of Shakespeare, the cumulative power of mainstream production, and the operation of that authority in the politics of culture. Elaine Feinstein, a writer who is perhaps better known for her novels and poetry, worked with the Women's Theatre Group, one of the first and most enduring of Britain's feminist companies, to co-create (that is, to collaborate and improvise on) the *Lear's Daughters* script.[14] This play is undoubtedly a 'herstory' – it produces the gaps and absences of Shakespeare's (and Bond's and Barker's) texts and, as Lizbeth Goodman has suggested, addresses itself to a female/feminist spectatorship. Goodman calls the play 'a landmark in feminist "reinventing" of Shakespeare. It takes as its premise the notion that . . . all of history as presented in standard texts may

51

resemble a genealogy of "false fathers"' (1993: 220). The effect is a deconstruction of 'the fairy-tale structure which underpins *King Lear*' (Griffin and Aston 1991: 11). *Lear's Daughters* is also very much the production of a counter or disruptive genealogy which recalls Foucault's assertion that the task of genealogy is 'to expose a body totally imprinted by history and the process of history's destruction of the body' (1977: 148).

The five characters in the Women's Theatre Group play are the three daughters, the Nanny (a new invention who takes over the girls' upbringing after their own mother's death after many miscarriages – trying to produce the much-desired and much-demanded male heir) and the Fool (an androgynous master/mistress of ceremonies who also represents the Queen/natural mother by draping a veil over his/her head). No King Lear. Moreover, in accord with the Women's Theatre Group's artistic policy and counter to the lead-driven productions of the mainstream (Laurence Olivier *is* King Lear or even Ruth Maleczech as the woman who *would be* king), *Lear's Daughters* employed a multi-racial cast. This cast was also a fluid and changing ensemble, each permutation of which made possible a new reading of the play. Goodman notes that in the first production Regan and Goneril were played by black women and Cordelia by a white woman and that, in the second, all three sisters were represented by black women while the Fool and the Nanny were white (1993: 222). Since both parents are absent, these casting decisions present themselves to the audience as problematic – in terms of *Lear's Daughters*, in terms of *King Lear*, and, of course, in terms of the theatrical realism that remains a benchmark or normative in an audience's expectations.[15] Assumptions about a received interpretation of the play, as well as about strategies for counter interpretation(s), are called into question, and, perhaps most importantly, are not replaced with an obvious and single set of assumptions or skills. That King Lear is rendered only as absence foregrounds the absence of his wife (or even an elaborated reference to his wife) in the source text.

The Women's Theatre Group production brings into the spotlight what Shakespeare's play ignores and refuses; this, I think, does more than provoke a doodle in the margins. It asks audiences to intervene in and to reconstruct Shakespeare's play in an active and critical way. Goodman suggests that *Lear's Daughters* 'questions the mainstream casting of Shakespeare as the "fit father" of the literary-dramatic canon' (1993: 220). Moreover, if, for example, a received interpretation of *King Lear* is that it deals with 'family values' (that much-beloved phrase of the New Right) – and a number of the productions discussed here would suggest that this reading has much currency for the 1980s and 1990s – then *Lear's Daughters* asks its audiences to consider other configurations of family (in its own representations) as well as the economic operation of traditional family structures (in Shakespeare's source text, in contemporary culture, in their own lives). And thus, like so many of the shifted Shakespeares in Britain in the 1980s, *Lear's Daughters* does not merely talk back to *King Lear*; it argues with a government that prohibits 'pretended' families and that uses Shakespeare as one of its tools by which to maintain and promote its own regressive political views. Griffin and Aston conclude their discussion of the play with this assessment:

> As the fool and the nurse are both paid for their respective services, they offer a materialist discourse, a critique of capitalism. They are both employees in the household of a dictator who is responsible for the poverty throughout the land, for establishing a regime of the haves and have-nots. This makes *Lear's Daughters* a play which speaks directly to audiences of the Thatcherite years.
>
> (1991: 13)

Unlike the other productions of *King Lear* considered already in this chapter, *Lear's Daughters* was primarily a touring production, targeted at small theatres and other community venues. It did play for London audiences, but not at a subsidized or commercial theatre directed at a mainstream theatre-going public. The production toured across Britain in 1987 and, according to the Women's Theatre Group's publicity, toured again the following year by popular demand. Why such a demand existed and the relationship of that demand to the position of Shakespeare and his plays in contemporary British society (and elsewhere) are areas clearly deserving of careful unpacking,[16] but, to use here merely a generalization, I want to note the presence of a reinvented Shakespeare text that asks those different (oppositional) questions and that seeks a different target audience – a popular audience that, unlike the three million television viewers who tuned into the BBC *King Lear*, is not asked to celebrate the received (or so-called universal) qualities of Shakespeare's work.

Another reinvention that sought to address a specific viewing economy was Barrie Keeffe's *King of England*. This version, staged at the Theatre Royal (Stratford East) in 1988, suggests to Michael Billington that:

> King Lear has lost none of its potency as myth. . . . [Keeffe] uses the framework of Shakespeare's story to explore racial attitudes. The result frequently strains credibility but it is fascinating to see how the borrowed majesty of the source – and its shifting moral balance – gives weight to Mr. Keeffe's work.
>
> (1988: 125)

In Keeffe's play, the protagonist, Thomas Gilbert King, is dividing up among his daughters the spoils of his thirty-five years living (and working) in England as a driver for the London Underground subway system before he himself returns to his place of birth, Trinidad. In the storm scene, at night on the railway tracks at the Underground's Stratford depot in east London, King rails against life working for London Transport to the play's 'fool,' a meths-drinking Scottish dogcatcher. As with Billington's review cited above and as with the 1980s revival of Bond's *Lear* in tandem with its Shakespearean counterpart, critical response to *King of England* (which ranged from wildly enthusiastic to mildly damning) is anchored again and again by the play's relation to the Shakespeare text:

> It doesn't work. Lear has language and scale, the voyage of a foolish old man to self-discovery, its poetry epic; an Everest of a play.
> This version is about a silly old man rambling the foothills of disappointment, its language contorted to convey the different attitudes of conformist immigrants and British-born children who are not humble with gratitude.
>
> (Nathan 1988: 122)

> There is, undeniably, a weird poetry in the way Keeffe deploys the parallel and in Philip Hedley's fluent direction of it, but the superimposition of Lear's mythic angularities on this material confuses and obscures a worthwhile topic that would be better tackled head-on.
>
> (Paul Taylor 1988: 123)

That King Lear should arrive in modern Britain by way of the Central Line is highly appropriate if you happen to live near the Theatre Royal, in Stratford East; that he should be a black tube driver on the eve of his retirement ... is a marvelously resonant conceit, regardless of setting.

(Armistead 1988: 124)

His [Keeffe's] main theme is the progressive souring of the West Indian community – from post-war hope to post-capitalist hate – but on that truism he has nothing new or fresh to say. This wouldn't matter if the drama were powerful, but the Shakespearian echoes raise expectations which Keeffe's leaden script (compounded by Philip Hedley's leaden direction) repeatedly fails to fulfil.

(Church 1988: 124)

Tampering with the Bard is obviously a dangerous ploy. Either Keeffe's play fails to live up to expectations which apparently need no explanation (since they are universally known and recognized) or it strays into the wrong mode since 'we' are supposed to know that the oppressed lives of working-class Britons (and perhaps especially if they also happen to be black) are material for stage (or film or television) realism, not 'great' poetic drama. What is of particular interest in *King of England*, however, is its (ab)use of the source text for a local theatre-going public. The play takes up the global cultural awareness of Shakespeare's plays and resituates it in the specific experience of a community audience.[17] *King of England* engages with issues and problems common to the Stratford East constituency and explores them on a scale that Brecht insisted was crucial to both the pleasure and engagement which would inspire a popular audience not only to attend but to think. Neil Bartlett's review for *Time Out* is suggestive of this effect:

On paper Barrie Keeffe's fable ... is that kind of 'State of the Nation' play that usually seems stranded in the dead theatre politics of the late 70s. Anywhere but in Stratford, this might seem like a lecture. But here, animated and argued by an ensemble of careful, committed performers, these crucial hours in the life of one angry, confused, black family have the audience buzzing with comment and unexpected laughter. Keeffe's big, beautiful speeches are heard out in passionate silence and the final meeting between father and daughter had me crying more openly and thinking harder than I wanted to.

(1988: 122).

Like the Women's Theatre Group's *Lear's Daughters*, this refashioned *Lear* takes as its focus the possibility of dialogue with its audience. Neither are so much concerned with the question 'what have we done to Shakespeare's play?' (although both clearly work with the pleasure in recognition of connection to, yet difference from, the Shakespeare text) but with another which asks 'how can this material be useful to us?'

In the decade under discussion, and with this notion of utility in mind, two other British reinventions for community audiences deserve attention. One is the production of *King Lear* by Footsbarn, a company of British theatre professionals based in France. Opening their *King Lear* in Italy (1983), Footsbarn worked in their usual very physical style. From its inception, the production was constructed around music, sound, masks, and mime, keeping only 25–30 per cent of Shakespeare's text, a strategy which provoked one London reviewer to decide 'they are operating under the sign of Ariane Mnouchkine' (Ratcliffe 1985: 22). Members of the group, however, account for the development of these performance strategies in their seeking-out of non-English-speaking audiences:

> It's been a wonderful training. For example, working on *King Lear* in Italy and France, you realize suddenly how much you've relied on the language in the theatre, and how it is so unnecessary, though beautiful. How it's far more impor-tant to do things with the body, to feel the whole meaning of the thing in the construction of the scene, to show the audience what is going on just by what the character is doing. . . . It made us much more physical, to work out of England.
>
> (cited in Cousin 1985: 123)

In the Footsbarn *King Lear*, Goneril and Cordelia were doubled. When the two had to be on stage at the same time, another actor simply stepped into the role of Goneril. Unlike the doubling of Cordelia and the Fool in the mainstream productions already described, such doubling is more pragmatic than interpretive: the Fool and Regan, Gloucester and Albany, Edgar and Cornwall, Kent and Edmund were also doubled – and all actors performed as part of a Greek chorus written into the performance text. To avoid an effect of mere confusion – and thus taking account of the particular cultural training/expectations audiences bring to productions of Shakespeare's plays – Footsbarn facilitate spectatorial engagement through masks and color-coded costumes. Characters inhabit their own narratives, which may comment on others' narratives, but the thrust of this *King Lear* is to let the audience respond to the many and different competing texts.

In these ways, Footsbarn works against the idea of one production offering a/the definitive reading of Shakespeare's text for that (or any) historical moment and against the power of extraneous factors to predetermine codes of 'proper' response. Their focus is, instead, on the *means* of production: how a text might and can be embodied. Such an approach, although quite different in philosophy and articulation from Kristin Linklater's commentary on voice, similarly makes explicit the parameters for the conventional training of actors to 'do' Shakespeare and equally for the training of spectators to 'see' Shakespeare. It is not only about what bodies receive permission to represent Shakespeare's text and how, but also about where those bodies can be visible. Footsbarn's *King Lear* is, in effect, the spectacle of Shakespeare rendered spectacular.

While audiences of almost 50,000 saw the 122 performances of Footsbarn's *King Lear* in 1983–4, no British audiences saw the play at that time. One member of the group comments:

> The company is now fourteen years old. It's no longer a kind of fringe alternative. It's a professional touring company, and it should by rights have a forum in England. . . . I think it would be very interesting for other groups and people in general to witness the development of this particular company.
>
> (in Cousin 1985: 125–126)

Paradoxically, when their version of *King Lear* played in London in 1985, one reviewer decided: 'This seriously thought-out production seems, in many ways, closer to the heart of the Bard than what we often see at Stratford [-on-Avon, the Royal Shakespeare Company's mid-England location]' (Gordon 1985: 22).[18] This observation remakes Footsbarn's point about the operation of cultural authority in the production of English theatre, especially if that theatre is constructed around the Shakespeare canon.

Far from the heart of the Bard, however, is *The Tragedy of King Real*, produced by Welfare State, another of Britain's alternative theatre groups with a long and radical history. Their work on this Lear project marked their first engagement in a seven-year residency in the northern English town of Barrow-in-Furness. Commissioning text from poet/playwright Adrian Mitchell and music from Pete Moser, Welfare State began the creation of a site-specific performance which would also be presented in a filmed version (then retitled as *King Real and the Hoodlums*). And, since the idea was to create work with and for the local population, their immediate economic geography gave shape to the project's concerns.

Barrow-in-Furness, with a population of around 70,000, had a single major employer (14,000 jobs) – Vickers Shipbuilding and Engineering Limited – which produced, among other things, nuclear submarines.[19] Like very many other English towns of its size outside the London area, Barrow-in-Furness also suffered from high unemployment in the 1980s and indeed 1990s. Against these two 'givens,' Welfare State planned to use their innovative mix of Brechtian and Bakhtinian techniques to create what they call 'critical carnival.' The writer for *King Real*, Mitchell, describes Welfare State as 'a practical, visionary group that I had no hesitation in asking to design and enact a nuclear war' (cited in Lowe 1985: 3). On his own debt to Shakespeare's play, Mitchell simply comments: '*King Lear* is the greatest piece of writing in the English language and I have used its story and many of its beautiful lines because I needed them' (cited in Lowe 1985: 3). But what Mitchell does with *King Lear* (or, for that matter, *King Real*) is and was only ever one component of this production. As Baz Kershaw puts it, '[w]here the film was made, and who it is made by, is as important to its significance as its use of *King Lear*' (1991: 252). Welfare State, then, sought to establish a co-creative process of production and reception with its local community and to facilitate the community's political (that is, oppositional) engagement through its collaboration on this nuclear age Lear. Notwithstanding the goals of Welfare State's critical carnival, it is important to contextualize such ambitions in what was not necessarily a hospitable environment:

> In fact, the 'politics' of *King Real and the Hoodlums* were so radical for the context that Welfare State almost came unstuck at the very beginning of their residency in the town. The rewrite of Shakespeare seemed deliberately to invite

the Barrovian cold-shoulder, even though, according to Welfare State, it was made in the best interests of the community.

(1991: 250)

Thus there was in no sense a pre-existent congruence between the theatre facilitators and their actors and audiences in the way that the collaborative development of *Lear's Daughters* might have relied on a women-centered commonality of interest.

It is of course possible to think of the audiences for mainstream theatres as local, yet the Welfare State project differs from all the other Lears discussed here in the degree of collaboration with its target audience. While the commissioned elements (Mitchell's script and Moser's music, with Shakespeare's text shadowing both) must have imposed particular directions on the making of the play/film, their enactment was achieved almost completely by local people becoming performers in order to realize the event/project.[20] About fifty Barrovians were employed, none of them professional actors and most of them drawn from the ranks of the unemployed. Moreover, the 'junk' submarine that formed the centerpiece of the production's procession through Barrow (where the size of the cast expanded considerably as others joined the Hoodlums in their march) was constructed by young apprentices from VSEL. Such strategies work to involve the community in obviously tangible ways: for example, they provide (and are recognized for) the talent that makes the performance happen and they use skills in ways that transgress what are otherwise limited and carefully regulated uses. In these two instances, Welfare State facilitate the self-empowerment of the actor/constituent in the drama. As Kershaw has pointed out, the creation of such a vehemently anti-nuclear production foregrounded a complexity of paradoxes with which Barrovians might engage. Among these were the fact that '[p]rior to the company's arrival, high-profile critical representations of the shipyard were always imported into the town from outside' (Kershaw 1992: 241); this was Barrow's own youth worrying out loud and in public about the manufacture of weapons and behaviors which can so easily produce mass devastation. And the production made explicit the town's own investment in an economy of death which if lost would lead to the town's own virtual demise with the inevitable closing of the shipyard (Kershaw 1992: 215–220). Of course, all of this adds up to leftist nostalgia: the attainment of socially responsible criticism through the production of site-specific community-relevant art. And I am conscious that my own preference for this possibility of resistance privileges these nostalgic interventions – like Kershaw and like Welfare State, what I record here is a wistful hope that art can indeed inspire social change.

To me, the most important elements both of the play itself (as text) and in its performance (as live action and the subsequent film) are their claiming of importance within and with a particular local geography. Clearly what interaction and creativity is gained in the process and immediacy of the production is mediated by the fixed and finished nature of the film[21] but Welfare State counter the cultural expectation and practice of passivity in the filmic spectator with a repositioning of representational codes. The 'stars' of the film are, with a single exception, drawn from the local community and the film is showcased as a cultural landmark and success of that community: '[t]he world-premiere showing was at the Astra, Barrow's only cinema, with all the silly razzmatazz of a feature film opening reproduced in satiric extravagance: with limousines and red carpets' (Coult & Kershaw 1990: 224). The point that needs making here is that both mainstream culture (the box-office smash movie) and counter-cultural representation (the Campaign for Nuclear Disarmament march) were heretofore imported forms.[22] In *The Tragedy of King Real/King Real and the Hoodlums*, Barrovians themselves become involved both in the making and the celebration of performance: they recognize (some of) themselves, they recognize their geography as subject and object of cultural practice, and they claim their right to make and celebrate art. It is on these multiple and micropolitical levels of recognition that this Lear can be particularly useful.

The indulgence of mainstream critical practice in playing the games of 'spot-the-connection' to Shakespeare's text, followed almost inevitably by an explanation of the production's inadequacies, does, indeed, seem to be academic pedantry. As much as Adrian Noble's red-nosed King Lear (which called to mind Brook, Beckett, Kurosawa and other cultural heavyweights) or Edward Bond's marxist Lear dared a redefinition of the power politics of Shakespeare's text, *King Real and the Hoodlums* assumes and exploits its audience's recognition of the authority of the source text, albeit here a distant source. It is because the Barrovians in their 'cultural desert' know what – or, better put, *how* – Shakespeare *means* in

60

contemporary culture, that the performance of a dissident Lear can be as expedient as it is.

Nevertheless it can be argued that this is an overly simple or naive response to Welfare State's mode of operation and certainly *King Real* was not happily or wholeheartedly embraced by the community it was a part of:

> To the conservatively-minded the attack on the nuclear powerbase was unjustified aggression towards a community that had no choice about which industry it relied on for is survival. To others it seemed that Welfare State was corrupting their young with enticing but brainwashing subversive fun. Yet even the most critical Barrovian had to admit that it was better that the unemployed young should be creatively engaged rather than roaming the streets, and after all Welfare State had brought a little money into the town with grants from the Arts Council and Marks and Spencer.
>
> (Coult and Kershaw 1990: 224)

From this assessment of Welfare State's inaugural project with the Barrow community it is clear that such obviously oppositional performance does not work to change behaviors or even opinions on a mass scale. The vocabulary employed by Coult and Kershaw in this assessment depends on a Right/Left binarism that I've already suggested characterizes academic (Shakespearean) criticism yet concludes with the mutual expression of more than a little of the 'venture capitalism' which characterized Thatcherite policy.

But the range of response is, I would argue, in itself a radical act. Kershaw uses the intertextuality 'operating in the *King Lear* – *The Tragedy of King Real* – *King Real and the Hoodlums* nexus' (1991: 258) to contradict the irritating and too generally held assumption that popular theatre means uncomplicated theatre: he argues that spectatorial awareness of all the texts at play here create a more complex and dynamic debate on issues of nuclear warfare. And certainly for the fifty or so Barrovians who produced the work (as well as their immediate community of friends and family), there was an engagement with the debate that no doubt had an intensity that they might not have encountered otherwise. Accounts of the project also point to other spinoffs: a couple of the actors went on to train professionally at college, Welfare State developed their interaction with the Barrow community, which only four years later included a performance at the city hall before an audience of 15,000 – more than the workforce total at VSEL – and so on.[23] Shakespeare in this particular service of job creation and audience building might be seen as a parodic refashioning of his most conservative impulses.

Welfare State's extended residency in Barrow functions, like this first project using *King Lear*, as a refusal of the dominant assumption that, for a community of this size and demography, art (and its critical reception) must necessarily come from elsewhere. The fact that the conversation on the production of art – who gets to make it and who pays for it – is raised in the work itself and in the local response to it, has, too, a potential for further development. In her review of *Politics of Performance* (1992), Kershaw's account of alternative/marginalized theatrical production in England, Loren Kruger concludes that it is necessary to 'read the moments of contradiction alongside those of argumentative force and evocative power . . . as signs of the fragility but also of the potential of cultural intervention through the theatre' (1993: 129). This is, I think, a useful summary which might also be applied to Welfare State's work. *The Tragedy of King Real/King Real and the Hoodlums* is loaded with contradiction, but it has, also in its creation and performance, the potential for cultural intervention. The success of this work (and, I would argue, it is a success simply on the terms of its involving a proportion of the community in the making of engaged art) validates Robins's argument that there is a counter-market to the global:

> the new geographies are, in fact, about the renaissance of locality and region. There has been a great surge of interest recently in local economies and local economic strategies. The case for the local or regional economy as the key unit of production has been forcefully made by the 'flexible specialization' thesis.
>
> (1991: 33)[24]

While Robins is surely right to see the local as 'a fluid and relational space, constituted only in and through its relation to the global' (1991: 36), the possibilities for 'flexible specialization' offer some seemingly resistant and resisting spaces.

Seventeen Lears in a decade. Many new ways to play old texts and many more old ways to make new texts. What I want to engage with is how all these productions – how the proliferation of a representation which can carry, uphold and occasionally subvert the weight and authority accorded to the figure of Lear whose traces occupy the proliferated editions of (some version of) Shakespeare's text – might provoke some different ways of thinking about our performance of the past. In short, I seek a more self-conscious realization of our own acts of disseminating that past in the present. But, before that task, I want to complicate a little more this account of the seventeen Lears.

RE-VIEWING ONE *KING LEAR* AND REVIEWING A *KING LEAR* THAT IS NOTHING

> PLUGGY: One is always disobedient in some way to something. . . .
> WM SHAKESPEARE JR V: Or obedient to something.
> PLUGGY: Yes. But disobedience is more interesting to study.
> WM SHAKESPEARE JR V: My orders are to bring the work of my ancestor to life. And I can't stop till the story's over.
> (Jean-Luc Godard, *King Lear*, 1987)

> 'The production frightened the life out of me. . . .
> King Lear was like my father, an old bigot. It was like home. All the fighting and noise.'
> 'Why did that old git there, the old man, frighten me like my father used to?'
> (Responses of patients at Broadmoor Secure Psychiatric Hospital, cited in Cox 1992: 137, 151)

My account of the seventeen Lears started in 1990 with Deborah Warner's production for the Royal Shakespeare Company, one I suggested rested heavily on productions of *King Lear* that had already been seen on the British stage in previous years. Just to make my description of this and the other productions probably a little obvious, let me insist that the account of these productions is not to downplay the abilities or the imaginations of Warner or any of the other directors who work with this text but to demonstrate the resilience of critical communities who make sense of a production by noticing primarily its resemblances to other productions. Warner's *King Lear*, then, comes with baggage that she, as director, may or may not want: alongside all the Shakespeareana, there is too her own reputation as a director, the actors' qualifications (previous Shakespearean roles in particular), the Royal Shakespeare Company as institution, the architecture and geography of their regular playing spaces in London and Stratford, and on and on. Theatre reviews come as much from the context as from the text or the production itself. What happens to a production when it is removed from much of this contextual apparatus stands here in the re-production of Warner's *King Lear* at the Broadmoor Secure Psychiatric Hospital. What happens to a production when it takes as its subject the contextual apparatus appears here in the metafilmic strategies of Jean-Luc Godard's *King Lear* (1987).

In a fascinating account, Murray Cox gathers testimonies, interviews and commentaries around the performance of Shakespeare's plays by the Royal Shakespeare, Royal National Theatre and other companies to inmates/patients at England's secure psychiatric hospital, Broadmoor:[25] one of the productions discussed is Warner's *King Lear*. Like Cox, I have to claim that this is not the place for a discussion of the function of drama/theatre in a custodial setting;[26] my discussion is to illustrate some of the shifts experienced by the actors and the director (the Warner *King Lear* had had over a hundred performances by the time it played at Broadmoor) and some of the responses of staff and patients documented in Cox's book.

Interviews with Brian Cox (King Lear) and Claire Higgins (Regan) point to the effects on their own performances of playing to an audience which they perceived to have different expectations from a mainstream theatre-going public.[27] For Higgins, playing a Shakespearean role at Broadmoor was not a first-time experience; she had earlier been there with Ron Daniels's production of *Hamlet* for the Royal Shakespeare Company. She talks of her performance of Gertrude:

> On a first night, you know that a well-heeled audience is coming in to watch you do a *Hamlet* . . . and there are a whole series of things that have already been set up: the show is being done for critics, it is being done for success. None of those levels were present at Broadmoor. This seemed to me to be the bottom line. I don't know how long it took for me to realise that the experience we were having was something extraordinary; but a feeling grew for me after I did my first scene, and sat down and started watching, that this was not like any audience I had ever played to: there seemed to be a whole layer of expectations that they simply did not have. And as the play progressed I realised that I was

in an arena that was much freer, and it became a liberating experience.

(Interview with Ann Barker; in Cox 1992: 66)

Brian Cox makes much the same sort of point about the emancipatory difference of performing to this extraordinary spectatorship. Interestingly, this enables him to imagine a purity in the field of production/reception that he identifies as resembling the original (that is, Shakespearean) experience:

> In a way the audience was like an Elizabethan audience. It was an audience of people whose brains were so sharp, because their sense of the language and imagery was so sharp. ... I sensed the Broadmoor audience had that kind of Elizabethan clarity, a kind of space which meant that everything had an extra reverberation because it was so direct.
>
> (Interview with Rob Ferris; in Cox 1992: 51–52)

While Brian Cox is certainly contributing to the obsessive valorization of the past experience (audiences were better then), what both actors point to is that when the usual conditions of production and reception are tampered with, rendered in some way unpredictable, the text and/or the performance comes to mean in different and occasionally surprising ways. At least when the actors *believe* that those conditions have been altered, the text and/or the performance comes to mean to them differently. This, in itself, suggests the tenacity of ideas around cultural privilege.

Responses recorded from the audience suggest the same pattern. The selection provided suggests that all kinds of expectations were brought into the Central Hall at Broadmoor: some of the spectators had experience of live theatre, others make comparison to television and film and, for some, this is clearly an entirely new phenomenon. In among all the praise ('More dramatic than I expected a Shakespeare play to be' [Cox 1992: 136]) and the brickbats ('It would have been a million times better if they had spoken in today's English' [Cox 1992: 142]), what is striking is a constant desire to take responses directly into their own realities:

> 'I found the production so powerful that I had to leave. It was like my own family – that's how they carry on. I thought I was losing my life.'
>
> (Cox 1992: 137)

> 'This made me think how unaware I was about other people's feelings when committing my crimes . . . I asked one of the actors how he put his heart into the role. He said to me "Understand the character and feel what he must have felt like." I had to think of my victims how they felt. It was an experience I will never forget.'
>
> (Cox 1992: 143)

> 'It's really strange for you to bring a play about madness to Broadmoor – we are so protected from it here.'
>
> (Cox 1992: 148)

and, perhaps most usefully,

> 'I have not been able to take in much of the production as I was preoccupied with my own problems.'
>
> (Cox 1992: 137)

It is not that Shakespeare appeals to universal themes, but that the language used to talk about certain ideas (of madness, of expiation) makes sense of some particular experience of the patient/spectator who encounters its representation.

In many ways, the record of the production and reception of *King Lear* at Broadmoor is an account of the economy of the 'real.' It is not that the patients are confused that what they are seeing is representation, but that it makes explicit a performance of the 'real' in their own lives which has been interpreted for them by and in the law. It is not, then, that this audience is profoundly 'different' from the audiences in mainstream theatres but that the context of their access to a production is explicitly so.

If dislocating *King Lear* (or, more precisely, its context) from prevailing assumptions and expectations about both Shakespeare and the performance of his (or others') plays produces, among other things, a collaborative production of what the text might mean (this production at Broadmoor or Welfare State's *King Real* in Barrow), then at the other end of the high/low continuum for viewing economies is Jean Luc Godard's film of the play. Like so many of the examples cited, this King Lear draws attention to its own precedents: Raymond Durgnat, reviewing Godard's film for *Monthly Film Bulletin*, notes that Shakespeare's play is 'notoriously the basis of *House of Strangers* [Joseph Mankiewicz, 1949], about an Italian-American bank director with three sons; of *Broken Lance* [Edward Dmytryk, 1954], about a Wild West cattle baron with sons of mixed race; and of *Ran'* (1988: 788). And as a further indication of the play's cultural currency and fluidity, Michael Billington's review of Keeffe's *King of England* opens with a cross-reference to Godard's film: the simultaneous availability of both in London proving that "*King Lear* has lost none its potency as myth" (1988: 125).

The story of Godard's *King Lear* (and, indeed, the film itself) starts with its own potent myth: the signing of a contract on the back of a napkin at a lunch that took place at the 1985 Cannes Film Festival between Godard and Cannon Film chiefs Menahem Golan and Yoram Globus. The film was to be a modern-day interpretation of the Shakespeare text, written by Norman Mailer, who would also take the lead role, with his daughter Kate in the role of Cordelia. In the opening shots of the film, Mailer is writing his screenplay but this scenario is soon interrupted by the director's voiceover: 'It was not Lear with three daughters but Kate with three fathers. Mailer as star, as father, me as a director. Too much indeed for this young lady from Provincetown.' Mailer and his daughter walk off the set as they had done literally, rumored to be as a result of Godard's insistence on an incestuous reading of the Lear/Cordelia relationship (something the film that does get made teases toward with images of heavily bloodstained sheets in the hotel bedroom and worn looks from Cordelia, now played by Molly Ringwald). Don Learo, a gangland version of Shakespeare's monarch, performs the symbolic Father role but it is not this issue which preoccupies Godard's film.

The film constantly refers to the apparatus by which it becomes filmic product, from the signing of the contract on the much-noted napkin to the suturing of film reels with a needle and thread, a performance by Woody Allen as Mr. Alien (wearing a very spiffy Picasso T-shirt). Such self-consciousness, not surprisingly, brings its critics. Kevin Thomas in the *Los Angeles Times* writes: 'It's a highly fragmented home movie-like meditation on the impossibility of revitalizing the classics, featuring a barrage of asides on the sound track and the most bizarre cast (coyly unbilled) since Orson Welles' *Touch of Evil'* (1988: 797). And Judith Williamson in the *New Statesman* comments: 'there is a kind of easy cynicism about Godard's relation to Cannon which pervades this whole film: whose self-referential comments on its immediate context consist merely of a repetitive harping about the constraints of working on "bankable projects" for "philistines"' (1988: 800).

What Godard's film for Cannon does to *King Lear* is to question the stability of the play's place in The (literary) Canon: William
Shakespeare Junior V reminds everyone he is 'on duty' for the
cultural division of Cannon; he might equally be seen to serve
the canonical division of culture. In the post-Chernobyl, post-
apocalypse world that Sellars's character stumbles through, there are
only the slightest traces of the literary world that once existed:
from Don Learo and Cordelia he retrieves some of Shakespeare's
lines; later in the film a copy of Virginia Woolf's *The Waves* is
washed up on the beach. What he (or 'we') make of those traces
is, the film argues, pure (re)invention. Peter Donaldson ventures
that the intervention of Woolf's text facilitates Godard's 'experiments in the "feminine" reinscription of patriarchal texts' (1990:
219). And to some extent this is true, but nonetheless the overall
landscape of the film is one in which patriarchal power (Don Learo)
is enlisted to recover Culture (William Shakespeare Junior V),
which is then reconstructed by the Artist (Godard, who plays
Professor Pluggy in the film, and Allen as Alien). Cordelia and
Virginia (Woolf?), Edgar's girlfriend, are no more than bit players
in the action. In other words, the depoliticization of aesthetics that
Donaldson's conjecture relies upon is, in reality, a patriarchial
sinecure on which Shakespeare's *King Lear*, Barker's *Seven Lears* and
Godard's film root their aesthetic claims.

It would easy to recuperate Godard's critical landscape for the dark
and bleak vision of the Jacobean (a subject explored at some length
in the next chapter) were it not for his insistence on keeping both
the economic and the filmic structures visible. Still shots of slogans
effect both a Brechtian *Verfremdungseffekt* and a poststructuralist
linguistic playfulness. As interventions they insist on the freedom to
construct our narratives as no more than a wishful fantasy that is
subject not only to the rules of language, but to the economic realities of film/text distribution. For all the wit of the film's assemblage,
it is, as David Sterritt has commented, 'an exercise in pure film-
making . . . less to entertain us than to get us thinking about issues
of art and power (symbolized by the odd marriage of Godard and
the Cannon company)' (1988: 796). In a very different context,
Judith Butler elucidates a political signifier as the sedimentation of
prior signifiers,

> drawing the phantasmatic promise of those prior signifiers,
> reworking them into the production and promise of 'the new,'

a 'new' that is itself only established through recourse to those embedded conventions, past conventions, that have conventionally been invested with the political power to signify the future.

(1993: 220)

Godard's *King Lear* reaches much the same conclusions. A phantasmatic promise of the past provokes Shakespeare Junior's quest for a 'new' that might in some or other way reinstate a power with which to anchor the future. Always doomed to fail, to discover the project incomplete, to mark its own nostalgic terrain, the film lays bare the conventional power of the privileged signifier and its expression in those agencies which disseminate sanctioned forms of cultural product.

THE HYBRID KING LEAR: CROSSING CULTURE, CROSSING GENDER

[I]t would be idle to pretend that the Kathakali King Lear is to most of us more than a ritualised, rainbow-hued spectacle.
(Billington 1990: 1,083)

MISS LA TROBE: I thought I'd bring you all out here under the trees to read this, in my opinion, Shakespeare's greatest tragedy. ... [I]t is the struggle between man and nature as well as between man and man, and between man and himself that make this, for me, his masterwork.
(Michael Gow, *Away in Brisbane* 1989: 336)

Michael Gow's 1986 play *Away*, a premiere production for the Griffin Theatre Company in Sydney, is framed by its school setting as yet another dissemination of privileged cultural/political signifiers. The wonderfully ridiculous schoolteacher Miss La Trobe functions at the close of his play to articulate all the colonial assumptions that the Australian education system imbues in and demands of its students.[28] Editor Katherine Brisbane notes that all Gow's plays 'are an attempt to make sense of a country burdened with an imported culture' (1989: xxi) and La Trobe's reading of *King Lear* is one that insists on the injunctions of imperial authority.[29] 'Shakespeare' in Gow's play demonstrates that 'Australia' (as a colonial practice rather than a physical geography) has made no cross-cultural demands on canonical texts. *King Lear* is resolutely

69

a masterwork. While Gow's tongue-in-cheek performance of Australian schoolchildren performing Shakespeare reiterates the durability of imperial tradition, other *King Lears* in the decade have attempted more complicated renditions of cultural hybridity.

Most attention has accrued to *Kathakali King Lear*, a South Indian dance-drama adaptation of Shakespeare's play, produced by a multinational cast for international production. Conceived by David McRuvie, an Australian who became director, and Annette Leday, a French actor/dancer, *Kathakali King Lear* was co-produced by their Association Keli, based in Paris, and the Kerala State Arts Academy in India. McRuvie provided a much edited version of Shakespeare's text, retaining only the father/daughter plot, which was then translated into Malayalam, the regional language of Kerala.[30] And this suggests a daring experiment in the fusion of two overcoded vocabularies of performance. Yet more ambition in the project is revealed by its global production: performances were staged first in Kerala then in Italy, the Netherlands, France, Spain, Singapore and Britain. As might be expected, the *Kathakali/* Shakespeare 'hybrid' provoked a diversity of responses, many of which were explicitly attached to specificities of cultural identification. Phillip Zarrilli offers a full and important account of its performance of 'the relationship between production, perception, and reception in a postmodern intercultural world' (1992. 10). He argues that its intent was not the creation of an exotic Other for the entertainment of the West but that it would 'speak equally to both its original audiences':

> For Malayalis the production was intended to provide a *kathakali* experience of one of Shakespeare's great plays and roles. Assuming that many in the European audience would know Shakespeare's play, the production was intended as an accessible way of experiencing *kathakali* and the aesthetic delight of *rasa*.
>
> (1992: 19)

In Britain (where it played first at the Edinburgh Festival and then in London), *Kathakali King Lear* met, obviously, with audiences (or at least critics) who had been well (over)exposed to *King Lear*. Critical opinion was, for the most part, negative, although with some wildly enthusiastic exceptions, such as Randall Stevenson: 'It wrings the heart and moves the performance forward into another dimension: towards the awesome, elemental world from which Shakespeare's original vision was compounded. Rhythmic, graceful, resonant, Kathakali has enormous potential for Western eyes and ears' (1990: 1,084). To some degree, this might mark the success of McRuvie and Leday's intercultural experiment; there is undoubted merit in producing an ability to see and hear anew. But even Stevenson's enthusiasm is grounded in a monoculturalism that pervades much of the production criticism. Less charitably, John   Percival   writes:

> None of this [Kathakali technique and movement] does much for Shakespeare. It does not throw new light on the characters or their situation, and the simplification of the plot, apparently necessary to meet Kathakali conventions of length and number of characters, is crippling.
>
> Does it, on the other hand, benefit the Kathakali tradition to get away from its usual subject matter of gods, kings and demons? Perhaps, for its audience in Kerala, but why not go the whole hog and tackle a modern, original subject? This *Lear* looks like a curiosity; a side issue rather than a new departure.
>
> (1990: 1,084)

And Michael Billington comments, 'I responded to the show's vibrancy and colour while remaining deeply frustrated: it was like landing in a foreign country where one doesn't speak a word of the language' (1990: 1083). Their touchstone is necessarily Shakespeare and, by extension, England. The reviews perform an unabashed colonialism that calls into question not only the possibility of intercultural theatre as a global phenomenon but also an unaware construction of their own British audiences as a white Anglo-Saxon monolith. As Rustom Bharucha points out in a critique of Patrice Pavis's theorization of intercultural performance (where 'source culture' is made intelligible to audiences from a 'target culture'):[31]

> one has to acknowledge that within the 'target audience' there could be members from a 'source culture' who would read the so-called 're-elaboration' [Pavis's term] of their culture in a significantly different way from the way a 'target audience' is expected to read it. Interculturalism has to account for different ways of seeing, otherwise it is yet another homogenized practice.
>
> (1993: 242)

If European audiences were bound, one way or another, to see 'their' text floating 'in some kind of make-believe India, somewhere between imagination and reality' (Bharucha 1993: 82),[32] then the reception in the reality of India, and specifically Kerala, was more blatantly controversial. Something of the project's complicity with a contemporary nostalgia for, and adherence to, the imperial project was ironically present in the semiotic field of its performance. Its premiere was staged 'on the proscenium stage of the Victorian styled V.J.T. Hall, Trivandrum, Kerala, India' (Zarrilli 1992: 17). It is as if the residue of colonialism – in its architectural/architextual monuments – must necessarily filter the indigenous cultural practices of the apparently post-colonial geography. Zarrilli suggests that the production stimulated 'a continuing "internal cultural debate" within the *kathakali* cultural community over the limits of experimentation within the tradition' (1992: 29).

More vehemently, the former chair of the National Drama School in Delhi, Suresh Awasthi, published (significantly in a British publication, the Cambridge University Press journal *New Theatre Quarterly*) an indictment of both the structuring and methodology of the work. He notes the impressive list of credits – translators, choreographers, musical director, artistic advisor, production directors and so on – and comments:

> Such a credit list is entirely alien to the Kathakali tradition and its performance structure. There is no choreographer, no music director, and no artistic or production director: rather, performers 'carry' in their bodily performance a score of role-typing and a performance implies decoding this score.
>
> (1993: 173)

In the strength of its own cultural tradition, this transgressive adaptation of *Kathakali* invokes a sense of a bodily violation written both on the performers and the 'source' audience.

Awasthi further enumerates the performance codes of *Kathakali* which he believes are destroyed by the meshing of Shakespeare's semantic layers. *Kathakali*, he notes, develops from a 'traditionally inherited performance score' which is defined and refined through 'intuitive improvisation' by each generation of practitioners:

> [i]t is because of this elaboration and embellishment that the performance time of Kathakali playscripts of some twenty pages, reading which would take no more than forty to fifty

minutes, in recitative verses and songs stretches to nine hours. Such a process of renewal and updating of tradition is integral to the aesthetic system of the Indian performance tradition.

(1993: 173)

In short, the experiment in interculturalism is, in Awasthi's reading, an unacceptable transgression of the traditions of performance time and aesthetic system. Zarrilli, a much more enthusiastic respondent to the experiment, concludes:

> Although *Kathakali King Lear* was conceived ideally as an intercultural project to be performed for Kerala and European audiences, the commercial realities . . . the Western Lear narrative, and McRuvie's directorial eye naturally shaped the production for a primarily Western theatregoing public. In doing so, it may not have been as well received by Malayali audiences as Western audiences. . . . Leday and McRuvie's project intentionally kept an active tension between a simplified Western narrative played in a fully codified theatrical and choreographic reelaboration of that narrative.
>
> (1992: 36)

The *Kathakali King Lear* is, ultimately, a rendition of the contradiction and conflict between two powerfully inscribed performance traditions, both carrying and demonstrating the weight of national histories. Rather than a performance which gestures towards an actual interculturalism, there is in its stead an articulation of the complexities of both orientalism and occidentalism, a double phenomenon which might be said to characterize the practices of contemporary global economies.

When Bharucha criticizes Brook's *Mahabharata* for its erasure of history 'and the endorsement it received from an international press of a "transcultural" sensibility somehow transcending the contradictions of our times' (1993: 245), he relocates the possibilities of proliferation in a context of multiple histories. In those histories we might recognize the very bases of power inequities which 'theatrical and choreographic reelaborations' might be said to mask. Or, as Bharucha summarizes it:

> [t]he body-culture of any actor cannot be separated from the history in which it is placed and the larger processes of politicization to which it is compelled to submit *and resist*. History,

unfortunately, is precisely what interculturalists for the most part have tacitly avoided.

(1993: 245, emphasis in original)

The *Kathakali King Lear* is, in this way, an informative example of experimentation with 'tradition' at the expense of the material histories of its subject(s). When Patrice Pavis asserts that 'Shakespeare remains the classic *par excellence*, the obligatory reference point for all scholars' (1993: 287), he enforces just that exclusion and denies, among other things, Awasthi's claim for a particular and equally long-standing Indian performance history.

Less well-known intercultural 'experiments' have raised related issues. Amal Allana's 1989 production of *King Lear* in an artificially constructed village complex on the site of the New Delhi Trade Fair took as its 'environmental scenography' the irreconcilable presence of the indigene and the tourist. The site was constructed in part for a tourist population; *King Lear* is similarly a site primed for the tourist visit. Balwant Gargi discusses the effect of fixing the audience in the performance environment and having the action of Allana's interpretation of *King Lear* surround them. It is as if the audience is secured in the territory and the performers must seek out the possibilities of their occupying that space. Moreover, Allana's production took account of the fact '[t]he father–daughter relationship in Indian society is very deep' (Gargi 1991: 96); she wove her version to speak to the cultural experience of her spectators. Unlike the Leday–McRuvie *King Lear* (or, for that matter Brook's *Mahabharata*), this *King Lear* seems to be offered as an open investigation of whether a canonical and colonial Western text might speak to its Other's realities. Allana's respect for the places and peoples of her 'target audience' suggests much more of an intention for dialogue.

It is undoubtedly true, however, that any encounter between Shakespeare, perhaps the definitive marker of the imperial archive, and those nations imagined as post-colonial, is lodged in an overdetermined matrix of submission and resistance which precludes a productive – or any – interculturalism. As Bharucha insists, we must always first play to 'historical contradictions' (1993: 250). This is the topic for my own investigation of the possibilities for the post-colonial body, chapter four in this book. Nonetheless, the determined proliferations of Shakespeare in a global economy are often made to stand in the name of intercultural practice. And with that comes a well-intentioned, if not so well-directed, optimism. In the United States, the 1988 adaptation of *King Lear* (as *The Tale of Lear*) by Japanese-born director Suzuki Tadashi attempted just such a manoeuvre in his first English-language production. Eric Hill, the actor who played Edmund (a role which involved a six-week workshop in the remote mountain village of Togamura, Japan), suggests the production's cross-historical, cross-cultural legibility:

> In the modern world, as in both the ancient Greek world and the Elizabethan world that spawned the chaotic vision of *King Lear*, destruction and extinction loom as constant threats. The menace can be devastating to the psychological well-being of an entire civilization. No one is more aware of this than the Japanese.
>
> (1988: 19)[33]

Once again, the desire for a stable present manifests itself through a nostalgia for a certain sort of history. The production of that desire, it seems, anchors itself not only in a remote pastness, but in the imagination of a cross-cultural relevance.

Finally, 1990 was not only a year saturated with *King Lear*s in Britain, but also the year which saw the long-awaited premiere performance in New York of Mabou Mines's cross-gender as well as cross-cultural *Lear*. That its research, rehearsal and preproduction publicity had garnered so much critical attention allows Iris Smith to name it quite persuasively 'a signature piece of the 1980s Mabou Mines' (1993: 281). There are two modalities of representation in this production which I'd like to consider: the first, the casting of Ruth Maleczech as Lear; and the second, the financial underwriting by American communications giant AT&T.

While roles were generally cast against gender, understandably most of the attention has focused on Maleczech's interpretation of Lear. As Smith indicates, 'for Maleczech gender has been the material obstacle between her and the chance to play Lear, and became, once the production was underway, the elemental link between Shakespeare's words and (her) contemporary American experience' (1993: 285). Maleczech herself reads her gender into a (gendered) history of production:

> Peter Brook said *Lear* [sic] was a mountain impossible to climb, and on the way up you trip over the corpses of Charles

Laughton here, Gielgud there, over yonder Olivier. Women
don't tackle this part, so I'm not likely to stumble over the
corpse of Eleanora Duse.

(cited in Holmberg 1988: 16)

If the representation of King Lear as a woman provided emancipatory critical distance to the act of that representation, Maleczech's
primary interest and motivation was apparently the character's
language. She comments: 'Lear's language seduces me. Why should
I, a woman, be denied access to such beautiful language? I wanted
to prove to myself that I could say those words out there in the
world' (cited in Holmberg 1988: 16); 'But for me it's still that
original impulse – to own the language, to own it for myself, and
then to give it to the audience from a woman's consciousness'
(cited in Wetzsteon 1990: 40).

Yet it is not only the beauty of the language, but the power that
adheres to it. That a woman might express such power in what is
recognized as a poetic frame creates no small shift in the paradigms
for 'doing' Shakespearean tragedy. Moreover, director Lee Breuer's
selection of the American South – a 'twangy accent of the back
country' of Georgia in the 1950s which Breuer suggests invokes
'a kind of cultural diaspora' (cited in Wetzsteon 1990: 39) – refracts
this in an interesting way.[34] Maleczech's Lear, then, was located at
the intersection of 'gender, geography *and* class' (Smith 1993: 286).
Not that Maleczech was the only cross-gender Lear produced by
a highly regarded director in the tradition of the avant-garde in
1990. This same year saw Robert Wilson's production in Frankfurt
with Marianne Hoppe in the eponymous role, a reading which
Patrice Pavis describes not as invested in any cross-cultural experimentation but as located 'in a postmodern no man's land' (1993:
275).[35]

But with Mabou Mines's *Lear*, the intersection of gender, geography, and class functioned also as the promotional angle for the
production. AT&T sponsored *Lear* (after many other potential
backers had failed to underwrite the costs – see Wetzsteon 1988)
and ran an advertisement for the New York premiere. The text
stated:

The woman who would be king.

   With the renowned Mabou Mines Company and director
Lee Breuer, performer Ruth Maleczech can be just that. The
avant-garde ensemble has adapted Shakespeare's *King Lear*,

redrawing the play's sexual, geographic and racial boundaries. This *Lear* takes place in contemporary America – with the roles reversed in gender, but with the verse and text intact. The ultimate drama of power, politics and mortality is now the story of a matriarch in a modern world, a tale to challenge the standards of a new decade. AT&T brings the premiere of this bold experiment to TriBeCa's Triplex Theater. For Mabou Mines, it's a crowning achievement. And for AT&T, it's the latest example of our 50-year commitment to the arts.[36]

Shakespeare as event. As globally relevant. As resolutely American. As high culture. As the avant-garde. As the past. As the present. As the future. Above all, Shakespeare as commodity, a strategic node at which to anchor the status of technological enterprise. By recognizing all the attributes of Shakespeare, AT&T acquires its own place on the stage of tradition. This, too, has much to say about power.

But if the New York premiere opened with such claims to the accretion of its cultural history, try-outs in New Jersey were altogether another phenomenon. As reviewer Eugenie Taub describes it, 'when the lights went up for intermission at the Saturday night performance of *Lear*, I was nearly trampled by members of the audience making a lemming-like rush for the exits' (cited in Smith 1993: 294). This would seem to suggest that, indeed, *King Lear/Lear* is all about class and that the New Jersey audiences found little shared community with Maleczech's representation of the central role. She, quite simply, failed their expectations.

This account of a decade of *King Lears* marks its limits as a 'great' play. In a traditional horizon of expectations, it performs a nostalgic identification with greatness – of the text, of Shakespeare, of the history of its mainstream productions and those who have directed and acted in the play, and of the audiences who recognize those values. The play provides an explicit illustration of the containing impulses of Shakespeare as cultural heritage. At another horizon (at its vanishing point?), the play's greatness derives from monumental status which impels, with more or less success, the polyvalent practice of transgression. It is tempting, too, to turn this contradictory and provocative performance history back to the fetishized text since Dollimore is surely right when he claims that this Shakespeare play is not a manifesto for essentialist humanism, nor a 'nihilistic and chaotic "vision" of Jacobean tragedy,' but an exploration of man 'in order to make visible social process and its forms of ideological misrecognition' (1984: 191). In very different ways, all of the proliferations of *King Lear* suggest the same; their importance lies in how they test such an exploration in the performative present of multivalent theatrical signification. My next chapter addresses transgression as foregrounded content in the articulation of not-Shakespeare.

3

NOT-SHAKESPEARE, OUR CONTEMPORARY

Transgression, Dissidence, and Desire

Already in the 1950s a vogue for Jacobean tragedy had fore-shadowed this attraction towards a rawer, uglier sex. That strange group of plays, written in a few years around 1600 – at the very beginning of the modern period – did indeed seem modern, filled with psychopathic violence and deviant desires.

(Elizabeth Wilson 1988: 3)

By dressing up in this manner, your enemies will simply assume I'm one of your whores.

(Sayers in Barrie Keeffe's A Mad World,
My Masters, 1977: 56)

This is a fascinating curiosity, a 400-year-old variation on a late 20th century theme.

(Benedict Nightingale 1990, on Middleton and
Rowley's The Old Law)

In an economy where innovation anchored to the traditions of the past sells, and sells well, one of the trends of the last decade or so has been a return to the sixteenth and seventeenth centuries for whatever other (not-Shakespeare) commodities might be re-circulated. This has seen any number of productions of con-temporaries of Shakespeare for the first time since the centuries of their premiere performance, and critical and other communi-ties tend to make sense of these exhumed texts in two particular ways: they mark the likeness of the play to one or other of Shakespeare's own and/or they mark the likeness to some appar-ently equivalent situation in the contemporary moment (as in Nightingale's review of *The Old Law* cited above). Wendy Griswold suggests:

any particular Renaissance genre, or individual play, stands
an improved chance of being revived when other types of
Renaissance drama are being revived, but this does not
explain what appear to be thematic distinctions whereby a
certain type of play dealing with certain issues finds excep-
tional favor.

(1986: 201)

Given the kinds and numbers of *King Lear* recorded in the last chapter, it might seem likely that other tragedies might be the obviously
favored fare. Yet this is not quite how the not-Shakespeare phenomenon has happened. This chapter will attempt to suggest that
obsession with the 'radical' in critical inquiry has a parallel expression in a revival of not-Shakespeares which flaunt 'thematic distinctions' concerned with transgression, dissidence, and desire.

An appendix in Griswold's study itemizing London revivals of
city comedies and revenge tragedies reveals the decades of 1660–9
and 1960–9 as the most intensive in their revival (although proportions differ: in the decade from the seventeenth century there were
eight comedies and seven tragedies; in the 1960s six comedies and
eight tragedies) (Griswold 1986: 218, 224). Yet it seems as if
Griswold completed her study a decade too early since the 1980s
show more concentration on city comedy and revenge tragedy (and
other generically sympathetic Renaissance texts) than at any other
time since the period of their first production. Along with *The
Old Law*, there were productions in London of *The Duchess of
Malfi*, *The Maid's Tragedy*, *The Witch of Edmonton*, *The Fawn*, *The
Custom of the Country*, *New Ways to Pay Old Debts*, *Women Beware
Women*, *Edward III*, *The Revenger's Tragedy*, *'Tis Pity She's A Whore*,
The Changeling, *Bussy D'Ambois*, *Bartholomew Fair*, *The Roaring Girl*,
The Fair Maid of the West and *The Dutch Courtesan* – several of
these texts saw more than one production and many garnered just
the same 'relevance' award as Nightingale handed down for the
Middleton and Rowley play. (Rosalind Carne, for example, says
of *The Maid's Tragedy* that 'Jacobean tragedy has a powerful fascination in our godless age' [1981: 556].) The effect of the inclusion
of these other texts is one of diversity in the proliferation of past
texts, a sense that not only Shakespeare can be brought into the
service of nostalgia. Moreover, these not-Shakespeares may have
different representations of different pasts to bring into collision
with the present that apparently resembles them.

In reviewing this development of canonical diversity, there are a number of specific locations which are worth attention. There is a renewed interest within the Shakespeare corpus; and, in this instance, we see what happens when some of the less well-known and less appreciated Shakespeare texts take to the contemporary stage. But perhaps even more interesting are those plays or productions which attract the appellation 'Jacobean.' Strictly speaking, Jacobean might refer only to those texts first produced during the reign of James I (1603–25) and, indeed, most playtexts that are familiarly known as Jacobean date from the first half of his reign. Nonetheless, I would argue that the terminology of Jacobean has come to mean both more and less than this original coinage. It doesn't connote all plays produced in that time frame (most explicitly, Shakespeare's plays written at that historical juncture are rarely either described as Jacobean or discussed in relation to those plays more readily identified as such). It does, however, come into use for many kinds of cultural production (deriving from any number of historical moments) which share some of the values that characterized the primary generic forms of Jacobean drama, the city comedy and the revenge tragedy. Jameson's correction to notions of periodicity is helpful here. He writes:

> period concepts finally correspond to no realities whatsoever, and . . . whether they are formulated in terms of generational logic, or by the names of reigning monarchs, or according to some other category or typological and classificatory system, the collective reality of the multitudinous lives encompassed by such terms is nonthinkable (or non-totalizable, to use a current expression) and can never be described, characterized, labeled, or conceptualized.
>
> (1989b: 520–521)

Recognition of this disjuncture between period concepts and lived realities frees up a term such as Jacobean to mean in different and sometimes contradictory modes. In this chapter I want to suggest several of the current applications of 'Jacobean' and to consider how these do shift Shakespeare and elaborate possibilities for the (dis)articulation of a monolithic past.

Elizabeth Wilson accounts for the re-emergence of the Jacobean in the 1960s both as a marker of political dissatisfaction and of the emergent 'sexual revolution.' She points to a commonality of experience:

we seem more and more to be living in an 'Italian' society of the Jacobean kind. Today, as then, despite religious gloss on sentiment and language, we live in a world that is wholly secular, so that much official Christianity has a hollow, cynical ring. And the more the assumed, taken for granted moral values of a society become hollow and decay from within – rather than being challenged in a positive sense by an *alternative* system of values – the more that society becomes cynical, and the more it will rely on violence rather than reason to maintain the status quo.

(1989: 74)[1]

This citation of the Jacobean illustrates both its merit (or, at the least, usefulness) and its shortcomings. The effect of performing nostalgia that Wilson suggests is one of a violent re-enactment. In this way, the return to the Jacobean forcibly maintains a sense of continuity through its anxious and excessive reproduction.

As John Frow indicates in his semiotics of nostalgia,

[t]he concept of cultural capital ("taste"), which is meant to place the discussion on the level of aesthetic competencies rather than on the level of social class, transparently fails to do so, since the aesthetic is immediately a code word for class.

(1991: 148)

To a large extent, the Jacobean is an aesthetic that attempts to mask not only class, but issues of gender, race and sexuality. Despite such an attempt, its recitation often exposes rather than veils the instability of these identities, and does so in order to challenge notions of cultural capital in the contemporary. Its aesthetic use most commonly, however, is as a denotation of (moral) decay, excess and violence – deficiencies we also find in our contemporary moment and for which this past can apparently give expression and meaning. What might be tested in reading these reproductions of texts already marked as transgressive is Dollimore's caution that 'it seems as if the existing social order might actively forestall resistance because somehow preceding and informing it; subversion and transgression are not merely defeated by law, but actually produced by law in a complex process of (re)legitimation' (1991: 80).

82

RADICAL CHIC: JACOBEAN IN/AS STYLE

Classic reinterpretation became sexy in the eighties, starry and glamorous.

(Simon Reade 1991: 119)

This is a road movie, supposedly. That wouldn't be worth noting except that the road traveled by Sailor Ripley and Lula Fortune is ultimately left littered with bodies, or parts of bodies. . . . Demolished heads and flaming bodies are leitmotifs.

(Devin McKinney, 1991: 1,583, on David Lynch's *Wild at Heart*)

What Frow identifies as 'touristic shame' might be reframed, in terms of dramatic production, as the recognition that the contemporary performance is only ever less than its antecedent (a concept well engraved in scholarship and also extensively disseminated through secondary education). In the failure of the Jacobean revival to imitate successfully its source text, however, there is – in a way quite different to the reproduction of *King Lear* – an activation of the purchase on transgression and dissidence that those Jacobean texts have come to represent. And this theatrical model stands in, nostalgically, for an expression in and of the everyday. Their appeal speaks to our desire for a past which subverts History at the same time as confirming its progressive trajectory.

This is not to insist that the classification of Jacobean always works in such a complicated manner. In some instances it does seem primarily to be an aesthetic marker, with little intention of unmasking the conditions of its production although this might well be an effect. An example here might be David Mamet's *Speed The Plow*, a play which likely takes its unusual title from George Chapman's *Bussy D'Ambois*, one of the first literary references to the old and somewhat ambiguous expression used as Mamet's title. Mamet's play does not develop particular connections to its Jacobean antecedent but merely flags that association in the title to produce, I suspect, an expectation of transgressive behaviors, decadent attitudes and, quite simply, money and sex. Robert Brustein cites Mamet in his assertion that '[p]erhaps in a time of ethical relativism and moral decay, it is, as Mamet suggests, sufficient simply to be good at your job' (1992: 65). 'Ethical relativism' and 'moral decay' are terms that derive directly from the Jacobean critical lexicon, and practices that Gould and Fox take for granted in *Speed The Plow*. It is the same kind of vocabulary as is reduplicated in reviews of David Lynch's *Wild at Heart*: violence, conspicuous excess, depravity, bestiality, gory sensationalism, evil, corruption, decadence.[2] In articulating a 'lack of restraint [as] precisely what is radical and thrilling about the movie,' Devin McKinney locates its effect as a surfeit of images, rather than in articulating any content or analysis in those images. In short, *Wild at Heart* is about style and not critique. As Jameson concludes in a reading of another Lynch film (*Blue Velvet*), 'despite the grotesque and horrendous tableaux of maimed bodies, this kind of evil is more distasteful than it is fearful, more disgusting than threatening: here evil has finally become an image' (1989b: 535).

Accordingly, the Jacobean can function as a performance shorthand for certain manifestations of behavior in certain cultural milieu, and its articulation in contemporary dramas is often mediated (and in this way made accessible) by a popular and widely recognized filmic genre, the thriller. The Glasgow Citizens Theatre opened its 1982–3 season with *The Roman Actor* (thought to be a Philip Massinger play), another one of those texts that had not seen a professional production for more than a century. Director Philip Prowse simplified the plot of his subject text but extended the operations of murders and revenge to assault (quite literally) the audience's sense:

> the front stalls were awash with blood which squirted out from concealed capsules and a highly visible throat-stabbing. In one extraordinary scene, two cultured senators were subjected to torture by electric drill; the victims laughed in the Emperor's face, providing a Black and Decker comedy of resistance to sadistic vandalism.
>
> (Coveney 1990: 167–168)[3]

Such a hybrid of Jacobean Italianate revenge plot/Godfather-like Italian mafia reprisal tactics has become almost a performance cliché: Godard's manipulation of *King Lear* transformed the mythic story to an account of the life of Don Learo (whom we see reading Albert Fried's *The Rise and Fall of the Jewish Gangster in America*); Peter Greenaway's self-defined Jacobean extravaganza *The Cook, The Thief, His Wife and Her Lover* showcases small-time gangster Albert Spica;[4] Derek Jarman's remake of Marlowe's *Edward II* makes use of 'gangster fashions' (O'Pray 1991: 8). The same figure also defines the production of John Webster's *The Duchess of Malfi* by the Red Shift Theatre Company (1982–4). As Kathleen

McLuskie and Jennifer Uglow describe it, the company sought out contemporary images which would give a particular currency to the play's rhetoric: 'The setting which brought these images together was the Italy of high finance, corruption and style created as an image in the cinematic styles of film noir and neo-realism and popularised by the success of the "Godfather" films' (1989: 59).

Unlike the generalized Italianate setting exploited by many of these texts/productions, Red Shift located their *The Duchess of Malfi* quite precisely in political events which were capturing the newspaper headlines of the day. The desired connectedness between past Machiavellian plotting and corruption, and present-day corporate maneuvering was unmissable. The production made use of

> explicit references from newspaper reports throughout the performance to the Calvi affair, in which the investigation into the death of a prominent banker exposed corrupt networks through Freemasonry reaching into the Vatican itself. The world of the play was secular but the church's potential for corruption was made clear by replacing the Cardinal with a character reminiscent, in both costume and bearing, of Archbishop Marcinkus, Calvi's Vatican connection.
>
> (McLuskie and Uglow 1989: 59–60)

Jonathan Holloway, Artistic Director of Red Shift, suggests that the objective of his play's style (the men were in dark dress suits with black ties, the women in identical short black cocktail dresses) was to provoke a socialist analysis (no date: 34). In his description, Holloway constantly refers his scenography to filmic equivalents (*The Thomas Crown Affair*, *Bring Me the Head of Alfredo Garcia*, etc.) and notes how the play was supported by 'a continuous filmic soundtrack played live' (no date: 36). Its success was evident both at the Edinburgh Festival and on a subsequent tour; Holloway writes:

> There is no doubt this second production of *The Duchess of Malfi* did more than any piece before or since to establish the company. The show looked fashionable. It contained filmic reference and use of disciplined stage technique reminiscent of Grotowski, Berkoff and Robert Wilson post-modernism. The application of all this to a play with a

reputation which probably outstrips the number of those who are actually familiar with the text, added up to an event which quickly gained a head of steam as the show to catch at the Festival. So successful was the piece that it secured most of a national tour for the spring of 1984 even before the Festival was over.

(no date: 37)

The Duchess of Malfi certainly seems to have been *the* Jacobean play of choice (McLuskie and Uglow list ten different productions, nine in Britain, one in New Zealand, for the years 1975–85) and one might speculate as to why its radical chic became definitive. In part this has to be because the play offers a strong, central role for a woman (although, as my students are always quick to point out, she is murdered at the end of the fourth act). There is some obvious appeal to this at a time when the achievements of feminism had insisted on more visibility and opportunity for women actors.[5] Yet the often-used claim of *The Duchess of Malfi* as a proto-feminist play seems to me entirely spurious. As Dollimore asserts, 'in Jacobean drama we find not a triumphant emancipation of women but at best an indication of the extent of their oppression' (1984: 240). He goes on to explain, by way of Natalie Zemon Davis's important and ground breaking work in the area, the significance of a disobedient female body 'as one aspect – and a crucial one – of a social order that thrived on exploitation' (1984: 240). And, as Holloway's rendition of the play makes explicit, such exploitation is rife at every level and intersection in contemporary Western society.

If this particular production of *The Duchess* gave conspicuous attention to the kinds of punishment effected on this transgressive body (then and now), it is nonetheless equally important to identify Holloway's reliance on what he calls the play's 'reputation.' Here is a visible indication of the reciprocity between the status of the text in the early 1980s and the marketing strategy of the company: 'classic' in a trading agreement with 'radical.' As Red Shift's second attempt at the play, the remarkable success of their re-revised *The Duchess of Malfi* is, I think, a particular combination of innovation and reputation – or reputation innovatively cast to (re)produce and (re)vision reputation itself (both for the play [again] and for the company [for the first time]). The company's subsequent production choices are worth noting here. After a disastrous adaptation of George Orwell's *1984*, Holloway took particular action: 'I resolved to repair the damage by mounting a concerted effort to achieve public funding and to revive the company's Edinburgh sell-out popularity through use of the deconstruction and overt political statement which had been so successful with *Malfi*' (no date: 43). Choice of Band-Aid? A Shakespeare play, and one of the best-known and most oft-produced at that: *Romeo and Juliet*. And this turned out to be a successful choice for the company, one which was instrumental in their obtaining some Arts Council funding.

A few years later, Red Shift returned to Shakespeare, this time to a much less obvious choice, *Timon of Athens*. *Timon* has seldom been performed in this century and almost always to pointedly negative criticism. Certainly it is a difficult text to make sense of and an even more difficult one to stage. With the context that Holloway provides, one can position this production as a decision on the part of Red Shift to put their artistic mandate on the line, to test in an extreme form the validity of their vision of radical deconstruction in performance. Holloway describes his attraction to the project as follows:

> The story [of *Timon of Athens*] struck me as appropriate to our own times in which the communal sense of social responsibility which was the cornerstone of the welfare state has been eroded. Thatcherite ideas pervade the selfish get-rich-quick culture of modern Britain. The attainment of wealth is mistaken for a litmus paper test of human worth. For me, the tragedy of Timon is the fact that he has no analysis to replace the fable when the scales fall from his eyes. . . .
> This interpretation of the play made the casting of a woman as Timon absolutely logical. Women are often at the centre of societal illusion.
>
> (no date: 69–70)

Perhaps the most daring (de/re)construction of Shakespeare's play was in their performance of Timon's death. In Red Shift's version, Timon has *her* brains 'bashed out by a group of assassins dressed in robes painted with emblems of the sensory organs':

> This shocking punctuation point was then undercut by 'an official version' in which Timon sank beneath the waves

made by fluttering clothes, while the cast intoned the original words used to describe Timon's passive wasting away.

(no date: 73)

Double-representations are a particular signature of Red Shift's
productions (they double-realized Tybalt's death in *Romeo and Juliet*
as well as Steven and Maggie's possible sexual union in *Mill on the
Floss*) and such repetitions work obviously to destabilize both
textual and production authority, as well as to mark the material
conditions in which both the characters themselves and our inter-
pretations of those characters are produced. The *Timon* project,
then, appears to have offered a very particular and (to me, at least)
quite tantalizing revision of one of those so-called 'problem plays.'

The reception history for *Timon of Athens* charts in telling ways
the implications of staging a non-canonical Shakespeare play, at the
same time as it marks a critical viewing public that read the
Jacobean largely for its stylistic apparatus.[6] Holloway relates the
history as an opposition between the London theatre critics and
audiences elsewhere in England:

> The London critics hated the show and the piece played five
> rather dismal weeks in the capital. . . . However, in its first
> two days on tour the production played to 250 people. This
> success continued virtually uninterrupted throughout the
> period of the tour [4 months, 34 venues]. Audience members
> seemed to react either very favourably (as most did) or were
> as annoyed as the London critics. Generally those who knew
> the play least were least worried.
>
> (no date: 73–74)

Reading Holloway's account suggests that spectators with a particularly 'knowing' horizon of expectations for the play (represented
here in the mainstream theatre critics) were bound to be disappointed, and in two specific ways: this is already marked as marginal
in its place in the Shakespeare canon *and* it is being produced as
if were not Shakespeare. Other spectators whose horizon of expectations perhaps did little more than bring them to the performance
(Shakespeare is worth seeing) seemed to be less inhibited by the
very qualities that undermined the production for the London
critics.

It seems as if transgressive rupturing of Shakespeare's text can
only be sanctioned (at least by the monotone voice of mainstream

review criticism and its close relative of arts funding agencies) if it succeeds merely as radical chic: when that style threatens to unravel more 'contestable ideology' (Armstrong 1989: 7), then a viewing contract seems to predetermine particular and conservative values for 'Shakespeare' that render the dissident production 'not-Shakespeare' and, by extension, not 'good' Art.[7] JoAnne Akalitis's production of another one of Shakespeare's difficult-to-realize plays, *Cymbeline* (Public Theatre, 1989), evoked similarly explicit critical ire, invoking both psychic and national boundaries. Elinor Fuchs remarks that it was 'as if Akalitis had burned the flag' (Fuchs and Leverett 1989: 24); David Norbrook writes 'New York's critics reacted to *Cymbeline* as if a totem had been violated' (in Fuchs and Leverett 1989: 27).[8]

Cast across race (including an African-American actor as Cloten, a decision that the critics particularly deplored because of the incredibility of Imogen's subsequent misrecognition)[9] and given a contextualization of Gothic melodrama, Akalitis made explicit the participation of 'Shakespeare' on a very particular historical continuum: 'Today's social injustice caused by prejudice became directly connected to the attitudes of Western cultural supremacy championed in Victorian England, which, in turn, had their roots in the colonialism of the Elizabethan era' (Nouryeh 1991: 187). The roots may go back four hundred years, but colonial insistence on the 'whiteness' of Shakespeare remains a contemporary phenomenon.

Amy Green's assessment of the multiple periodicity of production setting further suggests Akalitis's intervention along the fault lines of mainstream critical desire:

> The production depicted nineteenth-century, Shakespearean melodrama as only a contemporary imagination, fluent in the imagery of late-twentieth-century American culture, could conceive it. Its beauty lay in the way it seemed to exist, paradoxically, in at least three simultaneous theatrical time zones. . . .
>
> Akalitis's remarkable vision of the play blended nostalgia for old-fashioned, emotional Victorian melodrama with her own, high-tech theatrical vocabulary.
>
> (Green 1994: 93)

That New York audiences failed to appreciate the story that *Cymbeline* was made to tell, demonstrates, like Red Shift's production of *Timon of Athens*, an impatience with the marginal works in the Shakespeare's corpus.

This impatience translates into critical rejection especially if the production fails to (re)assure audiences of the greatness of the Bard and if the production notates the narrativity of History (marking the absence of a 'real' past) (see Stewart 1984: 23). *Cymbeline* is hardly a 'Jacobean' play, but Akalitis's manipulation of scenic modes and melodramatic flourishes gave her production an excess of effect. This, among other things, produced its critical failure, its designation as not-Shakespeare. The examples of Red Shift's *Timon of Athens* and Akalitis's *Cymbeline* underscore the difficulties in straying too far from the centre of even the Shakespeare canon. It is one thing to tamper with *King Lear* and altogether another to revive one of these less often produced Shakespearean texts.

There is a likeness between Andrea Nouryeh's description of *Cymbeline*'s revelation of social prejudice rooted in the precepts of colonialism and the shaping interests of recent productions of Middleton and Rowley's *The Changeling*. Its revival at the Royal National Theatre (Nouryeh 1988) relocated the text in a nineteenth-century Spanish slave colony, with the aristocratic char-acters represented as white colonizers while the servant class (most notably De Flores) were their black subjects. De Flores, the play's 'black mask,' embodied those qualities much more literally, his face bearing the tribal scarification of an exoticized other culture. To a text already imprinted with the flaunting of taboo, director Richard Eyre added miscegenation – as if the regulation and punishment of Beatrice-Joanna required more legitimation than the facts of her gender and sexuality. The RNT production garnered decidedly mixed reviews, but one is of especial interest here. Michael Coveney states: 'George Harris never develops De Flores into anything more luscious or lascivious than a routinely articulated Caliban with the hots for the boss's daughter' (1988: 860). The imperialist attraction to the figure of Caliban I will address in the next chapter, but this seems to me a breathtaking example of the racist reading not only of the texts themselves but also of the bodies who might inhabit them. In a similar vein, the debut performance of the British Chinese Theatre – one of two productions of *The Changeling* play-ing in London in January 1991 and set, on this occasion, in the familial hierarchy of a contemporary Chinese restaurant – attracts for De Flores the descriptor 'slinky Asian' (Rutherford 1991: 66). And since the Asian cast members were already coded as 'Other' to a hegemonic white gaze, this might have motivated the fact that De Flores's physical difference was heightened to excess with running sores all over his face.

Straying yet further from the source text, although still embedded in the discourses of colonialism, Brad Fraser's *The Ugly Man* (1993) retains little actual plot from *The Changeling*. In fact Fraser keeps only its most sensational features: the potion to test virginity, 'the bed trick' (where the maid slips into the wedding-night bed in lieu of her mistress) and a vengeful ghost.[10] Nonetheless, he is concerned to transfer to Prairie Canada the kinds of machinations of decadent and desperate characters that typified early seventeenth-century drama. Its setting, a ranch outside town, provides a culturally specific translation to what Nicholas Brooke describes for Beatrice in the Middleton and Rowley play as 'a narrowly exclusive world' (1979: 72). Fraser's objective is to foreground the Jacobean morality in his own society: according to one critic, this is achieved by the invention of 'telling motivations' for his central characters, Veronica and Forest (the latter, a present-day De Flores who bears his malevolence in physical form by way of a vast and disfiguring facial scar). It is suggested that their 'perverse horrors may be a response to repression or abuse inflicted upon them by others. . . . Here lies Fraser's central theme, and the one closest to his own heart: the accelerating cycle by which abuse is passed from one relationship, or from one generation, to the next' (Potter 1993: 152).

This may indeed be the goal of Fraser's play but, in performance, it is striking mainly as a display of sexual infidelity and taboo, both leading, seemingly inevitably, to murder, revenge, and death. In one sequence, Forest (who has agreed to murder Veronica's fiancé in exchange for her virginity) graphically executes the promised murder,[11] fucks the brother of the murdered man, starts to sever the body parts of the corpse with a workbench saw until he is interrupted by Veronica, whose payment for the murder (her virginity) he exacts after a powerful scene of seduction. The helter-skelter of sex and violence might well be induced by cycles of abuse. In the 'real' world, psychological studies have proven the frequence of repetition for patterns of abuse, but in the stage world of Fraser's play there is no depth of character which might ask questions of the violent and/or sexual rituals performed. Instead there is only the allure of the intensity of expression and, like David Lynch's films and Jacobean stage antecedents, Fraser's play favors 'the sensual over the sensical' (McKinney 1991: 1,558). The excess of the Jacobean mode is as seductive as Forest: ugly but irresistible – at least, that's what Fraser would have us believe. Confirming Jameson's reading of Lynch's *Blue Velvet* (1989b: 534ff), *The Ugly Man* concerns itself almost solely with evil as image.

What is more interesting in Fraser's text is his use of the Jacobean style to stage homoerotic desire. While the plot line seemingly puts the wealthy heiress–virgin at the centre of its play, the action of the text is primarily concerned with the four men: Forest, Acker, Cole (who is the man Veronica apparently really desires and who is identified as sexually insatiable), and Leslie (Acker's brother, once Cole's lover, now Forest's lover). Jonathan Dollimore suggests that in Jacobean drama

> masculine identity requires masculine ratification. At the same time, and within a heterosexual economy generally, there tends to be a profound separation between identification and desire, especially for males. Thus the male is required to identify with other males but he is not allowed to desire them; indeed, *identification with* should actually preclude *desire for*.
>
> (1991. 305)

Fraser's play blurs that separation and insists on marking the presence of desire in any process of identification. Indeed, the homoerotic impulses of masculine identification are literalized in Fraser's directions for performance. At the end of the play, however, Leslie exacts the revenge for his brother's murder. As the play's seemingly weakest character, Leslie is empowered by the injustice wreaked on his family: first he shoots Veronica and then exacts a slow and ritual torture of Forest:

> *Leslie moves toward Forest. He lights the torch and sterilizes the axe.*
> FOREST: Don't. Please.
> *Leslie kicks Forest's legs apart, wide. Forest screams in pain.*
> LESLIE: This is going to hurt a lot. But I want you to be very very quiet.
> FOREST: No.
> *Leslie hefts the axe in his hand.*
> LESLIE: Be very very quiet.

ACKER [his ghost]: Revenge!
Leslie suddenly brings the axe over his head, aiming it directly at Forest's leg. The lights snap to black.

(Fraser 1993: 149)

The final sequence of murders choreographs a brutal closure which I believe, despite perhaps quite other intentions, secures the heterosexual viewing contract: all the murders (the maid, the mother, Veronica, Acker and Forest) are, ultimately, punishments for sexual disobedience. Leslie, who executes much of this revenge, has requited his brother's demand, but is almost certain to find himself subject to the punishment of the law. The only free man (who literally walks away at the end of the play) is Cole, the handsome leading man who inherits Veronica's fortune and has his heterosexuality confirmed. It would seem that Fraser's text, for all its Jacobean parade of violence and desire, ultimately does no more than restate a compulsory heterosexuality not as critique but as a comfort to a mainstream theatre-going public that can applaud its own enjoyment of perversity as well as the necessary punishment of the same in the very terms of the text.

All of these productions, in differing degrees, appropriate a Jacobean text as novelty. More importantly, they appropriate these texts because these are novelties that sell, even when the reviewers warn against them and even if for no more complicated reason than the one that Griswold posits: more of the same. In most cases, however, layered on to the performance's novelty is the currency of the Jacobean, as a signifier bound to represent psychopathic violence and deviant desires. Beyond its marked signification, the Jacobean as performance realizes an intention to have the audience visualize the past in the present: to see its resemblance to our own world and to nourish our psychic desires for the past itself. Unlike the idealized authenticity and authority of Shakespeare's (great) texts, these Jacobean revivals point to a less than perfect past, but nonetheless one which can help us legitimize our own defective present. The designation's function, even as it marks transgression and dissidence, points to a continuous and repetitive history, the inevitability of which we can do no more than accept.

Yet, while citations of the Jacobean can and do exist simply on the level of resemblance, they can be more interrogatively staged. In her account of reading the past, Gillian Beer states: 'Radical reading is not a reading that simply assimilates past texts to our

93

concerns but rather an activity that tests and de-natures our assumptions in the light of the strange language and desires of past writing' (1989b: 80). The texts that follow perform precisely the activity of radical reading that might defamiliarize our own desires and dissatisfactions in the present.

DISSIDENT POLITICS AND DANGEROUS DESIRE: THE CONTEMPORARY JACOBEAN

> I ask her once again, and if she won't must stab her and say the violator did it. So I'll convert this farce into a tragedy, and win more pity than contempt. I'll be the black-clad mourner of all Europe, and all future cruelty will be explained away by pain.
>
> (The Duke, in Barker and Middleton's
> *Women Beware Women*, 1986: 34)

> Transgression opens onto a scintillating and constantly affirmed world, a world without shadow or twilight, without that serpentine 'no' that bites into fruits and lodges their contradictions at the core.
>
> (Foucault 1977: 37)

In this section I want to revisit the subgeneric categorizations of Jacobean drama: the city comedy and the revenge tragedy. In both, although the proportions (and, obviously, the methodologies) vary, there is an unmistakable, clamant partnering of politics and sex – somehow thought of as a leitmotif for our time. Griswold offers the following description of the subgenres in the context of the social metaphors which create their contemporary appeal:

> The social metaphor of city comedy is the genre's represen-tation of the collective concern with economic change, social mobility, and social stability. For revenge tragedy, the social metaphor expresses the collective worry regarding the central government's ability to provide both order and justice. When these concerns recur among those with the capacity to influence revival decisions, manager and audience, the genre representing them takes on a renewed salience, and its chances for revival increase.
>
> (1986: 208)

While the process for reviving either of these subgeneric catego-ries is rather more complicated than Griswold's conclusion infers (although what she says is certainly part of that process), both of these categories offer very particular and dissident commentaries on the generalized economy of transgression of which they are a part. The appeal of these categories is related to a location of the present as a time of crisis. Identification as crisis, according to Dollimore, is productive of contradictions which 'are especially revealing':

> they tell us that no matter how successful authority may be in its repressive strategies, there remains something potentially uncontrollable not only in authority's objects but in its enterprise, its rationale, and even its origin. In short: change, contest, and struggle are in part made possible by contradiction.
>
> (1991: 88)

The 'Jacobean' provides one site where the contradictory impulses of nostalgia perform themselves in a disruptive and occasionally emancipatory mode.

In this context it is possible to locate comedy as a genre that demands the performance of contradiction, and the two contemporary 'city comedies' discussed here stage contest and struggle as an expression of their respective authors' desire for change. Barrie Keeffe's *A Mad World, My Masters* and Peter Greenaway's *The Cook, The Thief, His Wife and Her Lover* both address very specifically the micropolitical, local community of London but do so, I think, in the understanding of the power that 'London' represents not only nationally, but internationally. Keeffe's play was originally produced in 1977 and revived again in the next decade (with some minor changes). In his introduction to the text, Keeffe describes William Gaskill's idea 'to make a modern Jacobean play, the sort of city comedy Thomas Middleton might write if he were still alive. He [Gaskill] and Joint Stock Theatre Company asked me to write it' (1977: 1). Employing the methodologies of collective creation, Keeffe and the commissioning company spent three weeks in a workshop to establish characters and to undertake exercises in practical and verbal conjuring.

As in its Jacobean forerunner, the appeal of Keeffe's *A Mad World, My Masters* is centered on the skills and the attractiveness of the trickster figures (in many ways the comic counterparts of a character such as Brad Fraser's Forest). The contemporary version reworked and complicated the basic double-action plot of Middleton's text, and the archetypal generational conflict (Follywit trying to gull his uncle Sir Bounteous Progress) along with the attempted seduction (the so-called 'citizen' plot involving Penitent Brothel and Mistress Harebrain) activates a complexity of social relations in the present historical moment. Generational conflict is exploited in the father/daughter relationship (described in the *dramatis personae* as Horace Claughton, a Gentleman of the City, and Janet Claughton, a friend of the poor and needy). The would-be Sir Horace is a cartoon-like representation of the extremes of New Right economic and value systems. Janet, referred to by her father as 'Madam Mao,' is a passionate reformer, in the tradition of Britain's Victorian women philanthropists. What is at stake in their relationship is not her father's wealth *per se* but that wealth as an instrument of power. Claughton's actions, however ridiculous and at whatever level, affect profoundly the lives of those whose crises Janet imagines she might solve.

Generational conflict, then, merely serves as a dramatic convention which can access the playwright's predominant concern, the oppressive practices of the ruling hegemony. Keeffe has insisted that he is 'much more interested in the effects of political decisions on people, than in people making political decisions' (Itzin 1980: 244). Thus Claughton's principal antagonists are an archetypal working-class family, the Sprightlys of Hackney, who collectively perform the tricks and disguises of the Follywit role. Interclass, rather than interfamilial, conflict predominates and Keeffe indicates the difficulties in contemporary social practice of challenging a largely invisible enemy who nevertheless almost effortlessly controls others' lives. Comic action is derived from the resourcefulness of the Sprightlys in devising plots to disempower the aspiring Claughton and their *lazzi* go far beyond the bravura performances of Middleton's Follywit. Moreover, the culmination of transgressive actions in the family's unmasking has much more tangible and painful consequences than the embarrassment Follywit experiences at his discovery that he has married his uncle's whore.

Like its seventeenth-century source text, Keeffe's play is centered on economic transaction. Corporate machinations (asset stripping, 'charitable donations' and so on) metamorphose into tricks and games which constitute comic plot. The effect of this almost incidental, but constant reference to the commercial benefits of the farcical disasters and ploys is to engage the unseen power of the corporate world with the trivial quotidian experiences of the Sprightlys. While Claughton (like Sir Bounteous Progress) appears as little more than a buffoon, Keeffe makes explicit the power that enables him to manipulate any action. The 'honest con' of the Sprightlys causes Harry's death and fails to bring the anticipated insurance pay-off from Claughton's company. Evidence that the 'con' has been executed is abundant, but significantly Claughton abrogates responsibility on a technicality: Harry forgot to clock on when he arrived for work at the docks. By contrast, when Claughton attempts to seduce Vi Sprightly, photographic and taped evidence is deftly intercepted by the ever present Superintendent Sayers. Simply put, Claughton assumes and demonstrably enjoys the protection of the institutions where the Sprightlys are constantly and increasingly vulnerable. As a fool figure, then, Claughton is dangerous but never so to himself. The Sprightlys are the collective victims of misapplied power as well as economic oppression. Even after Claughton loses his recommendation for a knighthood, he manages, by the end of the play, to recover and his fortunes are once again in the ascendant. Effectively Claughton represents a new, emergent aristocracy, the power of which has been confirmed by the reintroduction of Mrs. Thatcher's government of hereditary knighthoods and in the common practice in so many Western nations of patronage appointments.

Middleton's *A Mad World, My Masters* utilizes a series of dazzling disguises by which Follywit's comic endeavors are realized. And Keeffe's play also relies on a similar confusion of identities to bring the farcical events to a dramatic climax. When, in a complicated cross-plot confusion, Claughton consults with Doc O'Flaherty, the doctor chooses to disguise himself by adopting an Indian accent and revealing his 'real' name to be 'Tandoori . . . Shamee Kebab . . . Popadom. My friends call me Lime Pickle' (1977: 37, ellipses in the original). A few scenes later, Superintendent Sayers recites his skill at passing as Other to threaten Bill Sprightly:

> Master of disguise I am. Should have seen me when I was infiltrating the gang of vicious homosexual murderers. I dressed up in arse crushing tight white jeans and bangles and a poovey hair style. Loitering outside the Trafalgar Square urinals I picked up the esteemed Sir Robert Mark once. He mistook me for a slim hipped sixteen-year-old rent boy.
>
> (1977: 46)

And Sayers eventually cross-dresses to protect the powerful Claughton. In Middleton's text, Follywit disguises himself as a whore, a powerful visual signifier for a merger of sex, gender and economics. Sayers, likewise, has economic motivations for his cross-dressing (the hope of a mortgage to buy himself, ironically, a mock-Tudor house in the suburbs). When he is questioned by Claughton as to the suitability of the disguise, Sayers responds, 'By dressing up in this manner, your enemies will simply assume I'm one of your whores' (1977: 56), a comment which provokes little disagreement from Claughton.

It is not only in Sayers's case that sex, gender and money perform so interdependently. Vi Sprightly, in her seduction of Claughton, adopts a disguise which both upgrades and degrades her. She takes on the vocal signature and costume of a BBC newsreader, but turns this performance into a dance/strip performance.[12] What is disturbing in Keeffe's revision of the city comedy, as the examples of O'Flaherty, Sayers and Vi Sprightly all too clearly reveal, is its reliance on humor which is too often sexist, racist and/or homo-phobic. We do not necessarily endorse the characters who create and embody the jokes, but we are clearly expected to find the articulation and practice of their disguises entertaining. This, it seems to me, effects exactly the displacement of social crisis that Dollimore articulates as an aspect of theories of containment:

> Displacement often involves the demonizing of relatively powerless minorities, although it may be misleading to isolate this process from others. In abstraction there are at least three ways whereby the dominant identifies the subordinate (or the deviant) as threatening 'other.' The first is paranoid: the threat is imagined only; in actuality the subordinate is relatively powerless and unthreatening. The second is subversive: the threat is actually or potentially dangerous. The third involves the displacement of crisis and anxiety etc. onto the deviant. In practice some of these will typically coexist.
>
> (1991: 89–90)

This pattern identifies quite precisely the dynamic of Keeffe's version of a city comedy. The 'three ways' that Dollimore points to co-exist to produce a humor which relies on demonizing certain less powerful identities in its articulation of power as an expres-sion of class difference. Keeffe's play demonstrates a commitment to the issues and concerns of the property-less, but does not seem to recognize its own complicity in imperial values which would contain, if not erase, other expressions of alterity.

In Middleton's *A Mad World, My Masters* the comic satire is grounded or at least tempered by what one editor describes as Penitent Brothel's 'perfervid, if conventional, morality' (Henning 1965: xiii). In Keeffe's play, it is the absence of any position from which to present either a moral reading or serious challenge that marks a critical distance from the past to which his plot appeals. This absence is perhaps most tellingly revealed in the attempts of a third antagonist, Mr. Fox of the tabloid press.

As a representative of the popular media, Fox is perhaps most clearly a contemporary character and functions, at least in part, to demonstrate Keeffe's disapproval of the strategies of media coverage as well as an even greater dislike of a public that actively and avidly still consumes such material. This implicitly gestures towards a nostalgia for some objective, even if repressive, moral truth. Fox is quite unlike the bumbling Sprightlys; he is a professional in search of *the* story that will destroy Claughton's power. In a Volpone-like performance, the aptly named Fox tempts and implicates his victim at every turn. Fox, precisely because of his occupation, is seemingly most efficiently equipped to unmask Claughton's personal and corporate deceptions. Yet the final scene shows Fox, like Follywit, compromised and it is on this failure that Keeffe's play is concluded:

> FOX: I wrote it, the story of the decade. But my proprietor killed it, he thought it was too embarrassing to the Queen. He's after a knighthood you see. It looked good set up, before he destroyed the copy, the photographs and negatives. Ah well. I thought I might have exposed Claughton. Perhaps when he stands at the by-election. They adopted him last week.
>
> *He produces a bunch of flowers.*
> Grandma Sprightly lies beneath this tree
> Died celebrating the Silver Jubilee
> She tried to take on the upper class
> Now the worms are gnawing at her arse.
>
> (1977: 94)

Fox's inability to get the story into print renders patent the fact that his attack on the hierarchy of the institutions from his own position within one of those institutions was, at best, naive. As a gossip columnist, he is (like Sayers) merely a servant of an official 'voice' of dominant ideology. In other words, Fox could not beat Claughton and be in his pay at the same time.

Yet the play does not end with Fox's self-realization. Fox also imagines a future moment (the upcoming by-election), literalized with another of his conjuring tricks. The rhyming couplets which memorialize Grandma Sprightly echo the conventions of Jacobean plays where closure is enacted but where the too-easy rhyme of the verse indicates the very sham of that closure. Keeffe, in his ending, tries to suggest not only that Fox has learned something of his own naivety as well as the not to be underrated resilience of the interested parties. He thus anticipates tricks that might yet be performed.

Here, then, we might see a Jacobean text recycled not only to comment on the condition of present-day society but to test the limits that trangressions must cross over and back in search of a future moment where dissidence might be effectively enacted. Foucault notes:

> The limit and transgression depend on each other for whatever density of being they possess: a limit could not exist if it were absolutely uncrossable and, reciprocally, transgression would be pointless if it merely crossed a limit composed of illusions and shadows. . . .
>
> Transgression, then, is not related to the limit as black to white, the prohibited to the lawful, the outside to the inside, or as the open area of a building to its enclosed spaces. Rather, their relationship takes the form of a spiral which no simple infraction can exhaust.
>
> (1977: 34–35)

Keeffe's employment of city comedy to enact such a dependency of limit and transgression suggests not that the limit is 'uncrossable' but that it encourages the transgression – indeed, is nourished by it – in the assertion of its own fixity. For all the tricks at work in *A Mad World, My Masters*, the biggest trick of all is the security of power, challenged but ultimately also produced by the transgressive criss-crossing of limits, that serves the privileged few.

A more recent and perhaps more successful appeal to the strategies of city comedy comes in Peter Greenaway's film *The Cook, The Thief, His Wife and Her Lover* (1990). The opening sequence is dazzlingly metatheatrical: huge stage curtains are drawn back to reveal the film's sound set, a gesture which immediately recalls and renders as pastiche the beginning of Laurence Olivier's wartime film of *Henry V*. The sound stage serves as the street environment surrounding the restaurant where much of the film's action unfolds; we are at once refused the heightened realism of film and drawn instead to a more allegorical reading of Greenaway's text. The story, such as it is, involves boorish gangster Albert Spica (as critics have pointed out, Spica is a silly anagram of aspic, a culinary substance with some relevance to the character's ultimate fate) as a would-be gourmet who nightly takes his long-suffering wife to an extravagant French restaurant. Georgina, Albert's wife, catches the eye of another (lone) diner, with whom she soon has sex in the women's washroom. They commence a passionate affair, largely conducted during the course of dinner in one or other of the restaurant's kitchen storerooms. Eventually, Albert discovers his wife's infidelity and seeks revenge. If the plot signals revenge, the mood of the film is one of satiric humor – the kind of spirit that characterizes much Jacobean city comedy. And the characters, like their Jacobean counterparts, are not fully developed but more obviously functional in Greenaway's charting of 'the condition of England.' As one reviewer puts it, 'None of the characters have any internality: they are actors in a choreographed dance that Greenaway has meticulously designed' (Quart 1990: 45).[13]

Greenaway has made much of the film's being influenced by the Jacobeans and especially John Ford and his play *'Tis Pity She's A Whore* (revived twice in 1988 when Greenaway's film was likely in production – one production staged by Alan Ayckbourn for the Royal National Theatre and the other by Philip Prowse at the Glasgow Citizens Theatre).[14] Not that Greenaway's citation excuses the excess of his film for all his audience:

> Greenaway has mentioned Jacobean drama, and specifically *'Tis Pity She's A Whore*, as the model for his assault on taboo areas of sexuality and corporeality, and most reviews have taken this up, as if simply invoking the Jacobeans sufficed to account for *The Cook*. But if one were to try to explicate the film in these terms, awkward questions would have to be asked again about character, motivation and psychology.
>
> (Combs 1989: 323)[15]

Maybe this reviewer, Richard Combs, isn't too familiar with the criticism of Jacobean drama which tends to ask the same awkward questions to mark its distance from, and inferiority to, the Shakespearean benchmark.

Other critics are more ready to recognize the Jacobean connection, if not necessarily to applaud it. David Edelstein writes:

> For precedents, Greenaway cites bloody, tumultous Jacobean tragedies like Ford's ''Tis Pity She's A Whore' – a play in which individuals, swollen like monsters, rebel against the universe's moral laws and receive a terrible punishment. Reading of the comparison, I have to laugh. The Jacobeans might have given us gut-bucket travesties of Shakespeare and the Elizabethans, but the plays are nonetheless wrenching, and their heroes have a crazed stature. Spica is merely a sadistic gas-bag, and while he bellows incessantly, he doesn't have a single memorable line. In England, where the film was a mysterious hit, he was seen as a satire of Thatcherite piggery.
>
> (1990: 23)

Similarly, William Van Wert comments on the various temporalities addressed in Greenaway's text: 'What is English in this film is both Jacobean revenge tragedies and Margaret Thatcher's England' (1990–91: 42). In other words, the film provides two distinct (although perhaps not entirely different) points of entry for the spectator: one which relies on a nostalgia for the texts of the 'past,' the other which relies on a more contemporary nostalgia expressed in a present-day context.

Certainly the device of the Jacobean (and I will persist in my argument that, despite the revenge plot in the latter part of the film, its register is primarily that of the satiric city comedy) is engaged by the director to make the past speak as a thinly veiled allusion to the practices of English society under Thatcher. Albert Spica is seen as an excessive example of the self-serving, self-opinionated, consumerist nouveau riche who characterized, for her critics, the achievement of Thatcherite economic policy. Leonard Quart comments:

> Of course, since Greenaway's film is a fable with political implications, it need not provide detailed motivations for its characters. But viewed as a political parable, and Greenaway stated that *The Cook* is suffused with his 'anger and passion about the terrifying pejoratives done to the political life in Great Britain by this wretched Mrs. Thatcher,' the film is heavy-handed, and, paradoxically, lacking clarity. . . .

All of this is much too literal and facile. Viewing gross, working class Albert as a representative of the excesses of the Thatcher ethos lets the audience off the hook by allowing it to feel superior to this barbarian and psychopath. Thatcherism is clearly a more complex and subtle phenomenon than an ethos that gives license to uncontrolled and rapacious behavior on the part of the new rich.

(1990: 45)

Much of this criticism is well made. Greenaway's support for the cook (as artist), the wife (as sensually and sexually repressed in her marriage to Albert) and her lover (the sensitive man obsessed with his books and with his love for Georgina) is shared by the spectator but, as Quart notes, all three are equally tied up in the economy of consumer capitalism: the restaurant is the world that defines them for the film and for us.

But I think events in *The Cook*, like the actions in city comedy, dictate an ambivalent position from which we can respond to (and laugh at) a world that is both our own and an excessive exaggeration of it. In common with Keeffe's *A Mad World, My Masters*, this film frames all of its stories (or perhaps, since the choreography trope is a persuasive one, its dance steps) as economic transactions. We may be drawn to laugh in painful places, but we recognize our complicity in assigning an unambiguous financial price on all aspects of our experience. Combs suggests that

[a]s political allegory, *The Cook etc.* is both a vicious and a visceral indictment of the greed and conspicuous consumption of contemporary Britain. The only hope in the film, if it is a hope, is a reassertion of fairly traditional and conservative values about particular kinds of art.

(1989: 323)

And this is true. It is as if Greenaway produces a nostalgic craving for high art (Shakespeare? perhaps this could be considered particularly convincing since his next project was *Prospero's Books*), instead of the Jacobean model that serves his purpose of satire.

Nevertheless his concentration on bodily function within this film makes it a much more complicated text than a simple indictment of government policies. He realizes in filmic form bodies that transgress and desire at every turn, and it is in this mode that his work might be seen as thoroughly Jacobean:

103

The nature of chaos and the chaos of nature is after all one of Greenaway's major preoccupations. In *The Cook etc.* he cooks this raw material up into culture. The urgent sticky undertow of nature is always threatening to disrupt the cultural, in spite of our elaborate system of rituals and taboos. Albert Spica is a monster because he breaks those taboos. He pisses on his victims. He tells toilet jokes while eating. He is disgusting, greedy and excessive.

(Combs 1989: 43)

We, as viewers of this film, bracket Spica as Other: as he exceeds the limits of a transgressive field that we allow, he permits our identification with the artistic sensibility of knowledge that Greenaway also produces. It is, as Peter Stallybrass and Allon White describe, that

[t]he bourgeois subject continuously defined and re-defined itself through the exclusion of what it marked out as 'low' – as dirty, repulsive, noisy, contaminating. Yet that very act of exclusion was constitutive of its identity. The low was internalized under the sign of disgust.

(1986: 191)

Yet even as our rejection of Spica confirms our better selves, we are caught with our attraction to his performance: 'disgust always bears the imprint of desire. These low domains, apparently expelled as "Other," return as the object of nostalgia, longing and fascination' (Stallybrass and White 1986: 191).

That Spica is a parodic example of Thatcherite success is not, ultimately, the crux of Greenaway's film. It is more importantly about what we repress or fetishize in our attempt to succeed in the maintenance of a bourgeois subjectivity. The choreography of this film's excess and decay employs a Jacobean sensibility to structure a ' "poetics" of transgression [that] reveals the disgust, fear and desire which inform the dramatic self-representation of that culture through the "scene of its low Other" ' (Stallybrass and White 1986: 202). This poetics is one which is most dramatically realized in a device of two trucks filled with what soon becomes rotting meat. They are left unattended, the decay progressing to the point at which the carcasses are 'alive' with maggots and so on, until a vehicle is needed for Georgina and her lover's getaway (a grotesque parody of the obligatory movie car chase). Their despatch, amidst the decayed animal bodies (the finished nature of film even yet inspiring a sense of some horrific stench), speaks of a transgressive desire which makes us long for the love that Georgina and Michael express, at the same time as we manifest the disgust that always also 'bears the imprint of desire.' Greenaway's images are powerfully dissident: they give a visual imagination to the dark (Jacobean) recesses of psychical experience. *The Cook, The Thief, His Wife and Her Lover* is certainly a 'decay of the nation' film; it is also a compelling comedy which charts the return of the repressed.

Howard Barker's revision of the Jacobean – what he called a collaboration with Thomas Middleton on *Women Beware Women* – attempts to reinvigorate revenge tragedy as a late twentieth-century cultural expression. In a 'conversation' between Barker and Middleton that was published in *The Times* just before the play's premiere performance (1986 at the Royal Court Theatre), Barker discusses his attraction to the play for its 'obsessive linkage between money, power and sex' (Howard Barker 1986: 15). He, too, makes explicit the contemporary relevance of his project: 'England in this era is a money and squalor society, also' (1986: 15).

The new *Women Beware Women* retained the first three and a half acts of Middleton's original text and supplemented these with Barker's original writing. But before looking to this new conclusion and its implications in an optic of nostalgia and desire, it is perhaps useful to examine what is retained and to suggest how this seventeenth-century writing speaks as a contemporary Jacobean voice. The jarring of styles in Middleton's text (naturalistic scenes in Leantio's household; stylized formality in the chess game and masques) gives the play an almost postmodern hybridity which sets up a dissonance between visual and verbal signification. In the play's opening scene Leantio conveys his love for Bianca through images of her value; this scene is followed by the Duke's seduction, which implants the actuality of money as the basis for all relationships: Bianca dissolves her marriage in expressions of her distaste for the austerity of Leantio's house; Leantio is bribed first by the Duke with a captainship and then by Livia in a money-for-sex arrangement; and, in the subplot, Ward attempts a physical examination of his future bride, Isabella, which treats her only as a commodity. These actions demonstrate both what Leonard Tennenhouse has called the closing of 'the line between the two social bodies – the aristocratic body and that of the people'

(1989: 88) and the contemporary fetishization of sex in its economic register. In the first case, Tennenhouse goes on to suggest that the common lovers of aristocrats might appear to be capable (even perhaps deserving) of 'becoming part of the aristocratic body, but the fact of their transgression is acknowledged as they produce disease, filth, and obscenity that must be purged in order for there to be a pure community of aristocratic blood' (1989: 88). Thus, as in *A Mad World, My Masters* and *The Cook, The Thief, His Wife and Her Lover*, social anxiety located on the bodies of the dominant's Other materializes as a recognition of impurity, subject necessarily to discipline and punishment.

The most arresting demonstration of the power/sex/money triangle that Barker flags as the core of his interest in Middleton's text comes at the opening of the fourth act. This scene between Bianca and Leantio repeats the play's opening but acts as a distorting mirror. Alone on stage (once more citing and subverting Shakespeare's *Romeo and Juliet* with Bianca on the palace balcony and Leantio below), Bianca and Leantio trade lines on the material benefits of their commodified relationships, bringing the on-stage tension to a remarkable climax on Leantio's line 'Y'are a whore' (Barker and Middleton 1986: 18). It is not surprising that it is on this reading of the female body that Barker chooses to intervene with what he sees as the redemptive power of desire.

How these scenes perform as contemporary Jacobean text is revealed by Barker's editing strategies. Not only is the original text contracted to present a much tighter plot development, but the verse is rewritten as prose. Both tactics serve to contemporize Middleton's text. The paring of lines not only simplifies a typically tortuous Jacobean revenge plot, but makes an already fast-paced play dizzying in the speed with which characters capitulate to greed. In the more minimal presentation of motivation, the determined self-promotion is starkly apparent. Printed in its entirety as prose, the published version at least suggests Barker's intention, in some way, to alter the effect of the original poetic language. It might be said simply to cater to the taste of contemporary audiences, but the effects of Barker's cuts and shifts in emphasis are to create a *Women Beware Women* which sounds remarkably like the *film noir* echoed in so many Jacobean (re)productions.

In 'The Redemptive Power of Desire,' 'Middleton' tells his collaborator:

You are an irresponsible optimist. You have deprived the audience of its right to moral satisfaction. Admittedly you have provided a violent conclusion, but with only one murder, when I wrote five or six. I do think this is an encouragement for bad morals.

(Howard Barker 1986: 15)

Barker, in his 'response,' points to the centrality of desire in his refashioned ending. Certainly that conclusion rejects conventional closure, the masque and its carnage as testament to the inevitable result of sin. In Middleton's play, only four lines remain after the final on-stage death (Bianca's). To speak to contemporary times, Barker eschews closure and instead presents a fragmented, but surviving group. The Barker/Middleton collaboration rephrases the jarring of styles: the first half, the edited Middleton, seems curiously and consciously naturalistic while Barker's second half is determinedly imagistic.

In this second half, Barker foregrounds the dramatic realization of limits. He addresses the limits of sexual power and of political power in the context of the transgressions that must necessarily traverse them. In this negotiation, he attempts to locate a revolutionary discourse that might convey power in terms of desire – a possibility which fits well with Tamsin Spargo and Fred Botting's suggestion that '[l]ike power, desire demands the transgression and thus the affirmation and transformation of limits. It proposes a movement disruptive of any boundaries that attempt its final regulation' (1993: 381). Such a disruptive movement is posited in the transformation of Leantio and Livia's sexual desire into a potential for widescale political dissidence. As the director of the 1986 production indicates, 'whereas Middleton sees sex as part of the sin which leads to death, Barker sees it as a liberating revolutionary force in society' (cited in Trotter 1986: 194).[16]

The opening scene of the play's second and new half stages a graphic and disturbing account of Leantio and Livia's sexual relationship, their sexual histories, and the pervasiveness of sexual repressions. In part, Barker's strategy is to create a shock effect: the Jacobean signifying, as it always seems to, moral disobedience and excess. Yet the audience is bound to be dislocated by the shift in style and has, in effect, to construct a new set of receptive strategies with which to give signification to the revised events. Barker

107

dramatically counters the audience's habitual reliance on likeness (the text's resemblance to other Jacobean plays they've seen).

As a contrast to Livia's evocation of desire as revolution, the wedding plans for the Duke and Bianca suggest a cruel and oppressive manipulation of their relationship as only politically motivated and powerful:

> DUKE: My popularity was never higher, and she dangles from me, flashing like some encrusted gem, blinding discontent and dazzling the cynic. Duchess of Florence! How does the title please you?
> BIANCA: It enhances my beauty.
> DUKE: It does so, and your enhanced beauty in turn enhances me.
>
> (Barker and Middleton 1986: 26)

Moreover, the Duke sees their union not only in terms of political popularity but as an effective tool for regulating the behaviors of his subjects:

> You will see . . . that the dossers will applaud my wedding and go home warmer than they would be from a meal, there is great nourishment in pageantry. Later, the royal birth will have them gasping who cannot conceive themselves, and those that can will name their stinking brats after ours immaculate.
>
> (1986: 26)

If such an equation might be applied to any exhibition of vast political power, critics of the 1986 production have found it easy to connect the Duke's arrogance and appeal to pageantry with a British obsession with royal weddings and subsequent production of offspring.[17]

Notwithstanding the Duke's ugly aspirations, the royal wedding eventually marks the dissolution of the Duke's brutal control. In the Barker revision, Sordido (only a minor player in Middleton's original) − after separate encounters with Leantio and Livia − becomes the catalyst for sexual and political revenge. He is to rape Bianca on her wedding morning:

> LEANTIO: This is a futile picnic, dancing defiance from a distance . . .
> LIVIA (turning away): But laugh we must! Must laugh at wit

of dukes, who give decrepit forts to men with decent grudges!
SORDIDO: Laugh, yes, because our joke is better.
LEANTIO: What joke? The ruination of Bianca?
LIVIA: Ruination, why? We save her.
LEANTIO: Save her! By rape! Since when was rape salvation?
LIVIA: Leantio, whole cliffs of lies fall down in storms. By this catastrophe she'll grope for knowledge her ambition hides from her. And simultaneously, Sordido's crime will rock the state off its foundations, which is erected on such lies as ducal marriages.

(1986: 30)

Sordido, Barker comments, is the ideal opponent for the Duke and, through his new status, 'pushed the *nouveau riche* flavour of your [Middleton's] Florence, its vulgarity and accompanying poverty, into a cultural match for England' (Barker 1986: 15). In his resituation of the subplot characters (Ward, Isabella and Sordido), Barker insists they do more than comment on the main action of the play. Isabella's sudden inclusion in the wedding party (a device to facilitate Sordido's access to Bianca) is awkward dramaturgy but its effect, nonetheless, is to unite the women in a common realization of their own vulnerability to patriarchal power and, particularly, desire as an expression of that power. This is not, however, to negate the intention of rape. As Anthony Dawson has said:

In Middleton's version, an awareness of what rape means in the social and political economy, its relationship to sexual blackmail, social institutions, and political power, finds a place in the text but no effective way out. Barker's way out of the dilemma seems as bad as the original problem.

(1987: 318)

McLuskie is even more critical of Barker's representation of women:

Livia . . . celebrates the knowledge that this sex has given her. However, the knowledge is not arrived at by her own perception but by the overwhelming power of Leantio's phallic energy. Her language describes sexual experience in terms of male fantasies of the all-dominating phallus which hurts and tears, reaching the womb and the heart. The knowledge which this coitus brings fuels her determination for political change. However, the change is to be brought about by humiliating Bianca and destroying her as a false image of purity. The perpetrator of this act, Sordido, is presented as one whose lowly origins give him true knowledge, furthermore, as a homosexual, his rape of Bianca is a pure act, uncompromised by desire. Women, it seems, have to be raped into knowledge, men gain revolutionary knowledge and power by abstaining.

(1989: 21–22)

In marked contrast to the brief moral commentary that concluded Middleton's *Women Beware Women*, Barker's play ends with only tentative gestures. Leantio and Livia assume the rule of Florence but their power is obviously vulnerable and untested. Livia, Isabella and Bianca seem to make some steps towards an unexplored sisterhood which Barker would have us believe holds some potential – McLuskie's careful analysis suggests that this might reinstitute the same all too familiar oppressions. Transgression is certainly not necessarily the expression of desire – or, at least, it is a gender-coded desire which is made available to transgression – and the dissidence that Barker proposes seems to serve only a very particular group whose privilege is hardly in question. Like the other examples discussed in this chapter, dissidence seems largely to be an expression of heterosexual males whose panic in the face of sexual, racial and gender difference activates the grammar of Jacobean performance.

Like the Barker/Middleton *Women Beware Women*, Derek Jarman's film remake of Christopher Marlowe's *Edward II*[18] is breathtakingly misogynistic. But unlike *Women Beware Women*, this film has a clearly articulated dissident politics. In rewriting (or 'improving') his source, Jarman has repositioned a key text in an emergent canon of gay literature in the context of the specificities of contemporary cultural experience. The strength of Jarman's work is precisely in its referential multiplicity. I want to look here at particular moments in the filmic text where the 'pastness' of the world of Edward and his court is fractured by direct reference to the present, where characters and/or incidents are recodified. With this in mind, it is perhaps important to note briefly something of the play's original discursive formation.

In a clever approach to the cultural reception of Shakespeare's

sonnets and questions of sexual politics, Simon Shepherd offers a
helpful comparison between the cultural apparatus's privilege of
Shakespeare (in the frame of a hegemonic practice of tradition)
and its disdain for his contemporary, Marlowe:

> It is easier to concede that a supposedly lesser poet such as
> Marlowe may have been queer. In fact his homosexuality may
> be used to explain why he was a lesser poet: Wilbur Sanders
> says Marlowe's works are distorted by an ill-disciplined homo-
> sexual passion, where Shakespier was a consummate artist.
> Discussion of homosexuality in Shakspeer seems to be moti-
> vated not by an interest in Renaissance sexuality but by
> Shakespaire's national status. Criticism's task is to discover a
> fitting sexuality for the National Bard. The task is specifi-
> cally taken up by and shaped by *literary* criticism, for the
> literature is what is to be protected. The literature belongs
> to the nation.
>
> (1988: 97)[19]

Marlowe's plays, then, are explicitly marked as not-Shakespeare
(and, apparently, by association not-English) and designated thus
on an identification of sexual identity. Actual sexual preferences
and practices of the authors are neither important nor stable for
the efficiency of this designation. For Jarman, categorization of
Marlowe's plays primarily through the author's purported sexual
identity affords him an already coded and invested textuality on
which to overwrite his filmic images. In the screenplay to *Edward
II*, Jarman writes: 'I have a deep hatred of the Elizabethan past
used to castrate our vibrant present' (1991: 112).[20] Thus his use
for this classical text (even as a text located in a counter-classical
tradition) is to invigorate the present – to raise particular questions
relevant to contemporary social formations and to suggest a clearly
articulated political response to those questions. *Edward II*, an
exquisitely constructed film, demands that it be read not only in
its relation to what it does to the Marlowe source text, but as a
political intervention in its own historical moment.

There are a number of sequences which construct such a productive interplay between the dramatic imagination of Marlowe's text
and representations of homosexuality in the present. If Jarman is
often quite faithful to the lines from Marlowe's *Edward II* (and,
despite Jarman insisting 'fuck poetry' in his foreword to the screenplay, there is an aural intensity which more than matches Jarman's

always beautiful visual imagery), the characters visit their speeches on obviously contemporary artefacts. When Edward is persuaded to sign the order which effects Gaveston's deportation from England, the close-up shot reveals not any royal insignia but the logo of Britain's present-day rulers, the House of Commons, and the charter is visibly dated 1991 (1991: 60, Sequence 30). In this social index, Jarman deftly draws into frame the recent signing of Britain's pernicious Section 28 of the Local Government Act, which denies public money to any project that might be identified with what is defined by that Section as the promotion of homosexuality.[21] A little later in the film, the clash between the factions in Marlowe's play is resituated as an opposition between the police (fully armed in riot gear) and members of Britain's gay activist OutRage (dressed in T-shirts and carrying placards – the slogans from which serve as sequence headings in the published screenplay). The cacophony of the scene insists on that articulation of present-day censorship and resistance as part of an iconic tradition. As Jarman comments, 'In our film all the OutRage boys and girls are inheritors of Edward's story' (1991: 146). But it also insists on the specificities of ideological practices in a regressive social economy. Enacted protest resists the film's articulation of transgressive desire as merely historical. Jarman says, 'Filmed history is always a misinterpretation. The past is the past, as you try to make material out of it, things slip even further away. "Costume drama" is such a delusion based on a collective amnesia, ignorance and furnishing fabrics' (1991: 86). Moreover, what interests Jarman is not any sort of authentic representation of either past or present, even if that were a possible 'costume drama,' but the interplay between contradictory historical moments for the purpose of examining issues surrounding sexual identity: 'From the moment that Mortimer appears with the dress and bearing of an SAS officer in Northern Ireland, the equations between past and present, between state and sexuality, are clearly visible' (McCabe 1991: 12).

Not that audiences have readily embraced Jarman's use and abuse of History, his refusal to accept both collective amnesia and repressive nostalgia. Colin McCabe suggests that '[i]t is impossible for the audience to feel itself separate from the work - reaction is not only demanded (as it was always by the most neo-classical of forms), but is, of necessity, displayed in a genuinely new form of carnival (1991: 14). The excess and determination of that carnival has, undoubtedly, provoked extreme reaction to the film. When I first saw the film in Calgary (a city located in Canada's most vehemently conservative province), more people walked out of the art-house cinema than I've ever encountered in my cinema/theatre-going career – eventually leaving an audience of nine for the screening. How is it that the site/sight of Edward and Gaveston together, embracing on the throne, can still so affect a more or less monarchy-less world?

In what might be assumed to be a more sympathetic reception community, the gay press, critical reaction has, on occasion, been equally hostile: Bob Satuloff (writing in *Christopher Street*) calls the film 'stultifying, claustrophobic, and mean-spirited,' asking 'Does he want to kill the heterosexuals, lock them away, or merely separate us from them in some kind of sexual/affectional apartheid? Is that the purpose of the gay struggle? If it is, count me out' (1992: 4, 5). It is the explicit statement not so much of what he 'does' to Marlowe (since it's not-Shakespeare, the implication being 'who cares') but of Jarman's dissident purpose that would seem to transgress the parameters of the viewing contract. Jarman insists on the articulation of 'how this sexuality is linked to certain traditions of representation' (McCabe 1991: 14) and it is surely important in critical endeavors to calibrate the conditions under which his interrogation of such traditions becomes literally unwatchable.

Of all the examples cited in my text, Jarman's is perhaps the most successful in producing an interaction between multiple historical moments, an interaction that proposes a future which might look somewhat different. While his strategy does in some ways invite what McCabe calls 'a nostalgic Utopia' (1991: 14), it also, importantly, occupies a space that produces the limits of representation, yet imagines the possibility of exceeding those limits to produce other configurations of desire and power. Jonathan Goldberg has pointed out that:

> [t]he theater was permitted to rehearse the dark side of Elizabethan culture; it was a recreative spot where sedition could wear the face of play, where authors could make assertions as potent as monarchs'. In the theater, kings were the puppets of writers; greatness was mimed; atheists, rebels, magicians, and sodomites could be publicly displayed.
>
> (1991: 80)

Goldberg is concerned with how Elizabethan society produced a counter-identity, ascribing to Marlowe 'the rhetoric of his inventions. Marlowe is charged with *being* what he and his society allowed existence only as *negations* and *fictions*. Marlowe was not just playing' (1991: 81). And, in Jarman's film, Edward and Gaveston are not just playing either. The stakes in the world to which their story is being retold are incredibly high: Jarman writes against the fact of censorship on the basis of sexuality and, mostly poignantly in the screenplay, a diary of his own ongoing fight with AIDS. In all its aspects, *Edward II* seeks out an expression for sexual identity which cannot be easily contained or denied by hegemonic codes of heterosexual visibility.

Jarman's vision for a future is created, in part, through the trajectory in the film of Prince Edward. This character is represented in the film by a young boy, even though, as Jarman acknowledges in his screenplay, the *facts* of history indicate he would have been seventeen years old when he took England's throne.[22] The child delivers Marlowe's lines with a delightful innocence: in Sequence 32A as his father 'makes his way through a group of clergymen holding Prince Edward's hand,' Young Edward asks quite simply in response to his father's desperate speech to assert his kingship, 'Why should you love him who the world hates so?' (1991: 66). The clarity and simplicity of his question and its delivery is both moving and indicative of Young Edward's ability to see past all the diplomatic maneuverings of all the interest groups. His understanding of power and his incomprehension of love are starkly realized in this single moment.

Beyond his lines, however, Young Edward performs a multiplicity of gendered positions, each one in some way miming the identity of another character. We see him perform his father and his father's lover (dressed in the same Marks & Spencer pyjamas); at other times, he mimics Mortimer (in both formal military uniform and in more obviously terrorist garb). In Sequence 74, when an official photograph is being taken and he is on the verge of being declared King, his dark suit, white shirt and tie is an exact if scaled-down copy of Kent's to mark an allegiance counter to his mother's and Mortimer's claims. By the end of the film, his costume has been modified: he is still in the same dark suit but now, too, in his mother's silver earrings and make-up – and he is standing atop a cage containing Isabella and Mortimer. Jarman writes of the cage sequence:

The little boy is always there. He's a witness and a survivor.
... When he's dancing on the top of their cage later, it
reduces him to some sort of puppet. By using Tchaikovsky
[Young Edward is listening to the 'Dance of the Sugar Plum
Fairy' on his Walkman] I wanted to reinforce the idea of
them as wind-up dolls. I was thinking of Eisenstein's 'Ivan
the Terrible,' when he mounts the throne, that great moment
when child Ivan's feet dangle from the throne and don't reach
the ground. I couldn't get a quotation in like that, it would
have been too much. There is an element of young Edward
being me, but everyone identifies with the child.

(cited in O'Pray 1991: 11)[23]

Already the representation of Young Edward is too much. He tests
and exceeds the traditional iconography of power and of gender
identity. He shows them as only performatives. Judith Butler has
argued for the productive possibility of a range of disobedience:
'The law might not only be refused, but it might also be ruptured,
forced into a rearticulation that calls into question the monotheistic
force of its own unilateral operation' (1993: 122). And, indeed,
Edward's performative gestures speak to the generative potential of
such a site. *Edward II* is a hopeful film. Its insistence on a future
that might emerge at the interstices of transgression, dissidence and
desire confronts the shortcomings of its own historical moment
not, in the end, by looking back but by resolutely looking forward
and with some pleasure to all the dangers, to the inevitable and
costly conflicts, and, finally, to death.

(POST)COLONIAL (POST)SCRIPT I

My bones will rise from the earth and
drive you back into the sea.

(Nicholas Wright 1983: 52)

This chapter refers to one more play, as a kind of appendix to the
performance of the Jacobean. It is 1983 and I'd like to address two
productions which take as their starting point Fletcher and
Massinger's *The Custom of the Country*. For the Glasgow Citizens
Theatre, Robert David Macdonald resituated the 'picaresque study
of lust and love set in the stews of Lisbon after two brothers
and a virgin have left Italy to preserve the latter from the custom
of the country, i.e. the *droit de seigneur*, by which a nobleman can

sleep with any new bride married on his territory' (Coveney 1990: 168) in Hollywood, complete with a Sydney Greenstreet lookalike and an Oscar-toting Jean Harlow. Decadence resignified into the contemporary is most easily and accessibly represented by the movie business and America. At least from a British lens that might seem to be the case. Once again 'radical' is made to perform the role of chic. The second, and more interesting, reworking of *The Custom of the Country* was by Nicholas Wright for the Royal Shakespeare Company. Wright much more fully transposes his source text not only into a different time, but also repopulates his text with characters bearing only the slightest resemblance to their Jacobean predecessors.

Like Jarman's *Edward II*, Wright's play takes on the proliferation of identity. The play is set in the Republic of Transvaal in the 1890s, and the text reshapes the Jacobean comic plot to explore the tensions and fractures that necessarily occur at the intersections of identity positions. In the black female body of Tendai rests the prize of Empire – her sexual obedience ensures the extension and satisfaction of the colonial project. If she can be produced as a passive and obedient subject, then hers is the body which will function as passport to her home state's wealth of unmined gold. In the structure of comic farce, Wright explores the possibilities of claiming a self against a matrix of economic, gender and race regulation. And at the end of the play, after all the loose ends of comic plotting are at once unraveled and resolved, Tendai makes the stage her own:

> TENDAI: Good people, one moment.
> (*To ANTONIO:*) Honoured chief, you are a black man pos-
> sessed by the spirit of a white. Cast it out in the proper
> manner and you can mend the damage you have done.
> (*To HENRIETTA:*) Honoured mother, your husband is good
> for one thing only. If he does not do it enough, you must
> tell your neighbours, throw him out and keep your bride-
> price.
> (*To WILLEM:*) Little brother -
> (*To ROGER:*) – big brother –
> (*To JAMESON:*) – honoured healer –
> (*To BRINK:*) – bearded father -
> (*To PAUL:*) – husband of my heart, and all you white people
> Now I am married into your family you must love me.

116

Honour my father, respect my brothers, be generous and
kind to their wives, their children, their cousins, their most
far relatives. Live in our land in peace and we will protect
you. But treat us like dogs and we will rise. My bones
will rise from the earth and drive you back into the sea.

(1983: 51–52)

Her speech is a patently prophetic one: she speaks to the nation
of South Africa which, in the 1890s, was not yet founded; she
speaks to the imperialism of the English in that geography and
elsewhere, in that historical moment and in our own; she speaks
to black men to resist cooperation with the colonial project and
to avoid the kinds of damage we have since witnessed; and she
speaks to her spectators ('all you white people' – at the Royal
Shakespeare Company, one might assume a hegemonically white
viewing economy) to remind them of a widespread and punitive
racism that goes too often unchecked in contemporary society.
Since her warnings in the historical context of her performance
have gone unheeded, this monologue urges an increased urgency
to our own responses. We are made complicit in the dominant
cultural practices that demand abject bodies in the maintenance of
their/our own power. And we are charged, too, with the responsibility for change.

Thus, in the way of *Edward II*, *The Custom of the Country* looks
to a future. It may, too, be one of hope – that we will hear and
heed Tendai's words. Or it may be one of a dissidence that will
exact a high price from all the people whom it involves.

As Stallybrass and White remind us, '[c]ontrol of the major sites
of discourse is fundamental to political change' (1986: 202). Where
transgression, dissidence and desire can be employed to reveal the
fractures and the gaps in those sites, then there opens up a space
in which change becomes possible. Elsewhere, the endless production and reproduction of transgression, dissidence and desire merely
confirms the efficiency with which dominant economies claim
such subversive action for their own sustenance. The Jacobean calls
attention to its not-Shakespeare status, to its overdetermined signification as a plethora of decay-imbued adjectives, to its site at the
limits of tradition. For the most part, it performs itself as trope:
the Jacobean might fall under the very category that Stallybrass
and White define as 'the very subjects which it [the bourgeoisie]
politically excludes becoming exotic costumes which it assumes in

117

order to play out the disorders of its own identity' (1986: 200).[24] Few texts find the courage and the voice to wear those exotic costumes differently, to ask who seizes and who is given the right to wear such costumes, and for whom. And if the costume is a shifting signifier that contests the very conditions of cultural production and reception, it is also incumbent in such a reading to elucidate the bodies that Shakespeare is called upon to serve. It is this perhaps more primary stage that the ensuing discussion of *The Tempest* takes up.

4

THE POST-COLONIAL BODY?

Thinking through *The Tempest*

Can a Savage remayning a Savage be civill?
(Samuel Purchas, *Purchas His Pilgrimes*, 1625:
Vol. xix)

In our technological world where the humanities are crumbling
all around us the question remains – how shall we salvage
Shakespeare?
(G. Muliyil, 'Why Shakespeare for Us?' in
Narasimhaiah 1964: 11)

THE CRITICAL BODY AND THE COLONIAL BODY

No Western text has played a more visible role in the representation
and reconstruction of the colonial body than Shakespeare's *The
Tempest*. It is a play which has 'long functioned in the service of
ideologies that repress what they cannot accommodate and exploit
what they can' (Cartelli 1989: 112) and the bipolar and antagonistic
relationship of Prospero and Caliban persists as an originating
dramatization of the imperial master and the colonized indigene.
It is perhaps the case that the tired trope of Prospero and Caliban
(standing in for the equally tired trope of Same and Other) should
be retired and that other models for understanding the practices and
effects of 'imperialism without colonies' be developed.[1] Yet in the
complex and relational network of the discourses of colonialism
and the somewhat optimistic determination that 'we' now participate in an historical moment which is not only postmodern but post-
colonial, it in fact still seems premature to abandon this particularly
powerful staging of strategies for regulation across the boundaries of
gender, class, race, sexuality, and nation.

While there has been some attempt to correct the notion that at the time of *The Tempest's* first performance (1611) the discourse of colonialism was already entrenched and rigorous in its practice,[2] it is nevertheless the position of much subsequent critical practice (and, indeed, performance practice too) that the play is unquestioningly imbricated within that discourse (Barker and Hulme 1985: 204). In many ways, whatever its situatedness in the emergent colonial practices of early seventeenth-century England, *The Tempest* has come to function both in its textual and performative readings as a public testing of and response to Samuel Purchas's self-inscribed marginalia to his published account of William Strachey's *True Reportory of the Wracke* (the first of the two epigraphs which open this chapter). And, until very recently, the answer to Purchas's speculation was a virtually univocal 'No.'[3]

In the criticism of the last decade or so, however, the assumptions behind such a peremptory response have become the focalization of the criticism itself. Taking up an Althusserian position, Cultural Materialist (and to a lesser extent, New Historicist) analysis of *The Tempest* has argued that while readings of texts are always symptomatic of the ideologies which provoke them, this does not abrogate responsibility for the play itself since its reproduction 'has made seminal contributions to the development of the colonialist ideology through which it is read' (Cartelli 1989: 100–101).[4]

Through locations of the play's participation in existing and emergent maps of seventeenth-century colonial enterprise, it is argued that *The Tempest* stages anxieties concerning England's regulation not only of newly discovered properties (particularly Virginia, but also Bermuda and other islands of the Caribbean) but also of a much longer attempted 'possession,' Ireland. Peter Hulme reads the expression of 'hurricane' and 'cannibal,' then two relatively new words appearing as part of the colonizer's drive to chart discoveries in/through language, and posits 'a palimpsest on which there are two texts,' one a Mediterranean discourse (sources in Virgil, Homer, and Ovid) and the other a yet emergent Atlantic ('Caribbee') discourse:

> What is important is that in either case the two referential systems occupy different spaces except for that area which is the island and its first native, Caliban. What I'm suggesting is that, in the case of the geometrical metaphor, the figure

of Caliban functions as a central axis about which both planes swivel free of one another; or, in the case of the textual metaphor, that the original Mediterranean text has superimposed upon it an Atlantic text that is written almost entirely in the spaces between the Mediterranean words, the exception being Caliban who is therefore doubly inscribed, a state perhaps indicated by the need for the four words used to describe him on the list of characters: Caliban, salvage, deformed, slave; an overdetermination particularly at odds with his place of habitation which is described as an 'uninhabited island.'

(Hulme 1981: 72)

And while Hulme suggests this double-framing for constructing Caliban's character, Paul Brown suggests that Ireland as both 'an opportunity for the expansion of civility' and a site 'for the possible undoing of civilised man' (1985: 57) was also a significant part of his topography.[5] These multiple discursive frames for Caliban's insurgence in *The Tempest* mark a founding premise of colonialism: that the 'uncivil' may be dispossessed by the 'civil' on the justification of the latter's attempt to 'civilize' the former *as well as* the latter's vulnerability to a reverse procedure (Barker and Hulme 1985: 200). Thus, in the play, when Prospero is at his most civil, staging the masque entertainment for the newly betrothed Miranda and Ferdinand, it is the threat of Caliban's revolt – abetted by Stephano and Trinculo (who, as Brown indicates, fall into the masterless class which so troubled the English trying to harness Ireland [1985: 58]) – that causes the abrupt ending of the revels:

PROSPERO [*Aside*]: I had forgot that foul conspiracy
    Of the beast Caliban and his confederates
    Against my life: the minute of their plot
    Is almost come. [*To the spirits*] Well done! avoid; no more!
FERDINAND: This is strange: your father's in some passion
    That works him strongly.
MIRANDA: Never till this day
    Saw I him so touch'd with anger, so distemper'd.

(IV, i, 138–145)

Prospero's prescience testifies to the thorough and efficient surveillance of the colonizer and to the extent of his rage at the challenge from what, a few lines later, Prospero calls: 'A devil, a born devil, on whose nature/Nurture can never stick; on whom my pains,/Humanely taken, all, all lost, quite lost' (IV, i, 188–190). Kwame Anthony Appiah makes the point that it is not just colonialism that Prospero must justify, but 'the especial brutality of the colonization of nonwhite peoples' (1990: 278).

As Barker and Hulme indicate, the effect of both Caliban's attempted rebellion and Prospero's extreme reaction is to occlude Antonio's earlier deposal of his brother:

> This allows Prospero to annul the memory of his failure to prevent his expulsion from the dukedom, by repeating it as a mutiny that he will, this time, forestall. But, in addition, the playing out of the colonialist narrative is thereby completed: Caliban's attempt – tarred with the brush of Antonio's supposedly self-evident viciousness – is produced as final and irrevocable confirmation of the natural treachery of savages.
>
> (1985: 201)

Yet such a playing out inevitably foregrounds the anxieties of that colonialist narrative at the same time as it seems to confirm its power (Brown 1985: 48) and *The Tempest* thus stages a remarkable ambivalence toward the violent dispossessions in the Atlantic colonies or, for that matter, in Ireland.[6]

Violence, however, is only a spectacular aspect of colonial regulation and, as Prospero attempted to teach Caliban and as the nineteenth-century English perhaps more successfully indoctrinated their children in preschool readers such as *ABC for Baby Patriots* and *Pictures for Little Englanders*,[7] language was a more subtle but no less effective tactic for the production of what Foucault terms 'docile bodies.' Stephen Greenblatt's *Learning to Curse* pays particular attention to the opposition of Prospero as 'a European whose entire source of power is his library and a savage who had no speech' (1990: 23).[8] Pointing to the conclusion to Samuel Daniel's *Musophilus* (1599) which interpellates the New World as 'a vast, rich field for the plantation of the English language' (1990: 16), Greenblatt accounts for the soon formed and long tenacious belief on the part of the imperial project that the indigenous peoples of the New World did not have either language or culture 'even in the face of overwhelming contradictory evidence' (1990: 17). It is not, of course, that Caliban is without language; it is that his own language is rendered silent – 'unhearable' – in the face of a discourse supremely confident of its own 'culture.' That Prospero, as colonizer, rules by his linguistic competence is perhaps most compellingly realized in Peter Greenaway's recent film version of Shakespeare's play, *Prospero's Books*. In this film, Prospero is played by John Gielgud, an actor whose presence is already overcoded as the last survivor of a group of English (male) actors whose apparent supremacy/authenticity with Shakespeare's English afforded them – and the plays and films they performed – a tremendous global currency. Moreover, the Greenaway/Gielgud Prospero speaks almost all of the characters' lines, thereby literalizing the idea that all Prospero's subjects must accede to his version of the past.[9] Equally compelling interpolations of a script in the process of being written by hand – what Greenaway calls '[w]ords making text, and text making pages, and pages making books from which knowledge is fabricated in pictorial form' (1991: 9) – combine with Gielgud/Prospero's often singular and always predominant voice to leave no doubt as to where power might be located.[10]

Certainly the textual body of Shakespeare's plays has been a prevalent and enduring component of Western colonial practice. Articles such as Alan Sinfield's witty but disturbing 'Give an account of Shakespeare and Education, showing why you think they are effective and what you have appreciated about them. Support your comments with precise references' (Dollimore and Sinfield 1985, 134–157) have demonstrated the usefulness of Shakespeare's texts to the conservative ideologies of institutional practice, although if we imagine that this is merely the product of English chauvinism, then the Editor's note to *Shakespeare Came to India* is a salutary reminder of the enduring pervasiveness of the Bard's 'moral wisdom.' C.D. Narasimhaiah writes of his volume:

> The title is not so fanciful as it appears to be when we remember that of the many things that came to India from England few in the long run are really as important as Shakespeare. For the England of trade, commerce, imperialism and the penal code has not endured but the imperishable Empire of Shakespeare will always be with us. And that is something to be grateful for.
>
> (1964: v)[11]

The examples of Greenaway's *Prospero's Books* and C.D. Narasimhaiah's introduction offer two different and contradictory trajectories for the dissemination of Shakespeare in the recent past, and, as a development of the kinds of synchronic histories provided by Hulme and Brown, critical readings of *The Tempest* through a diachronic matrix indicate 'many who would quarrel with the notion of a *Tempest* that speaks the predatory language of colonialism on behalf of the governing structures of western power and ideals. But there is another, nonwestern interpretive community for whom *The Tempest* has long served as the embodiment of colonial presumption' (Cartelli 1989: 101). Both Cartelli and Rob Nixon dwell on appropriations of *The Tempest* by African writers (a topic I return to in discussion of Aimé Césaire's *Une Tempête* and other 'anti-colonial bodies') and point to such appropriations' reliance on their source text as 'a foundational paradigm in the history of European colonialism' (Cartelli 1989: 101). Cartelli discusses *A Grain of Wheat* (1967) by Kenyan writer Ngugi Wa Thiong'o and his protagonist's intersections both with his source script (he is working on a book called 'Prospero in Africa') and the 'other' foundational colonial text, Conrad's *Heart of Darkness* (Cartelli 1989: 101-107). Ngugi's stance, Cartelli suggests, is that

> a historically or critically 'correct' reading of *The Tempest* that isolates the play 'at its originating moment of production' would serve merely an antiquarian's interest, documenting an alleged 'intervention' in colonialist discourse that made no discernibly positive impact on the subsequent development of colonial practices.
>
> (1989: 107)

So for all the anxieties and ambivalences traced in accounts of the play's 'originating moments,' it is evident that the text has had rather a different after-life, and other – equally extensive – critical attention has focused on producing a reception history.

Such analyses, along with the many and plural primary texts rewriting and appropriating the Shakespeare play, afford not only Howard Felperin the confidence to speak of *The Tempest* as 'post-colonial' (1990: 173). As Felperin points out, Caliban in the last 150 years has been represented as an Australian aboriginal, an American Indian, a West Indian, an Indian, an African, a Boer, a 'red republican', a 'missing link', a 'Hun', and an Irishman (1990: 175).[12] As well as these diverse performance identities, Caliban has accumulated a cultural history sufficiently detailed and complex to render him the subject of a 290-page book (Vaughan and Vaughan

1991). Its authors see Caliban as an inexhaustible signifier, a prolif-
eration which they somewhat unfortunately recuperate for
'Shakespeare's unmatched universality' (1992: 171). More usefully,
Felperin concludes:

> if the disclosure and deconstruction of colonial discourse has
> changed our reading of *The Tempest*, it has certainly not
> *stopped* our reading of *The Tempest*, or theatrical production
> of it, or the teaching of it at every level of the curriculum,
> or any of the interconnected institutional and cultural prac-
> tices that constitute and perpetuate canonicity.
>
> (1990: 180–181)

This is, without doubt, true and it is this web of relations – and
particularly the tenacity of Shakespeare's so-called original texts in
the light of such prolific rewritings – which critical commentaries
must more carefully traverse. And, moreover, we need to be particularly attentive to what, in the intense scrutiny of Same/Other
staged as the bodies of Prospero and Caliban, is elided as a result
of that construction.

Felperin notes that the 'oppressed group to whom Caliban has
not yet been assimilated is that of women – an idea whose time
might have come, and (let us hope) gone' (1990: 175). I can, if
only just, resist reading the 'us' that Felperin imagines himself a
party to, but his comment is nonetheless significant for its attention to the inattention paid to women in the play.[13] The potency
of the Prospero/Caliban tropology has served to mask the sites in
The Tempest of patriarchal colonization and the play's women
(Miranda and the textually absent/silent Sycorax) have not been
much read for their participation in (and destabilization of) what
otherwise becomes a hegemonically male contest. Even these
women, Stephen Orgel suggests, are part of 'Prospero's creation of
surrogates and a ghostly family' and result from '[t]he absent presence of the wife and mother in the play' (1986: 51).

As Brown understands the anxieties and ambivalences of
Shakespeare's text, it points to the implication of sexual behaviors
in colonial government. He usefully identifies that the indigene's
lack of civility includes an 'untrammelled libidinality' (1985: 50)
and that the colonizer included in its regulatory scope the
ordering of 'potentially truant sexual desire' (1985: 51). And this
is, of course, enacted in *The Tempest* in the narration of Caliban's
attempted rape of Prospero's daughter, Miranda:

There is Miranda, miraculous courtly lady, virgin prospect (cf. Virginia itself) and there is Caliban, scrambled 'cannibal', savage incarnate. Presiding over them is the cabalist Prospero, whose function it is to divide and demarcate these potentialities, arrogating to the male all that is debased and rapacious, to the female all that is cultured and needs protection.

(Brown 1985: 62)

In the first tripartite encounter between Prospero, Miranda and Caliban, the master asserts the necessity of physical and violent regulation of the intended subject:

> Thou most lying slave,
> Whom stripes may move, not kindness! I have us'd thee,
> Filth as thou art, with human care; and lodg'd thee
> In mine own cell, till thou didst seek to violate
> The honour of my child.

(I, ii, 346–350)

Cartelli is right to notice that Prospero's anger derives from the immediately preceding speech, where Caliban claims his right to sovereignty of the island and that this anger is merely compounded by an attempted rape which Caliban does not try to disclaim (1989: 110). In this way, then, the rape only has significance insofar as it proves the savagery of the colonial subject: Caliban's irresponsiveness to 'human care' and his own predisposition to sexual truancy. Eric Cheyfitz suggests we pay attention to the scene's figuration not as one of violence, but one 'of failed education, in which the savage, naturally enough, cannot cross the frontier of translation to attain the eloquence of the imperial orator' (1991: 172). Yet if we limit readings of this exchange to the implications for the Caliban/Prospero trope then we fail to identify another regularly staged Renaissance anxiety, the threat of contamination to an already weakened aristocratic bloodline. The prevailing uncertainties about succession and the threat of an increasingly economically powerful merchant class were manifested (among other ways) as an obsession, both on and off stage, with the female (reproductive) body.[14]

The action of *The Tempest* is, of course, to demonstrate unquestioningly Prospero's right to dominion over the geographical territory in the face of two classes of trangressors (the indigene and the shipwrecked insurgents from his own Milan) and to establish and ratify his authority through the subjugation of both slave and daughter. Only when power is guaranteed is the colonizer prepared to evacuate the hitherto virgin territory (the island, his daughter's body). Miranda, then, is as much a colonial territory as the island she has been brought up on, and her reproductive body ensures for her father the re-production of his own power back in Milan. Peter Stallybrass has convincingly outlined the idea that within the discourses of early modern England, the 'woman's body could be both symbolic map of the "civilized" and the dangerous terrain that had to be colonized' (1986: 133). The intersection of the ideological assumptions exercised on each of these 'territories,' as well as the ambiguity of her body as symbolic map, would seem a significant and somewhat neglected area deserving of further enquiry.

Laura Donaldson's provocative study, *Race, Gender and Empire-Building*, takes up what she calls 'The Miranda Complex.' She suggests that the 'crucial question raised by the coupling of Miranda with Caliban . . . is why these two victims of colonialist Prosperity cannot "see" each other' (1992: 16). For Donaldson, Caliban's attempted rape of the colonizer's legal property offers him both 'poetic justice' and 'vicarious patronymic power,' with the effect that 'Caliban's overdetermined participation in imperialism and masculinism as both victim and victimizer radically questions any construction of him as the homogenous colonized Other' (1992: 17). This seems a long overdue complication and corrective to the binary of Same/Other that the Prospero/Caliban antagonism has been made to serve, and scrutiny of Miranda's similarly doubled role is equally necessary. If she is subject to the sexual objectification of both colonizer and colonized, she is very much contained by and complicit with her father's (and future husband's) tools of mastery. It is crucial that when Caliban responds to the charge of rape 'O ho, O ho! would't had been done!/ Thou didst prevent me; I had peopled else/This isle with Calibans' (I, ii, 351-353), it is Miranda who answers his defence:

> Abhorred slave
> Which any print of goodness wilt not take,
> Being capable of all ill! I pitied thee,
> Took pains to make thee speak, taught thee each hour

One thing or other: when thou didst not, savage,
Know thine own meaning, but wouldst gabble like
A thing most brutish, I endow'd thy purposes
With words that made them known.

(I, ii, 353–359)[15]

It seems entirely appropriate that Miranda should function as the vehicle for nurturing civility through language (and, as such, a rather prophetic statement of the gendered practice of education in the even more avidly colonial age of Victorian England) and her emphasis is once again on Caliban's 'gabble' which can only be heard when translated into her own discourse; 'Miranda thus conforms to the dual requirements of femininity within the master-culture: by taking on aspects of the white man's burden the white woman only confirmed her own subordination' (Loomba 1989: 155).[16]

In short, the relation of Miranda–Caliban foregrounds ambivalence not only about the play's other(ed) characters but about the reader/viewer's complicity in privileging singular aspects of that relation. The consequences of such a self-consciousness form the topic of Ann Thompson's discussion of Miranda's role. She suggests that 'reading the play as a woman and a feminist,' she might 'consider the conscious and unconscious sexism of its critical and stage history. Reading as a white British person, my conscience is less clear: women as well as men benefited (and still benefit) from the kind of colonialism idealized in *The Tempest*' (1991: 54). This statement of complicity provokes for Thompson two questions:

> [I]s it possible for a staging of *The Tempest* to convey anything approaching a feminist reading of the text (without rewriting it or adding something like Leininger's epilogue), and, secondly, what kind of pleasure can a woman and a feminist take in this text beyond the rather grim one of mapping its various patterns of exploitation?
>
> (1991: 54)[17]

The framing of positive responses to her second question is, I think, decidedly fraught, especially when, in her first question, she tries to restrict the degree of 'rewriting' that can legitimately be done (inferring 'this is a *Shakespeare* text'). It would seem to me that a woman and a feminist might derive a great deal of pleasure precisely from the literal act of rewriting the text. The possibility of an affirmative response to the first question accentuates the omission of almost all of the critical analyses referred to here: the intervention of the performing body. In the conclusion to their discussion of *The Tempest* as colonialist text, Barker and Hulme remind their readers that

> the mode of the theatre will also inflect it [discourse, specifically colonialist discourse] in particular ways, tending, for example, through the inevitable (because structural) absence of any direct authorial comment, to create an effect of distantiation, which exists in a complex relationship with the countervailing (and equally structural) tendency for audiences to identify with the characters presented – through the language and conventions of theatre – as heroes and heroines. Much work remains to be done on the articulation between discursive performance and mode of presentation.
>
> (1985: 204–205)

The diligent attention of Cultural Materialist and New Historicist criticism to discursive performance has, as a very real deficiency, the consequence of almost always ignoring, and so explicitly or implicitly negating the implications of an intervented presentation: 'what has been elided – or acknowledged only in the condemnatory form of the charge of sensationalism – is the theatricality of this theatre' (Francis Barker 1984: 17). In our present moment conventions of spectatorship for the Shakespearean text insist, as they have for some time now, on the privileged signification of the word (even, I suspect, when the word is rendered as an absence – since the cultural apparatus of Shakespeare lies powerfully behind any form of its reproduction) and the viewing contract miscarries when the mode of presentation exceeds its prescribed limits.[18] In one of the more extreme manifestations of such a prescription, here in critical practice, Hulme argues that Caliban 'can exist only within discourse: he is fundamentally and essentially beyond the bounds of representation' (1981: 72)[19] – an odd claim about a character whose intended mode of constitution is by an actor in a play.

THE SPECTACULAR BODY

For this, be sure, to-night thou shalt have cramps,
Side-stiches that shall pen thy breath up; urchins
Shall, for that vast of night that they may work,
All exercise on thee; thou shalt be pinch'd
As thick as honeycomb, each pinch more stinging
Than bees that made 'em.

(Prospero, in *The Tempest*, I, ii, 327–331)

46.6 Miranda – in the gown that scarcely hides her nakedness –
is beautiful – top-lit by the high morning sun – which throws a
deep shadow under her breasts and under her belly. Her hair blows.
And she is flanked and backed by the horde of mythological
figures, who are staring and smiling in expectation – one or two
of them making the slightest of sexual gestures. The golden harvest
dust blows stronger.

46.7 We [sic] watch the incomprehension on Ferdinand's face.
Ariel – carrying *The Book of Love* – in which he quickly checks
some fact – flies around behind him and takes off Ferdinand's
broad-brimmed hat . . . and whispers in his left ear (courtesy of
Prospero feeding him his lines):
    PROSPERO (playing Ariel): O, you wonder!
With dawning realization – Ferdinand repeats Ariel's lines – we
see him mouth them . . . though – again – it is Prospero speaking.

(Peter Greenaway, *Prospero's Books* 1991: 104)[20]

As both quotations demonstrate, the relationship between discursive
performance and mode of presentation is not only complex but
crucial. To think about representation of the colonial body through
The Tempest, a text conceived as performance, we might refer to
ideas of the body in circulation at the time of its original realization. Foucault confidently states at the beginning of *The History
of Sexuality* (volume I) that the seventeenth century was 'a time of
direct gestures, shameless discourse, and open transgressions . . . it
was a period when bodies "made a display of themselves"' (1978:
3). And, if *The Tempest* lacks some of the more extreme exhibitions
of the body (common in many of its Jacobean contemporaries), it
is nevertheless a play which draws constant reference to the anatomy
and its inextricable jointing to the discursive performances of the
characters it represents. In the 'interview' scene between father
and daughter (I, ii), for example – the play's first representations
of Prospero and Miranda – the language used by Prospero draws
constant attention to the body he addresses: 'tell your piteous
heart/There's no harm done' (14–15); 'Lend thy hand,/And pluck

130

my magic garment from me' (23–24); 'Wipe thou thine eyes; have comfort' (25); 'The hour's now come;/The very minute bids thee ope thine ear;/Obey, and be attentive' (36–38).[21] Such an intensity of reference to the physical serves the cause of production in several ways: it provides for the actors a code of gesture and physical representation; it supplies the spectator with an itinerary for the gaze; and, most significantly, it alerts us to the spectacle of the female body which 'in a white, masculine, western political and sexual economy is peculiarly the battlefield on which quite other struggles than women's own have been waged' (Jacobus et al. 1990: 2). Underlying Prospero's story is his assumption of Miranda's filial duty to him represented by her commodified physical body. It is as much this female body as his own knowledge which will ensure his restitution to power at the colonial centre.

Francis Barker maintains that the regulated body in the seventeenth century 'is the crucial fulcrum and crossing point of the lines of force, discursive and physical, which form this world as the place of danger and aspiration to which the Jacobean texts repeatedly attest' (1984: 23). From its first moment of representation, Miranda's is the body made consciously visible so that the stakes of 'danger and aspiration' are immediately and continuously available to the audience. But, in what sense(s), are we (as contemporary viewers) able to read this? Barker's caution about an inability in twentieth-century representational practices to encode and realize such visibility is perhaps worth quoting at length:

> The Jacobean body – the object, certainly, of terrible pleasures – is distributed irreducibly throughout a theatre whose political and cultural centrality can only be measured against the marginality of the theatre today; and beyond the theatre it exists in a world whose most subtle inner organization is so different from that of our own not least because of the part played by this body in it. In the fullest sense which it is now possible to conceive, from the other side of our own carnal guilt, it is a *corporeal* body, which, if it is already touched by the metaphysic of its later erasure, still contains a charge which, set off by the violent hands laid on it, will illuminate the scene, incite difference, and ignite poetry. This spectacular visible body is the proper gauge of what the bourgeoisie has had to forget.
>
> (1984: 25)

If Miranda's body has in post-seventeenth-century stage productions remained more or less exclusively the subject and object of
a romantic love encoded in the precepts of a liberal humanism,
then filmic representations of the same body have attempted more
consciously to render her spectacularly visible. The cited frames
from Greenaway's screenplay reveal a body which is unmistakably
made object, the recipient not only of the audience's gaze but of
Ferdinand's and her father's too. Only Ariel is distracted in his
reference to the text he must use in order to give that body its
discursive performance, an intervention which breaks frame and
points to the conditions of her reception.

In the same sequence in Derek Jarman's film version of *The
Tempest* (1980), Miranda and Ferdinand encounter each other as
naked bodies and with the suggestion of a sexual desire that
Prospero must work hard to regulate and control to his own ends.
Notwithstanding the determined staging of Ferdinand's and
Miranda's simultaneous and exclusive readings of each other's
bodies, it remains evident that this serves the perpetuation of domi-
nance. Jarman attempts, however, a critique of the inevitability of
Ferdinand and Miranda's corporeal 'charge' being recuperated for
'romantic love' both in his casting of Toyah Wilcox and in his own
'signature' as producer of homoerotic films for a predominantly
gay spectatorship. Wilcox as Miranda produces a particularly interesting effect since in 1980 she was a popular (and thus visible)
punk singer-performer. Connected to a movement whose identification was with aberrant, often violent social behaviors as a
rejection of mainstream values, her body (as the primary site for
her designation as a punk artist) works against the romanticization
of Miranda and against the apparent naturalness of the match with
Ferdinand.

Two mirrored scenes in *The Tempest* stage the discipline enacted
on the body when its sexuality is perceived as misplaced or mis-
timed. In a doubled representation of what Foucault terms 'the
political technology of the body' (1979: 26), we see the extent to
which Prospero's power hinges on the successful discipline of all
subject bodies. The second scene of the second act opens with
Caliban carrying 'a burthen of wood' and speaking directly to the
audience:

All the infections that the sun sucks up
From bogs, fens, flats, on Prosper fall, and make him

By inch-meal a disease! his spirits hear me,
And yet I needs must curse. But they'll nor pinch,
Fright me with urchin-shows, pitch me i'th'mire,
Nor lead me, like a firebrand, in the dark
Out of my way unless he bid 'em: but
For every trifle are they set upon me;
Sometime like apes, that mow and chatter at me,
And after bite me; then like hedgehogs, which
Lie tumbling in my barefoot way, and mount
Their pricks at my footfall; sometime am I
All wound with adders, who with cloven tongues
Do hiss me into madness.

(II, ii, 1–14)

The tortured body, or even the threat of the tortured body, ensures Caliban's participation in Prospero's regime and the imposition of a timetabled discipline

> increases the forces of the body (in economic terms of utility) and diminishes these same forces (in political terms of obedience). In short, it dissociates power from the body; on the one hand, it turns it into an "aptitude", a "capacity", which it seeks to increase; on the other hand, it reverses the course of the energy, the power that might result from it, and turns it into a relation of strict subjection.
>
> (Foucault 1979: 138)[22]

The following scene (III, i) opens with Ferdinand 'bearing a log.' Not only is the task the same (and similarly commanded/regulated by Prospero) but so too are Ferdinand's responses ('mean,' 'heavy,' 'odious'). Yet Ferdinand is all too willing to retrieve his pains as 'aptitude' once the task is mediated by the physical presence of Miranda:

Hear my soul speak:
The very instant that I saw you, did
My heart fly to your service; there resides,
To make me slave to it; and for your sake
Am I this patient log-man.

(III, i, 63-67)

And as we witness the repeated task – the former, denied access to the sexual body of Miranda, is performed unwillingly but inevitably; the latter, with the promise of the sexual body of Miranda, is performed willingly – there is once again a remarkable ambivalence around the power–knowledge axis staged precisely through the representation of the three disciplined bodies (Caliban, Ferdinand, Miranda). If we are inclined to make sense of Ferdinand's readiness to serve as also self-serving, we might remember that the soul he claims as the site of truth is more accurately 'the prison of the body' (Foucault 1979: 30).

Display of the subjected body is, then, a continuing site for assertion and confirmation of Prospero's power. Moreover, the persistence of the indigene in rebelling against imperial regulation is a necessary energy for the success of that colonial project. Even at moments when the language of the play seems to suggest a more concerned and humanistic engagement, the production of performing bodies insists on making explicit the assumptions under which such discourse is articulated. If this seventeenth-century text discloses the incipient corporeal regulation demanded by colonization, it is hardly surprising that the same text attracted so much attention in the construction of an anti-colonial body.

THE ANTI-COLONIAL BODY

[W]e, the *mestizo* inhabitants of these same isles where Caliban lived, see with particular clarity: Prospero invaded the islands, killed our ancestors, enslaved Caliban, and taught him his language to make himself understood. What else can Caliban do but use that same language – today he has no other. . . . I know no other metaphor more expressive of our cultural situation, of our reality.

(Roberto Fernández Retamar, 'Caliban,' 1971: 14)

CALIBAN: Call me X. That would be best. Like a man without a name. Or, to be more precise, a man whose name has been *stolen*. You talk about history . . . well, that's history, and everyone knows it! Every time you call me it reminds me of a basic fact, the fact that you've stolen everything from me, even my identity! Uhuru!

(Aimé Césaire, *Une Tempête*, 1969: 18)

The appropriation of *The Tempest* by writers from colonized (or once colonized) nations has been well documented. It is not my intention to repeat that history in much detail here; I am more concerned with entering a representation of anti-colonial bodies into my own mapping and with responding to the notion that the anti-colonial has been superseded and replaced by the post-colonial.

As Rob Nixon and others have shown, *The Tempest* has been a foundational text for writers of both fiction and non-fiction in Third World countries and especially in Africa and the Caribbean.[23] As Nixon suggests, these critical rewritings were produced out of specific geopolitical and historical conditions prevailing from the late 1950s to the early 1970s:

> Between 1957 and 1973 the vast majority of African and the larger Caribbean colonies won their independence; the same period witnessed the Cuban and Algerian revolutions, the latter phase of the Kenyan 'Mau Mau' revolt, the Katanga crisis in the Congo, the Trinidadian Black Power uprising and, equally important for the atmosphere of militant defiance, the civil rights movement in the United States, the student revolts of 1968, and the humbling of the United States during the Vietnam War. This period was distinguished, among Caribbean and African intellectuals, by a pervasive mood of optimistic outrage.
>
> (1987: 557)

The Tempest, then, was made subject to such a mood and generally involved in the foregrounding of Caliban at the same time as the laying bare of the colonialist assumptions which motivated Prospero's 'nurture.' In many instances, the process of revision was not simply a direct encounter with the Shakespeare text but a response as well to Octave Mannoni's *Psychologie de la Colonisation* (1950) – significantly named in its English translations *Prospero and Caliban: The Psychology of Colonization* (1956, 1964). Working from an analysis of the Madagascar crisis in 1947–48, Mannoni proposes a thesis of colonialism grounded on oppositional complexes: Prospero = inferiority; Caliban = dependence. His conclusion was that 'the Madagascan revolt was fueled less by a desire to sunder an oppressive master-servant bond than by the people's resentment of the colonizers' failure to uphold that bond more rigorously and provide them with the security they craved' (Nixon 1987: 563). Of course, Mannoni himself was positioned along the more powerful of the thesis' axes since he was a social scientist who worked for France's General Information Department in Madagascar and it is hardly surprising that the subjects that

Mannoni imagined to be 'eager partner[s] in [their] own colonization' (Nixon 1987: 564–565) were as anxious to revise this
text as the Shakespeare play from which it drew the paradigm.

Since the focus of this chapter is a performing body, I want to
look at what is perhaps the best known of the fictionalized
responses to Shakespeare via Mannoni, Aimé Césaire's *Une Tempête*.
Césaire, from Martinique (like Madagascar, an island colonized by
the French), sets up a framework for *A Tempest* which is – like
the title – close but not identical to that of its source text, *The
Tempest*.

CHARACTERS
As in Shakespeare
Two alterations: ARIEL A mulatto slave
                          CALIBAN A black slave
An addition: ESHU A black devil-god

Césaire's refocusing is, then, evident even in the pre-text. In the
play itself, it is the Prospero/Caliban tropology which occupies
almost all of the stage time and interest, with Césaire asserting:

> Caliban is the man who is still close to his beginnings, whose
> link with the natural world has not yet been broken. Caliban
> can still *participate* in a world of marvels, whereas his master
> can merely 'create' them through his acquired knowledge.
>
> (cited in Belhassen 1972: 176)

And this is foregrounded in the performance of the masque for
Miranda and Ferdinand's wedding where the gods and goddesses
of Western mythology which Prospero conjures up are interrupted,
insulted, and driven away by the counter-performance of Eshu.

In *Une Tempête*, Caliban's first words are not those of compli-
ance to the master but are the cry of African freedom: 'Uhuru!
Uhuru!' (13), and (in the quotation which opens this section)
Caliban refuses his naming in English by Prospero and demands
instead only the designation 'X.' As the play refutes the presence
of a Western mythology so it challenges the imposition of a
Western history, again to replace the colonizing narrative with
an oppositional tradition which is enacted in performance. Yet
Césaire's ending is, as S. Belhassen suggests, an 'equivocal' one.
Prospero leaves the rule of Milan in the hands of Antonio until
Miranda and Ferdinand can 'take effective possession' (1972: 74)
and stays behind with Caliban: 'Very simply put ... Prospero and

Caliban are *necessary* to each other. "Prospero can no more live apart from Caliban than whites and blacks can exist independently in today's world," says Césaire' (Belhassen 1972: 177).

If *Une Tempête* seems a somewhat obvious parable of African/Caribbean liberation,[24] its rewriting of Ariel's and Caliban's physical descriptions works to embody the arguments within an active decolonization. Represented as 'a black slave,' Caliban pursues a hard-line and aggressive opposition to his colonizer. Ariel as 'a mulatto' represents the internalized contamination of the colonizer which seemingly provokes Ariel's much more conciliatory stance (one that is shown by Caliban to be misplaced and naive). The opening scene of Act II stages a hierarchy of blackness which reinforces the necessity of Caliban's confrontational approach and renders ludicrous Ariel's optimism. In this sense, Ariel performs the Caliban envisaged by Mannoni's text as well as demonstrating his own blindness to his master's narratives of the individualized human subject: 'I'm not fighting just for *my* freedom, for *our* freedom, but for Prospero too, so that Prospero can acquire a conscience' (Césaire 1985: 26).

In writing back to *The Tempest*, Césaire creates a multivalent anti-colonial body: native tradition figured in Eshu, passive resistance figured in Ariel, and violent confrontation most forcefully figured in Caliban/X. Nonetheless, *how* an anti-colonial movement might resolve (or not) the compatibility of these various elements was beyond the scope of the text's historical impetus.

Nixon concludes his survey with the assertion: '*The Tempest*'s value for African and Caribbean intellectuals faded once the plot ran out. The play lacks a sixth act which might have been enlisted for representing relations among Caliban, Ariel, and Prospero once they entered a postcolonial era' (1987: 576). To some extent, this is the case, although the play's global history as an anti-colonial text is clearly far from over. When Cuban writer Roberto Fernández Retamar returns in 1986 to his original 'Caliban' – an essay written in 1971 and described by Fredric Jameson as 'the Latin American equivalent of Said's *Orientalism*' (1989a: viii) – he concludes:

> My wish is not, and never was, to present Latin America and the Caribbean as a region cut off from the rest of the world but rather to view it precisely as a part of the world – a part that should be looked at with the same attention and respect as the rest, not as a merely paraphrastic expression of the West. . . .

The tempest has not subsided. But *The Tempest*'s shipwrecked sailors, Crusoe and Gulliver, can been seen, rising
out of the waters, from terra firma. There, not only Prospero,
Ariel and Caliban, Don Quixote, Friday and Faust await
them, but Sofia and Oliveira, and Colonel Aureliano Buendia
as well, and – halfway between history and dream – Marx
and Lenin, Bolivar and Marti, Sandino and Che Guevara.

(Fernández Retamar 1989: 55)

Fernández Retamar's return to *The Tempest* claims a place for the
competing narratives which have troubled the once 'univocal
voice-over' – History (Kruger and Mariani 1989: ix) and speaks
to the need I suggested at the beginning of this chapter to remain
vigilant as to the uses to which *The Tempest* might yet be put.
Neither should we imagine that Caliban has found a definitively
anti-colonial presence in his performance or textual history. In
a critique of Henry Louis Gates's *'Race,' Writing, and Difference*,
Houston Baker determines 'a firm inscription of the duality
suggested by the venerable Western trope of Prospero and Caliban.
. . . For me, the signal shortcoming of *'Race,' Writing and Difference*
is the paucity of Caliban's sound' (Baker 1986, 190). If Caliban
has now achieved a space from which to speak (a stage history as
it were), it is not yet altogether clear what he can say. The paradox
remains that for Caliban to speak back to the imperial power
(whoever, in the present moment, that turns out to be), he must
do so in his master's voice. If we recollect Miranda's initial charge
that 'thou didst not, savage,/Know thine own meaning, but
wouldst gabble like/A thing most brutish' (I, ii, 357–359), it is
evident that it remains difficult, perhaps impossible, to speak,
recognize, or respect that 'gabble' as language. National identities
and mappings have redrawn the colonizer's map; the English
language maintains the colonizer's rules not only of speech but of
conduct.

And if these more recent critical writings suggest that Nixon
is too quick to sign away rights to *The Tempest*, we might also
remember Loomba's caution that the colonized subject who effected
these anti-colonial resistances was exclusively male.[25] For the
reader/viewer who is both a woman and a feminist – the subject of
Ann Thompson's questions cited earlier – the mapping continues,
indeed, to be grim. In these male-authored challenges to colonial
authority, the representation of the female body (Miranda, but also
Sycorax) is yet more passive, ever more silent.

THE POST-COLONIAL BODY

[T]he concept [of the post-colonial] proves most useful not when it is used synonymously with a post-independence historical period in once-colonized nations but rather when it locates a specifically ... *post*-colonial *discursive* purchase in culture, one which begins in the moment that colonial power inscribes itself onto the body and space of its Others.

(Stephen Slemon 1990: 3)

DINNY: That's better, Willy. When you give over the shouting you're a different man. We can talk now. I mean *I* can talk. Oh, I know: because I was invisible, as you keep putting it, you thought I couldn't talk back. That suited you, eh? A little invisible friend who would go on listening and never talk back?
WILLY: I thought you were Dinny.
DINNY: Stop thinking, Willy. Listen.

(David Malouf, *Blood Relations*, 1988: 81)

Notwithstanding Stephen Slemon's argument for a complicated, primarily oppositional usage of the term 'post-colonial,' the term demands a first reading which suggests a moment and a space *after* colonization, a moment and a space which we presently occupy. But what is that space and what bodies perform in it? It is the space not of a singular alterity but of cultural hybridity where markers of race, gender, class, sexuality and nation are contingent and unstable. And the bodies that perform (in) it demand – like the Australian aboriginal Dinny/Caliban in David Malouf's *Blood Relations* (1988) – an inversion in the hierarchy of production and reception. The colonizer at last learns to listen to his own language and sees it represented in a myriad of ways he could not predict or prevent. But as the post-colonial demands a rift in the trope of Same/Other, it does not, of course, content itself with such a reversal. It does not perform simply for its former colonizer(s) or even for itself. The post-colonial body must perform (for) its own past and to other peoples for whom the possibility of 'post' is far less tangible. In a discussion of 'nation,' Homi Bhabha describes 'the narrative movement of the post-colonial people':

Its implicit critique of the fixed and stable forms of the nationalist narrative makes it imperative to question those western theories of the horizontal, homogeneous empty time of the nation's narrative. Does the language of culture's

139

'occult instability' have a relevance outside the situation of anti-colonial struggle?

(1990: 303)

Such post-colonial bodies occupy the space in-between hearing and speaking along the axes of contradictory and uncertain pasts. Yet if these are the performances that 'post-colonial' seeks out, Loomba's cautionary reminder is crucial: 'Whereas in *The Tempest* Caliban is simply left on his island, we know that in reality Prospero rarely simply sails away' (1989: 157). Lewis Baumander's production of *The Tempest* (Toronto 1987 and 1989) considers precisely that reality. This version of Shakespeare's play 'situated Prospero on the Queen Charlotte Islands off the coast of British Columbia, set the action during the late eighteenth-century voyages of Captain James Cook, the period of the area's colonization, and cast Ariel and Caliban as Haida Indians' (Peters 1993: 14).[26] This casting explicitly tested the feasibility as well as the visibility of a post-colonial body in late twentieth-century Canada. Critical response suggests that Baumander's strategy was not, in fact, entirely workable. As Helen Peters describes it:

> [Billy] Merasty's Caliban presents at best the pathos that many of today's Aboriginal people in Canada hold in the eyes of more fortunate fellow Canadians. His drunken buffoonery does not appear to challenge the authority of the imperial power, to mock it successfully so as to convince us of its folly of tyranny, or to threaten its overthrow.
>
> (1993: 15)

In many ways, the representation of Caliban in this particular production gives weight to Rey Chow's assertion of the West's 'logic of visuality that bifurcates "subjects" and "objects" into the incompatible positions of intellectuality and spectacularity' (105). Notwithstanding the spectacularity of Merasty's Caliban, Peters claims Baumander's production adopts a post-colonial view of History and a postmodern view in theatre (1993: 17). For my own part, I think it might be more accurate to read the production's consciousness of a neo-colonial Canada, represented not in Merasty's Caliban but in the queer perversity of Monique Mojica's Ariel. Choreographed by Rene Highway, her trickster-inspired Ariel laid bare in Prospero his otherwise uncontested assumptions of symbolic legitimacy and intelligibility. Her unexpressive face and

140

multifaceted representation of spiritual power refused the abjected and delegitimated script assigned for her. In that refusal, she exposed the constructedness of Prospero's own sources of power, the ongoing legacy and efficacy of imperialism. When, at the end of the production, she is ordered to free Prospero's captives, she is the agent of an apparently post-colonial moment; at the same time, however, her inherent bodily script – the identity markers of Native and of woman – denotes a semiotic field which acknowledges the colonialism that the post-colonial is bound to carry.

The visuality of the post-colonial body was, too, an explicit premise of a London production of *The Tempest* staged between Baumander's two stagings of his own version. In fact, in 1988, Jonathan Miller's 'po-co' *Tempest* was one of four playing in England: both the major subsidized state theatres offered a production, as did Miller at the Old Vic and Declan Donellan's Cheek by Jowl (a company well known for its revisions of Shakespeare's text). Miller's overt attention to the colonial impulses of *The Tempest* and the destructive legacies it constructs were facilitated primarily through casting. Caliban and Ariel were both played by black actors, the dogs made human as 'Natives' and Ceres, Juno and Iris similarly so, dressed in grass skirts. The cumulative effect caused one reviewer (Jim Hiley in *The Listener*) to diminish the production as 'sitcom West Indian caricature' (1988: 1,426). In showing the new dictators to be just the same as the old, it would seem as if Miller's production indulged in some nostalgia for the 'humanism' of old colonial practice in the face of the exigencies and turmoil of post-coloniality.[27]

The post-colonial body continues, certainly, to be over-inscribed with the discourses of the colonialism(s) it imagines it can exceed. It is resigned to the sedimentation of habitual memory (Connerton 1989: 72). But what else? That same body is imbricated by two other discourses: one that it endeavors to recall and include, another for which it too often provides the mask.

THE PRE-COLONIAL BODY

This island's mine, by Sycorax my mother,
Which thou tak'st from me.
(Caliban, in *The Tempest*, I, ii, 333–334)

Caliban's assertion of his right to possession of the island through succession is ignored by Prospero, but the reference to that pre-colonial government serves as an uneasy reminder of the obscured Other culture of *The Tempest*. Denied a bodily presence in Shakespeare's play, his mother Sycorax can represent no counter-model by which to displace the colonial imperative of Prospero, to rewrite the idealized female body of Miranda.[28] Jarman's *The Tempest*, however, does offer a filmic representation of the island's one-time ruler: smoking a hookah (a clichéd North African semi-otic), Sycorax feeds her adult son at her breast. The transgression of Western codes of social behavior in the staging of the female grotesque body has, in materialist feminist criticism, been identified as an important visibility in challenging dominant codes of beauty/mechanisms of desire (Russo 1986: 221; Stallybrass 1986: 142; Woolf 1990: 129). The presence of Sycorax's 'grotesque' body also draws attention to the pointed absence (even in name) of Miranda's mother, once more stressing the mother (of Caliban, of the island) as potential threat and subversion. She not only performs cultural difference but further develops Jarman's attack on 'dominant ideological perceptions of sexual identity' (Collick 1989: 98).

More generally, however, the pre-colonial body is objectified as the site of an uncontaminated cultural identity of the people who must now labor with the hybridities of post-coloniality. As Nixon writes of Césaire's *Une Tempête*,

> the island's captive kind christens himself 'X' in a Black Muslim gesture that commemorates his lost name. . . . The play supposes, in sum, that Caribbean colonial subjects can best fortify their revolt by reviving, wherever possible, cultural forms dating back to before that wracking sea-change which was the Middle Passage.
>
> (1987: 572)

Similarly, David Wallace's *Do You Love Me Master?* (Zambia 1971) uses three African languages to celebrate the dis-mantling of Prospero.[29] In these instances, then, traces of a pre-colonial heritage are available to inform and support a self-consciously anti-colonial performance.

It is revealing that it is white Anglo-Celtic theorists in the so-called settler nations such as Canada and Australia who have been most tempted to conjure up an authentic original culture beneath the sediments of the colonial project, which can apparently be made available to determine the expression of post-coloniality. Rhonda Cobham makes, I believe, a timely attack on such calls for the reconstruction of the ontological and epistemological bases of traditional cultures. Post-colonial theory has often claimed that reconstruction is a strategy 'to subvert the political and textual authority of the imperial European perspective with a view to cultural reclamation, the breaking of a mould to reveal a new potential wholeness based on, if not entirely composed of the resus- citated materials of the original culture' (Tiffin 1988: 175). In response, Cobham comments:

> Although I agree with Tiffin's critique of the uses Western theorists have made of the notion of the colonial Other, the final portion of her argument runs the risk of fixing the African/Third World reality in some form of original prelap- sarian innocence which can only ultimately infantilize the African subject.
>
> (1992: 56)

Like Bhabha, she suggests both the necessity of breaking from 'a Western paradigm of linearity and consolidation' (Cobham 1992: 57) and the complexity of the relations which occupy the remaining space.

In this same regard, Judith Butler's cautions about the operations of those laws that constitute gender are apposite. She points out that repressive laws ground themselves 'in a story about what it was like *before* the advent of the law, and how it came about that the law emerged in its present and necessary form' (1990: 36). This seems to me to mark one effect of Miller's didacticism in his 1988 production. Butler continues with a warning to those who find

> in the prejuridical past traces of a utopian future, a potential resource for subversion or insurrection that promises to lead to the destruction of the law and the instatement of a new order. But if the imaginary 'before' is inevitably figured within the terms of a prehistorical narrative that serves to legitimate the present state of the law or, alternatively, the imaginary future beyond the law, then this 'before' is always already imbued with the self-justificatory fabrications of present and future interests.
>
> (1990: 36)

Butler is, of course, addressing the performativity of gender and/on the body but her analysis is relevant in the context of other colonizations of the body. That the 'before' is always already an imaginary field suggests that representation of the pre-colonial body is also always already bound to fantasize the future. However desired, the pre-juridicial past can only reside in the inauthenticity of nostalgia.

If the pre-colonial body runs the risk of being represented in the post-colonial as a figure of depoliticized nostalgia, then a more insidious nostalgia figures in another body that the post-colonial often elides.

THE NEO-COLONIAL BODY

> The SFD [Shakespeare Festival of Dallas] program notes that Redd is 'a champion of non-traditional, multi-cultural casting,' and certainly Hyman's presence (and the casting of SMU graduate student Dolores Godinez, an Hispanic as Miranda) served those ends admirably, it not thematically, for nothing was made of their ethnicity.
>
> (Michael L. Greenwald 1992: 116)

> Canadian writers appear reluctant to deal openly with Caliban, perhaps because they set their imperial/colonial encounters on home ground, where the exact nature of the conflict is harder to see
>
> (Diana Brydon 1984: 87)

Brydon's rationalization of the absence of rewritten Calibans in the Canadian literary corpus rather misses its own neo-colonialist point. Her statement neglects the First Nations and Metis people for whom the colonial experience is not only very real, but continuing, as Baumander's *The Tempest* tried to make visible.[30] In Greenwald's review of the Shakespeare Festival of Dallas's 1991 production of *The Tempest* and their use of the much-lauded strategy of non-traditional casting, he elaborates how it is, in this case at least, ironically blind to its own effects:

> Redd also incorporated members of Dallas Black Theatre (a 15 year old enterprise) to play the sprites, fairies, and 'divers spirits in shape of dogs and hounds' without lines: Ariel was a lithe and mellifluous Caucasian woman. Despite the director's *best intentions*, this, for me, led to one of the production's most unsettling moments: at III.3.31–33 Gonzalo describes the sprites as being of 'monstrous shape,

144

yet note/Their manners are more gentle, kind, than of/Our
human generation'. . . . Despite SFD's *commendable intentions*,
it may well be that the final impression fostered by this
Tempest is that Shakespeare is still pretty much by, for, and
about white folks, even when minorities are used in the cast.

(Greenwald 1992: 116, my emphasis)[31]

This may well be. To reproduce a classical text of the European
imperial archive is always to risk its willing and wistfully nostalgic
assent to (re)claim its own authority. Those texts are simply so
heavily overcoded, value laden, that the production and reception
of the 'new' text necessarily becomes bound to the tradition that
encompasses and promotes the old 'authentic' version. This remains
the argument against the revival/rewriting of *The Tempest* or any
other classical text: that containment is an inevitable effect.

Intentionality is certainly no guarantee of achieving a radical
revision. If the 'blind' casting of Cliff Redd revealed a neo-
colonial blindness to the production of an overt racism, then the
importation of *The Tempest* to another's culture using the representational strategies of that other's culture is an obviously more
precarious venture. In David George's director's log for an
Australian production of *The Tempest* which toured in Bali, the
dangers are explicitly stated:

[C]an a Western performer so casually pick up performance
techniques which take 'the natives' twenty years to master;
can these then be read correctly or even usefully by a Western
audience: if not, is this mere exoticism, archaeologism, or
cultural rape? . . .

Though we originally used Balinese theatre to revive a
Shakespearian [sic] play for a Western audience, that was but
a prelude: the ultimate goal was reached when the production was taken 'back' to Bali. That is a quite different matter,
for instead of the performances saying: 'Look how another
culture might present one of our plays,' the offer now became:
'Look what we have learned from you and have made of it.'

(1989-90: 22–23)

As in Greenwald's review, George's recourse is to intention.
Cognizant of strained political and social relations between
Asia and his home nation Australia, he reassures his reader that
'our intentions were to demonstrate cultural respect, [even if]

145

Australia remains the source of greatest threat to Bali' (1989–90: 23–24).

But the company's cultural tourism is inescapable as is George's inattention to a hierarchy of knowledge that he assumes for his multicultural company. They decide to consult a 'pawang' who can ask the gods to spare the outdoor performance from rain: this is George's description:

> He goes into a light trance, chants, invokes, and suddenly reaches back and whips a flower from behind his ear and throws it at the altar, rapidly sprinkling water after it, then sits, meditating. . . . Is that it? Yes. He is at pains to show us his receipt for this job: 100,000 Rupiah. He does not want us to think he is cheating us as foreigners or that this is something about which one can bargain.
>
> Peter – our Prospero – watched the whole thing and was silent, withdrawn: confronted now by a real-life version of what until then had been an exotic fiction, he began to experience what we all had to go through: genuine terror at the audacity of imitating the Balinese to themselves. Darrell – our Caliban – scoffed, knowing fakirs and shams from Sri Lanka.
>
> (1989–90: 29–30)

Peter, presumably, is a white Australian since his racial or ethnic background needs no explanation. Darrell is, however, twice in the director's log identified as Sri Lankan (not Australian, this despite the company's identification as a multicultural Australian one). The representation of Stephano and Trinculo, those 'masterless' clowns with whom Caliban aligns himself in the aborted overthrow of Prospero, as an Australian tourist and an American film producer, complicates the matrices of reception yet further. If the *intention* of producing this remodeled *Tempest* is to 'give back' something to the Balinese audience, one wonders what, in fact, that can be. The neo-colonial assumptions that manifest themselves both within the company and within the performance serve to peel away the masks of a multiculturalism and post-coloniality that Australia so often postures for itself. Once again, indigenous culture is made to serve a colonial master, to function as a tool in its own discipline.

Moreover, the reproduction within a 'post-colonial' nation by a company drawn from within the nation itself provides, as Loomba reminds us, no more of a guarantee of its being read against the grain. She persuasively argues that

> [i]n India ... the Aryan myth was invoked to disguise the specifically racist aspects of Empire, and can be seen to "persuade" the readers/spectators of *The Tempest*, already holding strong colour prejudices that permeate caste and communal politics within India, and unfortunately perceiving themselves as somehow less black than Africans, that in fact they are closer to noble, white Prospero than monstrous, black Caliban.
>
> (Loomba 1989: 147)

Finally, if we imagine that the production of classical European text, however radically revised, is not only bound to be contained by the colonialism that first produced it but is in danger of pre-empting the production of the original texts of indigenous peoples, then we run the risk of collapsing the neo-colonial impulse of such production into the pre-colonial nostalgia which hovers near its margins.

RE-MEMBERING THE POST-COLONIAL BODY

> Reproduction is the guarantee of a history – both human biological reproduction (through the succession of generations) and mechanical reproduction (through the succession of memories). Knowledge is anchored to both.
>
> (Mary Ann Doane 1990: 172)

> DIRECTOR: Rehearsals are not going well:
> Selwyn, darling,
> Caliban is a primitive,
> He tried to rape Miranda,
> So don't try and give us the noble savage,
> It just won't work,
> It's an oversimplification
> It will destroy the balance of the play.
> Prospero is the hero,
> Not Caliban.
> SELWYN: Who is Selwyn to argue with England's greatest playwright?
>
> (Philip Osment, *This Island's Mine*, 1988: 91)

The complexity of the interrelated and intersected bodies of pre-colonialism, neo-colonialism and post-colonialism raises the question of whether the post-colonial body – in either its literal or a more expanded sense – can actually be represented. And, indeed, whether it is desirable to do so. The post-colonial body is constantly susceptible in its gestures, in its languages, of cultural expropriation. It is the body which colludes with postmodernism in a global economy that appropriates and markets exotic practices in a showcase called multiculturalism. Yet it is also the body which holds out the hope of exceeding the regulated performances of the past.

Philip Osment's *This Island's Mine* (1988) for London's Gay Sweatshop returns to the Prospero/Caliban trope to stage the apparently obligatory exile of those who contravene the codes of race, gender, class, sexuality, or nation. In reproducing some of the key passages from *The Tempest*, Osment's play intervenes not only by its production of dissident bodies (both positively and nega-tively framed: Prospero/Stephen is an American businessman whose company has been exposed for selling contaminated blood to the Third World; Miranda/Marianne is a lesbian living with a woman of color; Selwyn is a gay black actor rehearsing his upcoming role as Caliban) but also in its very contemporary resis-tance to the British Conservative Government's curtailment of gay and lesbian rights through Section 28.[32] Each character in Osment's text (not only those doubled with a Shakespearean referent) points to the commodified nature of identity as well as to the problems attached to claiming visibility. For the most part, characters quote their own lines (speaking their bodies' actions in the third person) as well as Shakespeare's and this serves to illustrate the gap between knowledge and performance, to rehearse the possibility of a body that can proceed beyond and apart from the agencies which (still) attempt to control it. As the Director puts it, 'the rehearsals are not going well.'

The play's claim – 'this island's mine' – savages Shakespeare's original assertion and aggressively returns those words to the colo-nizing nation. The question is whether they can be heard. England may well have lost its Empire, but, as Osment's play powerfully demonstrates, the Prosperos have not lost their will for imperi-alism. The right to speak one's 'own language' – and what that language might be – remains at the heart of the struggle: Mark (Selwyn's lover) loses his job for coming out; Selwyn, who is rehearsing Caliban's 'You taught me language' speech, is reminded by the Director, 'Where's the West Indian accent?' (1988: 115).

This Island's Mine stages bodies and languages that cannot be reconciled[33] and asserts its resistance by way of this contradiction. The play recognizes the hybridity and fragmentation of post-coloniality but ultimately suggests that the oppressions it confronts are much the same as they were in a more obviously colonial setting. The dissident body will be disciplined; it must follow the master's direction: otherwise only invisibility and silence remain.

So is it possible to re-member a post-colonial body that can produce an insurgence that the colonizer cannot predict? Osment's play makes it all too clear that the body remains subject to all kinds of rigorously enforced colonizations, but it claims too the desire of many of us to produce and inhabit a body that is actively post-colonial: this island's mine. The most useful – and, indeed, optimistic – argument for post-colonialism has, I think, come from Sneja Gunew, who, working from Jean-François Lyotard's definition of 'post'[34] suggests: 'we ourselves are condemned to repeat modernism forever unless we go back and work through its "forgotten" aspects, its moments of forgetfulness, as in, for example its relations to those beyond the boundaries of the so-called West' (1991: 5). In this way, Gunew retrieves post-colonialism (and perhaps those other 'posts': post-modernism, post-feminism, post-identity) as a statement of 'the conditions of its possibility; a going back . . . in order not to repeat but to get somewhere else. It is also of course an analysis of the absences, what has been forgotten or displaced' (1991: 6). Such a definition offers an engaged and pragmatic outline for pursuing the performance of a powerfully post-colonial body. And, in this connection – finally – I want to return to the second epigraph which opened this chapter and to think, one last time, through *The Tempest*. In what is obviously intended as the conservative and restrictive preservation of the classical Western text, G. Muliyil asks (of the reader? of India?) 'how shall we salvage Shakespeare?' One strategy – constructed out of a dissidence that Muliyil's question seeks to arrest – is to replace 'salvage' with its semantic content in its *Tempest* use: 'savage.'[35] We can best salvage the Shakespearean text when we savage it, when we plunder it for its gaps and blind spots.

We turn to the past to stage our desires in the present. We return to the post-colonial body we desire but cannot yet configure. Thinking through the reproduction of *The Tempest* lays bare the absences of that past and offers up some knowledge of the bodies it has struggled to contain. Some of the performing bodies cited here enact not a violence which customarily erases difference, but one which insists on it. Their spectacularity registers the bodily elements of Shakespeare's play as a corrective to the authority of the spoken text. The Caliban rewritten by Malouf's Dinny, the Ariel danced by Mojica, and the assertive (if ultimately romantic) characters of Osment's island are all, in effect, dissident bodies. Such dissidence might reposition the performativity of designation to open up, as Judith Butler hopes at the end of *Bodies That Matter*, 'a difficult future terrain of community, one in which the hope of ever fully recognizing oneself in the terms by which one signifies is sure to be disappointed' (1993: 242). In performances such as these – performances which take as their task the return to *and* deviation from and beyond such powerfully regulatory texts – comes the offer of new maps with which to chart the possibilities of 'post.' As the impossibility of full recognition is realized as nostalgic desire, the slippages between source characters and their simultaneously deficient and excessive re-enactments produce dissident bodies on stage. If the 'post' prefix is re-membered as a return to someplace else, we perhaps begin to realize the cultural effects of difference.

Producing these bodies in the performance space creates a generative potential for realizing a representation of excess and for realizing alliances precisely at the moment and place that excess emerges. These social, spectacular, visible bodies remind us – at their best, at their most savage – of what the bourgeoisie has, indeed, 'had to forget' (Francis Barker 1984: 25).

5

ASIDES

At most historic sites it is nostalgia that pays the bills.
(David Lowenthal 1985: 345)

The return re-iterates questions of desire; its repetitive movement
activates differences. The text at which the return is directed is
no longer recognizable as the image of the reading position;
refusing to comply with the demand that anticipates meaning, the
text to which one returns is reinscribed with the marks of desire.
(Tamsin Spargo and Fred Botting 1993: 379)

The different concerns considered in this book demand and display
a deregulation of the past. They perform a past that need have no
visible limits. Instead History becomes a collection of texts which
open up, fly apart, and reconstruct at the whim of those who
would perform them in the present. What is crucial is the seeking
out of a multiplicity of strategies for reading those performances.
Tradition has made a powerful claim for representations of the past
that confirm a continuous untroubled narrative, for the Shakespeare
that is not for an age but for all time. But the texts discussed here
that constitute a shifted Shakespeare mark a counter-tradition
which believes 'we shall better discover our own fixing assumptions if we value the *unlikeness* of the past' (Beer 1989a: 5). And
in the breath that claims 'our own fixing assumptions,' 'we' must
recognize the diversity of voices which might articulate 'a difficult
future terrain of community' (Butler 1993: 242).

This is a book which, as an effect of its topic, centres on cultural
productions emanating for the most part from Britain. As noted
in the first chapter, this in itself creates particular and limited
performance conditions both for the texts themselves and for my
own arguments about them. I have tried, where possible, to extend

the scope of reference in terms of canonical identities. I have looked outside Shakespeare's nation, outside the mainstream theatres, outside theatre to all those other sites where performances of the past by way of Shakespeare can and do take place. It is true to say that Shakespeare has played and continues to play a part in all English-speaking countries and beyond. His iconography, perhaps more than any other, has a global (if shifting) set of meanings. By engaging with such a diffuse text as Shakespeare, what is seen in the broadest scope might find some useful translation in the micropolitical circumstances of local geographies.

Part of my interest in Shakespeare is concerned with determining the parameters of the project itself. In *Rewriting Shakespeare, Rewriting Ourselves*, Peter Erickson provides a counterbalance: on the one side, he discusses Shakespeare's representations of women; on the other, women writers' representations of Shakespeare. This fascinating opposition enables Erickson to read his own critical position in 'Identity Politics, Multicultural Society' (the title of his Afterword). Foreclosing the first-person-plural voice of his text, he shifts to examine his 'own specific situation as a white male critic,' a positionality which involves 'my relation as a specifically white male critic to Shakespeare on the one hand, and, on the other, to contemporary twentieth-century writers, exemplified by the black women writers previously discussed. I speak for my particular self here' (1991: 169). When we take up the unexpected perspective (as Erickson fruitfully does), the potential to learn about the text, about ourselves, and about our responsibilities is happily expanded.

Yet it is not easy to overlook the vast (over?)production of scholarship and its historical disregard for the fact of performance. As I hope this book in part illustrates, many of the problems and questions that occupy serious scholarship have generative and equally engaged counterparts in contemporary performance. To restate one of the claims of my opening chapter, it is crucial that we expand the field of contemporary performance to enact these kinds of collisions between genre, gender, race, nation and other positionalities. And it remains, for me, powerfully ironic that Shakespeare is such an effective device for realizing this aim. In my own writing of this book, I have turned again and again to Trinh T. Minh-Ha's assertion that

[o]ne has to be excessively preoccupied with the master's concerns, indeed, to try to explain why women cannot have

written 'the plays of Shakespeare in the age of Shakespeare' as Virginia Woolf did. Such a waste of energy is perhaps unavoidable at certain stages of the struggle; it need not, however, become an end point in itself.

(1989: 85)

In part, Trinh's statement has moved me because there have been so few women to be found when thinking about these particular performances of the past. Yet this is less of a surprise and more a reminder of the powerful past of Western (theatrical) tradition, which has excluded women from its performance spaces and dramatic texts. Women have been mute and immobile, rarely (and relatively recently) actors on our public stages. Trinh's comments also suggest to me that this might be a certain stage of the struggle, the struggle to bring Shakespeare into a different arena where other questions might be asked of his dissemination and power. This might be a particularly engaging moment for the 'post' of going back, to bring to centre stage the gaps and omissions of History's performance calendar.

I also want to register another crucial aside to this project. For almost every moment of performance to which it refers, the study erases the processes which have made that movement, gesture, utterance possible. Inhabiting each performing body is a complex and particular training. Much has been written about the dissemination of Shakespeare in the education systems of the world: about the editing processes which make certain kinds of texts available to serve certain cultural expressions (for instance, the relevance and utility of the Globe Shakespeares to an imperial project that would assume ownership of the globe); about education systems which accord Shakespeare a transhistorical and overdetermined authority in literary/cultural studies; about post-secondary theatre training which disseminates a technical apparatus that both informs and is informed by an assumption of Shakespeare's overarching importance in the performance canon; and about theatre repertories and theatre festivals everywhere in the world which dedicate large percentages of their space, time, and energy to the creation of so-called authentic representations of the Bard's text. Much work is being done to identify the assumptions behind and implications of many of these processes. Much more is needed. It is important, for example, to understand better the implications of traditional actor training for the limits of representation that can be witnessed

153

on contemporary stages. To what extent does the designation 'professional' limit the kinds of performances an actor can and will realize?

And the centrality of Shakespeare to all aspects of education, whether as a performance or a literary text, is a topic that is far from exhausted. Consider, for example, Michael Vanden Heuvel's discussion of Robert Wilson's avant-garde performance, in which he draws the following conclusion:

> First, it is questionable whether another director or auteur would be willing to stage Wilson's work, since it is so bound up with the processes of its own production and the sensibilities of its producer and his collaborators: one trembles at the image of a Wilson piece being done on a shoestring budget in a regional theater, or at the hands of a well-meaning MFA [Master of Fine Arts] student at an American university.
>
> (1991: 191)

The point Vanden Heuvel makes here is certainly understood. But it raises a number of other questions about what does not make us tremble in the least. Innumerable directors at any given time are bound up in the task of producing a Shakespeare play and much of the cause for this phenomenon is the global currency that I've already discussed. And, as David Lowenthal notes, 'it is nostalgia that pays the bills' (1985: 345). But what is it about our relation to that nostalgia or, equally, about our confidence in the processes that constitute secondary and post-secondary education which not only cause us *not* to tremble at the thought of Shakespeare appearing at regional theatre on a minimal budget or at the thought of an MFA student doing *King Lear*, but which, in fact, lead us to expect this? Should we not tremble equally at these manifestations? Should we not be asking more searching questions about these 'fixing assumptions?'

Gauri Viswanathan concludes the important *Masks of Conquest: Literary Study and British Rule in India* with this assertion:

> we can no longer afford to regard the uses to which literary works were put in the service of British imperialism as extraneous to the way these texts are to be read. The involvement of colonialism with literary culture is too deep, too pervasive for the disciplinary development of English literary pedagogy to be studied with Britain as its only or primary focus.
>
> (1989: 169)

Given the utility of Shakespeare not only in literary studies and in theatre schools but, as many of the critics cited here have claimed, in society in its broadest sense, I cannot help but wonder if Shakespeare is bound inextricably and persistently to exercise a colonial will that its performance might not often resist. The transnational, high and low cultural performances which form the focus of this book offer some suggestions of where and how that will is made visible. They gesture, too, towards an ease with which they can support the exercise of that will. Occasionally they mark a refusal to submit to its conditions. It is my hope that readers might read the performance of the nostalgia in their own topographies with some of those same uses in mind. There are certainly more (other) questions to be asked of the nostalgic impulse to produce seminal texts, all the time that we claim a fanciful longing for a contemporary (often staged as a future) dissidence.

(POST)COLONIAL (POST)SCRIPT II

> This is a cautionary tale, but not with the moral that Shakespeare or even the particular play, *Hamlet*, has no meaning or relevance outside Shakespeare's cultural environment. (Indeed *Hamlet* is a very popular play in Africa both as a school text and on the stage). No. There may be several other morals however. The first is: Don't (if you can avoid it) retell Shakespeare's plots. The second is: Don't attempt impromptu translations. The play is the thing . . . the whole construct of words creating pictures and direct impressions, the clash of characters and, ideally, the visual spectacle with which the story bodies forth.
>
> (Eldred D. Jones 1986: 3)

> The modern sign dreams of the signs of the past.
>
> (Jean Baudrillard 1983: 85)

The play is the thing, the thing that has been so readily put into the service of colonial power – and not just the power of nationhood, but of any number of other positionalities. It is such a proposition that provides the context for Ann-Marie Macdonald's *Goodnight Desdemona, Good Morning Juliet*. At every level this play attempts to mark its critical distance from tradition, from the hegemonic Shakespeare that serves conservatism and the past. In her introduction to the text, Banuta Rubess notes: 'Ann-Marie MacDonald was trained as an actor and after some brushes with establishment theatre, plunged into collective and collaborative ventures' (in MacDonald 1990: 8). We can infer that what MacDonald learned was neither useful nor satisfying and that part of the impetus for *Goodnight Desdemona* is MacDonald's desire to retrain herself and Shakespeare. The collective process by which the play was first produced at Toronto's Nightwood Theatre (which has a long, remarkable history of fostering and developing women's theatre work) represents an alternative methodology to the one that is usually called upon to 'do' Shakespeare. As Ric Knowles describes it, '*Goodnight Desdemona* is a feminist revisioning of Shakespeare, a sophisticated deconstruction of the authority of authorship and an enactment of resisting reading' (1993–94: 276). And, beyond its dissidence on gender identification, the play also staged an engaged tension between ideas of Canadian nationhood and the colonial imprint of the English (literature). So, as *Goodnight Desdemona* found an audience in Toronto, it must have been difficult for anyone involved with the production (or, for that matter, its reception) to forget the presence of Canada's Stratford Shakespeare Festival, not so very many miles down the road and long a cornerstone in Canada's national artistic pride.

The central character in MacDonald's play is a hapless and sometimes helpless junior English professor (Constance Ledbelly), struggling to finish a doctoral dissertation involving a particularly esoteric reading of Shakespeare's texts: her thesis is that 'the Gustav Manuscript, when finally decoded, will prove the prior existence of two comedies by an unknown author; comedies that Shakespere plundered and made over into ersatz tragedies!' (1990: 21). MacDonald's own thesis is that none of this has much to do with the performance of Shakespeare's texts. Pulling her academic protagonist through a ridiculous warp into the action of her subject plays, *Othello* and *Romeo and Juliet*, MacDonald teaches Constance about herself and we learn as much about the assumptions under which Shakespeare is produced. Here Ric Knowles's argument about the different effects of two productions of *Goodnight Desdemona* in Toronto is revealing. He suggests that the first afforded community engagement between producers and receivers (rather like, perhaps, audiences for the Women's Theatre Group's version of *King Lear*); the second, according to Knowles, was radically different: '[a]pparently containment occurred in the new settings: what had been empowerment devices in the first productions became ways of constructing a kind of unity and universality that effaced difference' (1993-94: 278).[1] What the changes in

production context wrought, then, was another matrix of intelligibility which rendered the text merely a comedic parody of its
cornerstone, Shakespeare. If both her methods and her results are
very different, MacDonald nonetheless articulates a position not
unlike that of Eldred Jones in his account cited as a header to this
section.

And it is interesting, too, that Jones punctuates his articulation
of the utility of Shakespeare's texts to the contemporary political
unrest in Africa with an account of the playwright's universality.
That universality is expressed, not surprisingly, in the context of
the academic world:

> I once examined a doctoral thesis putting forward analogical
> interpretation of the major tragedies using as a point of
> entry the scapegoat rituals of West Africa, not in order to
> demonstrate that Shakespeare (that remarkable man) had
> somehow become au fait with African folk-ritual . . . but to
> show that the myth of the dying god (Lear) or the ritual of
> the scapegoat carrier (to whom Hamlet was likened) or the
> taboo scapegoat (Macbeth), or the pure sacrificial victim
> (Desdemona) were universal types.
>
> (1986: 5)

As MacDonald makes evident and Jones reveals, there are particular ways, shaped and imposed by specific cultural contexts, of
learning to read Shakespeare and he is almost always bound to be
produced according to those prescribed reading strategies.

A more specific example of this can be seen in Ania Loomba's
account of *Hamlet* in Mirozam. She notes that '[t]he almost obsessive Mizo playing of *Hamlet* has to do with the relationship between
theater, power, and subversion; with the politics of subaltern
appropriations of "master-texts"; and most importantly, with the
intersection of gender relations with other social differentials'
(1993: 227). This *Hamlet* is a very particular shifting Shakespeare,
one that has, outside the intention of the performance yet at a
more or less synchronous historical juncture, a number of different
viewing economies – her non-Mizo students, the BBC funding of
the film, and so on. Loomba's kinds of careful counter-reading
prepare a complicated matrix by which we can understand the
vulnerability of performance, even of something so inscribed in
the Western tradition, to cultural forces which remain unexpected
and unaccepted.

Moreover, a study such as Lawrence Levine's *Highbrow/Lowbrow: The Emergence of Cultural Hierarchy in America* (1988) gives us a diachronic reading of the production of Shakespeare in a national context which shows quite precisely how this apparatus has shifted in status between the nineteenth and twentieth centuries, as well as outlining the interventions that have made such shifts possible. Sketched in Levine's text is the remarkable impact Shakespeare has had on American definitions of selfhood and independence.[2] Still, Levine does well to remember that even as Shakespeare was being grasped as a definitive marker for the high cultural experience, his cross-genre productions (as in filmed versions of the plays) insisted on a 'generally porous' cultural line that can and, as we have seen, will be transgressed (Levine 1988: 234).

To summarize, '[w]e need a stronger sense of how texts are nego-tiated in reception, for it is what you do with a book or record that counts' (Sinfield 1989: 302). And especially so if 'a book' is as over-coded as the Shakespearean text. But not all transgressions of the colonial script are necessarily contained along a British/American contour of imperialism. One of the effects of the fall of the Soviet empire is the opening up of the institutions of its former subject nations to the spectatorship and critical scrutiny of the West. The Theater am Schiffbauerdamm, home of the Berliner Ensemble, has, for example, been through some remarkable shifts in its operating practices: the artistic director has been removed and replaced by a five-person directoriat and they have 'reconfigured Brecht's theatre with an Elizabethan influence: A new thrust onstage is being built into the auditorium, and the audience will stand in the top balconies and sit on and around the stage itself' (Sprung 1993: C1). And the premiere production for the newly organized company was, perhaps by now predictably, a Shakespeare play. At the same time, at the East Berlin Volksbühne (people's theatre), a newly appointed director opened with *King Lear*. This latter production was described by a Canadian reviewer in this way:

> The three daughters start off on their knees washing the stage with cloth and bucket. Lear, wearing what seems to be a bordello dressing gown, says goodbye to Cordelia with some deep throat kissing and gropings at her crotch. Cordelia, left alone, drops her knickers and urinates loudly into a bucket, not once, but four times. Her suitor, the King of France, drinks from it, presumably to show his devotion.

The gags continue endlessly. I thought for a while the director was attempting to demonstrate to his German audience that it will accept any kind of nonsense with absolute passivity. . . . I waited eagerly for some sign of outrage to break out. But they sat enthralled applauding during scenes and standing at the curtain call.

Perhaps if I too had had to endure 45 years of state theatre, I might have been less angry at the abuse of the Bard.

(Sprung 1993: C3)

Whose limits are here transgressed? What is it (other than the putative reason offered in the last quoted sentence) that causes the German audiences to enthuse over the vandalized Shakespeare and the reviewer to label the performance abusive? What is it that Sprung wants to re-member and that the German audience seems content to forget? At such a point, colonialism and Shakespeare establish a complicated matrix where its possible enunciative and receptive conditions hardly return the text of *King Lear* to a singular British History. The performativity of nation itself comes into play and indicates the density of different agencies of memory which enable the contradictory production and reception of not just this Shakespearean text.

To some extent, what these transgressive and proliferated productions create is a queer nostalgia, in the sense that the identity-forming discourses of the past are both confirmed and fractured at the moment of performance. As Eve Sedgwick has recently suggested, recent work around the notion of queer has put some different spins on the term which cannot 'be subsumed under gender and sexuality at all' (1993: 9). And, if Jarman's *Edward II* and Osment's *This Island's Mine* explicitly queer the past in order to comment on the disjunctures of identity-formation in the present, many of the other examples here queer that same past to very different effect and interests.

Queer nostalgia, then, takes place at the limits that transgression is bound to cross and double-cross and our desire for desire, too, finds itself unmistakably queer. At the recognition of the inauthenticity of the authentic past we long to consume, all the time we continue to seek out the production of our own myth of the past, all the time we long to have it confirm our own historical moment. Dollimore comments:

159

Transgressive reinscription will always remain controversial, if only because it raises such disturbing questions about desire itself, making it profoundly social and thereby asking equally disturbing questions about culture, representation, and social process. This is even more so when . . . so many dimensions of a culture have been displaced and/or condensed into the identity of the transgressor. But then there is no transgression from the position of the subordinate that is not controversial; it is a virtually inevitable consequence of the disempowered mounting a challenge at all.

(1991: 323)

What these various approaches point out is that while remembering will most likely serve 'to legitimate a present social order' (Connerton 1989: 3), it won't always. The colonial script has as part of its condition the possibility of its slippage to post-colonial, its reinvention as a postscript to itself. Spargo and Botting remind us that returns 'are also departures, movements away that happen in the process of going back' (1993: 379). The shards of History that return in the performance of the present insist on staging the unthinkable. If, then, the contemporary sign is doomed to dream of signs of the past, its signification need not be bound to the narratives of a single History. So shifting Shakespeare is both easy and not so easy. His texts are and have always been subject to the modifications of the cultures that produce them. But, in the end, shifting Shakespeare is precisely what makes space for all kinds of future performances.

NOTES

1 NEW WAYS TO PLAY OLD TEXTS
Discourses of the Past

1 First coined, I believe, in his programme notes for the 1986 Royal Court production of Howard Barker's *Women Beware Women* – a play that Barker argued he had collaborated on with Thomas Middleton. See Barker and Middleton (1986), 15a.

2 Davis explains: 'Coined by the Swiss physician Johannes Hofer in the late seventeenth century, the term [nostalgia] was meant to designate a familiar, if not especially frequent, condition of extreme homesickness among Swiss mercenaries fighting far from their native land. . . . The 'symptoms' of those so afflicted were said by Hofer and other learned physicians of the time to be despondency, melancholia, lability of emotion, including profound bouts of weeping, anorexia, a generalized 'wasting away,' and, not infrequently, attempts at suicide' (1979: 1–2). Davis goes on to note how the medical profession invested a 'straightforward' term 'homesickness' with the characteristics of a disease in the naming of nostalgia and suggests that the term has now been thoroughly demedicalized. This may not, in fact, be the case: it would be revealing, I think, to consider the relation between the kind of macro-nostalgia under discussion in this chapter and the prevalence of the same symptoms on the contemporary body as well as the contexts in which they are presently diagnosed.

3 See Frow (1991: 135–137) for a discussion of the relationship between the emergent history of the (medicalized) concept of nostalgia and discourses of modernity. Patrick Wright's discussion of 'the nostalgia of everyday life' is also helpful here (1985: 19–24).

4 That the Left is as 'guilty' of commitment should not be any surprise: nostalgia is an intrinsic part of our psychic and social make-up. Moreover, whether a collective nostalgia is invoked by the Right or the Left or any other invested group, it is, by virtue of its condition, conservative. It insists on the preservation of a specified version of a constructed past.

5 In their introduction, Doane and Hodges start from the pervasive use

of nostalgia in the politics of the New Right in America and suggest that '[n]ostalgic writers locate that [the woman's] place in a past in which women "naturally" function in the home to provide a haven of stability' (1987: 3–14). While they are absolutely right about this – and the analyses of 'nostalgic' texts in their book are useful potential interventions – I'd argue that we cannot afford to see nostalgia as a unidirectional symptom exercised under the discretion of particular positionalities. It would seem that nostalgia, as the desire for desire, is part of how our psychic life is structured and to understand very specific manifestations – where that symptom is legible on the body – is a task which has to take place much more inclusively.

6   While I have added 'sic' to draw attention to Lowenthal's assumption of a male traditionalist, there is some good reason for his gendered pronouns. It is more or less the case that the contestation over the past is a male-identified enterprise. Both in the theories and histories written and in the performance texts located, there are far fewer interventions by women writers. To some extent this must denote a lack of interest, but it also speaks persuasively, I believe, to the rigidity of a codification which sanctions only certain sorts of trespass.

7   Simon Barker also notes that these coffee-table books 'are liberally sprinkled with quotations from Shakespeare, who best records the enduring experience of these values' (1984: 18).

8   The term is Jonathan Dollimore's. See 1991: 88–91.

9   Stephen Eddy Snow's recent *Performing the Pilgrims: A Study of Ethnohistorical Role Playing at Plimouth Plantation* (University of Mississippi Press, 1993) is an indication that this area might now be attracting more attention and more complex readings than it has to date.

10   Publicity on these 'American Elizabethans' flaunts that the 'troupe from the U.S. will make British history come alive to a most demanding public. Using environmental-theatre techniques to portray British history with *an exceptionally high standard of authenticity*, the group will "inhabit" several historic properties, demonstrating domestic life, authentic handicrafts, and "divers entertainments" from the 16th Century' (promotional material in Delta Airlines *Sky Magazine* August 1992, my emphasis).

11   See Patrick Wright's second chapter in *On Living in an Old Country* (1985: 33–92).

12   Foucault argues elsewhere that history has effected the 'destruction of the body' (1977: 148). In this case, it is interesting to imagine what kind(s) of bodies performance, in its insistence on the present, might construct (even if only from the rubble of H/history).

13   The discussions of their funding arrangements for the English Shakespeare Company are detailed and revealing. It is clear how the Arts Council's directive gave shape to Bogdanov and Pennington's plans, that their desire was for what Pennington describes as 'big, popular Shakespeare' (1990: 5).

14   See, for example, my discussion of their *King Lear* in Chapter Two.

15   Alan Sinfield provides a useful and important discussion of arts produc-

tion in relation to the political practices of the New Right in Britain. The arts, he suggests, are marked as 'an obvious place for the New Right to discover and develop tradition, Englishness, elitism and social stability. But this also is ideologically complex, for "good" culture has been defined by its uneasy relationship with the market' (1989: 297). His account of the withdrawal of state funding for the arts under Thatcherism draws attention to the conjunctive risk of diminishing the authority of that same tradition, Englishness and elitism. An example of the complexity of market-driven economics and the heritage-feeding arts comes, not surprisingly, through 'Shakespeare':

> Chancellor Nigel Lawson asserts that Shakespeare is all about order and conservatism, but he still has to persuade much of the accredited Shakespeare apparatus. The interchange between cultural and financial value when Shakespeare's image appears on banknotes and credit cards still strikes many people as incongruous. Far more is at issue than the cost to the stage (which is tiny): the granting or refusal of public funding stakes out an ideological position.
>
> (Sinfield 1989: 299)

16 However irresistible the pun may seem, Paul Taylor's selection of this 'French' expression is far more appropriate than I suspect he realizes. As Rosalind Krauss has pointed out, *nostalgie de la boue* is not a French idiom at all 'being instead a purely Anglophonic invocation of the English notion of slumming transposed into the magically resonant frame of a supposedly French turn of phrase' (1991: 112).

17 All reviews of British productions (except where otherwise indicated) have been taken from *London Theatre Record*. References to the particular issue can be located in the Bibliography under the name of the reviewer given in the body of my text. It should be noted that I do not propose any of these reviews (or others cited in the following pages) as 'objective' readings of any of the performances. Merely they enter, in what is a particular privileged public discourse for and of the arts, a trajectory of 'the past' which can be, like the performance itself, an agent in the process of 'shifting.'

18 In the current tensions between Canadian federalism and Québec as a separate nation-state, this is perhaps in itself a rather nostalgic claim.

19 A useful account of the complexity of this comes in Patrice Pavis's essay 'Wilson, Brook, Zadek: an intercultural encounter?' in Kennedy (1993a: 270–289). Of especial note is Pavis's assertion that 'Brook relativizes all Eurocentric claims to release the enigma of the text. At the same time, Shakespeare is for him so mysterious and complex that one cannot interpret him with words and ideas' (Kennedy 1993a: 280).

20 I'm grateful to my colleague Gerry Thurston for his account of the Congress.

21 It is not surprising, given the determination of British theatre critics to cling to more traditional markers for Shakespearean performance, that a recurring criticism in their reviews of Lepage's *Dream* is that

French Canadian actor Angela Laurier 'negotiates English verse with all the nimbleness of Inspector Clouseau' (Paul Taylor 1992).

22 Claire Armistead's account talks of another response to the Compagnia de Collettivo's 'tampering' with Shakespeare, 'that Terry Hands, director of the Royal Shakespeare Company, is said to have responded with a relieved memo to his company that they represented no threat' (1994: 162).

23 While my reference here is to 1992 and *Les Atrides*, Mnouchkine and the Théâtre du Soleil have earlier had their own career with revivals of Shakespeare's plays – see Adrian Kiernander's *Ariane Mnouchkine* for Cambridge University Press's 'Directors in Perspective' series (1993) and some discussion of her *Richard II* later in this chapter.

24 My vocabulary here is drawn from Robert Wallace's account of the group's work in *Producing Marginality: Theatre and Criticism in Canada* (Saskatoon: Fifth House Publishers, 1990). See particularly 206–207. Feingold's review of Mnouchkine's work (cited in part below) uses very much the same language of director as visionary.

25 Hawkes's use of 'we' is somewhat disconcerting, as is a reference a line or two earlier to 'our culture.' Hawkes might enjoy the privilege of participation in an academic and, more generally, cultural mainstream, as do the texts, critics and performances he discusses in *Meaning By Shakespeare*. It is what remains peripheral and/or insignificant to such a confident statement of 'culture' which concerns my own text even though I, too, have resorted to a first-person-plural voice with which to suggest the pervasiveness of the past and the inevitability of nostalgia.

26 Martha Rosler's 'Notes on Quotes' is concerned with practices in the visual arts in the twentieth century but her argument for a resisting feminist (visual) art has much in common with my own for a radical re-examination of deployment of the past.

27 How McDonald might read plays such as Timberlake Wertenbakers's *The Love of the Nightingale*, Deborah Porter's *No More Medea*, Franca Rame's *Medea* and Jackie Crosland's *Collateral Damage* against some of the performance-based revisions she does describe would, I think, provide a much clearer sense of how this particular past occupies a multiplicity of positions in the present.

28 Two recent examples can serve for the many: Bruce King's collection of essays entitled *Contemporary American Theatre* (London: Macmillan, 1991) and Susan Rusinko's *British Drama from 1950* (Boston: Twayne, 1989). I recognize that an umbrella categorization has often been crucial in bringing to our attention work that has otherwise been undervalued or ignored. Here we might recall groundbreaking texts such as Sue-Ellen Case's *Feminism and Theatre* (London: Macmillan, 1988) and anthologies published by Methuen under series such as 'Plays by Women,' 'Black Plays,' 'Gay Plays,' 'Lesbian Plays.' It is nevertheless troubling if each category is only recorded by virtue of its distinct, apparently essential, features.

29 For an historical overview of theories of intertextuality, see the Introduction by the editors to Judith Still and Michael Worton's *Intertextuality: Theories and Practices* (Manchester: Manchester Univer-

sity Press, 1990) and particularly their commentary on Derrida and iterability, 23ff.

30 Notwithstanding this goal, it is true that the majority of examples discussed in this text originate in the United Kingdom. This is discussed further in the final section of the book.

31 I have more or less restricted myself to the English-speaking world (some examples being drawn from the former British colonies who were rigorously forced to speak English). Much of my argument, I think, holds true for European performances of the past (and especially for their rewritings of Shakespeare) and for other countries which have become fascinated by Western cultural practice (particularly, I suppose, Japan).

32 There are many revisions of the Renaissance and again especially Shakespeare which do not appear in this book. Some of these revisions are the topics of other books, others are no doubt subjects for future books. It is part of the marketability of cultural heritage with Shakespeare as a particularly fast-selling item that books on Shakespeare in the novel, in poetry, in dance, in music, in opera, on television, on film proliferate. Secondary developments like the market for 'educational video' – recreations of the past, or of how to recreate past – are, to judge from my own mailbox, a growth industry. See, in this context, Nigel Wheale's 'Scratching Shakespeare: video-teaching the Bard" in *Shakespeare in the Changing Curriculum* ed. Lesley Aers and Nigel Wheale (London: Routledge, 1991) 204–221.

33 'The Structure of *King Lear*' by Fredson Bowers in the Spring 1980 issue (31.1 7–20); 'Shakespeare's *The Tempest*: The Wise Man as Hero' by Paul A. Cantor, also Spring 1980 (31.1 64–75); 'Logic Versus the Slovenly World in Shakespearean Comedy' by O.B. Hardison, Jr. in the Autumn 1980 issue (31.3 311–322); and, 'Thematic Contraries and the Dramaturgy of *Henry V*' by Brownell Salomon in Autumn 1980 (31.3 343–356)

34 ' "Knock me here soundly": Comic Misprision and Class Consciousness in Shakespeare' by Thomas Moisan (276–290); ' "Documents in Madness": Reading Madness and Gender in Shakespeare's Tragedies and Early Modern Culture' by Carol Thomas Neely (315–338); and 'Where Are the Mothers in Shakespeare? Options for Gender Representation in the English Renaissance' by Mary Beth Rose (291–314). All essays in *Shakespeare Quarterly* 42.3 (Fall 1991).

35 See Brantlinger 1990: 12ff.

36 And Simon Barker's account (1984) of images of the sixteenth and seventeenth centuries in circulation in contemporary Britain would suggest that Shakespeare not only functions as a kind of cultural Esperanto but as a kind of metonymic shorthand. Most dramatically and perhaps most transparently in Britain, Shakespeare stands in for those centuries and for all ideas of tradition and the past which would insist on continuity and conservatism. This effect is, however, not confined to Britain, nor is it unentangled with the project of Empire: 'Moreover, to those depressed by a sense of national decline the reasons for which they don't understand, it means something that his plays still

NOTES

work in theatre and film in every part of the globe. Shakespeare has become part of the way that literally millions of people, consciously or unconsciously, imagine and fantasise and think about the world' (Heinemann 1985: 204).

37 It's interesting to note further, in the framework of my own project, that Cohen makes the assertion that 'if new historicist reductions of Shakespeare to an agent of royal power are hard to defend in the context of the Renaissance, they acquire a certain logic and justification in the context of the present' (1987: 36).

38 And this functions as a trope for the past/present continuum. As many of the reviewers of the play suggested, its remote setting was unmistakably a commentary on Thatcherite policies and especially those at the heart of the controversies of her last months in office (her resistance to full integration with Europe). Jeffreys suggests not only the inappropriateness of nostalgia – no one finds Thomas alone funny – but also the very real risks in insisting on a performative present. Lucius is doomed to die; Thomas goes on to establish a new career outside comedy.

39 Other projects of intercultural performance which locate as one of their axes a Shakespearean text are discussed in my following chapter, as are some of the debates (Pavis, Bharucha) surrounding the performance potentials and impediments of cross-cultural expression.

40 Frost sets up her article as a response to, broadly, Edward Said's arguments directed at western orientalism and, more specifically, to Jyostna Singh's article 'Different Shakespeares: the Bard in Colonial/Postcolonial India,' *Theatre Journal* 41 (1989). Her argument is a more or less conservative one, arguing for moments in the theatre 'where political and racial barriers could be transcended' (Frost 1992: 98). While I would find it hard to imagine conditions of transcendence, I do think the performance histories she describes are significant in their *making visible* those political and racial barriers and impelling their audiences to engage with the precise terms of their social formation.

41 And in another essay, directed against the possibility of definitive productions of Shakespeare's plays, Marowitz offers another invective on the practices of scholarship: Shakespeare 'must never become . . . the exclusive property of academics. I would make Shakespeare available to everyone – except the traditional academics, those semiotic vampires whose vocation is to suck him dry, and index him out of existence' (1991: 30). Yet while this is in some ways an understandable position (even as it relies on a dangerous anti-intellectualism), the essay's title 'How to rape Shakespeare' represents a kind of violence that makes it impossible (at least for this scholar) to endorse the kind of project Marowitz has in mind. Rape, as every woman knows, is all about differentials of power and not in the least about the kind of interpretive freedom Marowitz wants to inspire. Frankly, the gendered, sexualized and violent metaphors of his rally cry are terrifying; that essay concludes: 'His "greatness" is nothing more than the sperm bank from which we must spawn present and future off-springs. Earlier I discussed the myths embedded in his works, but the greatest myth

166

of all is that we cannot transcend him. Once we kill that myth, we will have launched our own renaissance, one that, theatrically speaking, is long overdue' (1991: 31).

42 For a full and often entertaining account of the Campaign, see Christine Eccles's *The Rose Theatre*, published by Nick Hern Books in 1990.

43 In a parallel and earlier version to Garber's, Margot Heinemann has mapped a similar ventriloquism by British politicians (1985: 202–203).

2 PRODUCTION AND PROLIFERATION

Seventeen Lears

1 As Dympna Callahan rightly points out, it is not at all useful and intensely problematic to separate directors' practices by virtue of their biological sex (Marsden 1991: 164). But it is the case that critical reception of Deborah Warner's work does that – it is enough that she is a woman to impose some mark of the radical on her productions. As my following examples of mainstream productions of *King Lear* suggest, the radical is generally limited to (and thus contained by) the aesthetic. For a production of *King Lear* outside the time frame of this chapter's discussion (for the Royal Shakespeare Company, 1974), see Callahan's essay 'Buzz Goodbody: Directing for Change' (in Marsden 1991: 163–181). Here Callahan provides a fine analysis of Goodbody's production of *King Lear* as an intervention in the cultural politics of Shakespearean production. This suggests that dissidence is not an impossibility in mainstream (re)production of Shakespeare; yet it suggests too how hostile the critical establishment is to such interventions.

2 Anthony Sher cites the red nose as 'liberating,' but as John Kerrigan has persuasively argued, that nose (as with all noses) comes with its own specificities in the history of comedy. As he notes in an introductory discussion of Wilhelm Fliess and Sigmund Freud's collective anxiety over Emma Eckstein's nose as hysteric symptom (more accurately, the shine on her nose) and a later account of medieval clowning, the nose is overdetermined as a marker of sexual activity. The redness of the nose, now perhaps best recognized as occupying the semiotic field of drunkenness, connotes too a predisposition for aggression (see Kerrigan 1994: 254 and especially on Cromwell's roseate acne). Thus the parade of red noses on Lear and in *Lear* draw up a coincidence of sexual (mis)behaviour and political (mis)management.

3 And as a note of academic pedantry, T.J. King in his recent book on the casting of Shakespeare's plays concludes that these two characters were not doubled in the original production (1992: 270, note 64).

4 See Samuel Crowl's discussion in his book on Shakespeare on the stage and screen (1992: 124–131); the section on Noble's *King Lear* concludes: "'This production brings me closer to Lear than I have ever been; from now on, I not only know him but can place him in his harsh and unforgiving world." That comment serves well as a summary

response to Adrian Noble's *King Lear*. It happens to be twenty-five years old and was the final sentence in Kenneth Tynan's review of Peter Brook's *King Lear*' (1992: 131).

5 For a full discussion of the connections between the two productions, see chapter IX in Leggatt's discussion of the play (120–131). Not only does the 1983 television production echo Olivier's earlier 'classic' reading of the text, but it recalls (according to Stanley Wells, who is quoted by Leggatt) Irving, Wolfit, and Laughton, and (for Leggatt himself) Charles Kean and his 1858 production of the play. Another, and of course inevitable, intertext is the contemporary BBC Shakespeare *King Lear*, directed by Jonathan Miller. One significantly made comparison is the degree of funding: Olivier's for Granada Television had three times more studio hours and more than five times the budget (US \$2 million – then the most expensive production in British television history) (Willis 1991: 131).

6 Linklater's engagement with what she calls '[m]ono-cultural Shakespeare' (1992: 201) is interesting as she tries to reconcile the agenda (and effects) of blind or non-traditional casting with her own unshakable belief in the humanistic core of Shakespeare's texts. Her rationale for liberating the words from monoculturalism is argued as follows:

> If an African-American or Asian-American or Hispanic actor goes to London, learns to speak with an English accent and studies with the Royal Shakespeare Company how to play Shakespeare in the very best way that England can teach, s/he will have acquired the style but not the substance of the plays. If that same actor, recognizing the unique artistic excitement to be found in playing Shakespeare, is willing to undergo the rigorous training it takes to free her/his voice from inhibition and limitation so that it has the two or three octaves necessary to express the full gamut of emotion and all the subtleties and nuances of thought, and is then able to explore the anatomy of words and the forms of language not as the outer clothing of style but as the inner guide to understanding, s/he will marry Shakespeare's words to the roots of African-American English, Asian-American English, Hispanic-American English or Native American English, and will liberate Shakespeare from the shackles of a narrow Anglo-Saxon tradition into the wide universal arena where his archetypal works find new life.
>
> (1992: 202)

While it seems that there is an irreconcilable contradiction regarding the 'truth' of voice/text implicit in this argument (and such a contradiction seems to me a potentially productive one), her point of view is a clear indicator of the assumptions that are upheld when it comes to the teaching of the performance of the past as represented in Shakespeare's classic works.

7 It is at this point that the reader may well sympathize with the seeming exhaustion of reviewer Martin Hoyle (for the *Financial Times*), who

writes in his piece on Branagh's production 'the third important *Lear* in a month – and an Indian version takes the Festival stage next week' (1990: 1,069). As a more concise response to the saturation in 1990 of *King Lears*, Charles Spencer, in his report from the Edinburgh Festival, says 'Lear we go again' (1990: 1,084).

8   For a discussion of Miller's production choices for his television *King Lear*, see Willis (1991: 127ff). Also, in *Subsequent Performances*, Miller writes: '*King Lear* seems to show how families fall apart when parents abdicate their responsibility and their powers, and how the state similarly fragments if its symbolic head abdicates responsibility' (1986: 131).

9   Armstrong is responding to the idea of 'contestable' values raised by Alan Sinfield in his essay 'Royal Shakespeare: theatre and the making of ideology' (in Dollimore and Sinfield 1985, 158–181).

10 The list of commandments reads as follows:

   (1) No production of Shakespeare to be directed by Oxbridge graduates;
   (2) Compulsory 'how to stress an iambic pentameter' classes for all actors in Shakespeare productions;
   (3) A maximum of three professional productions in any one year of *Hamlet* and *The Tempest*;
   (4) No, repeat no, productions of *King Lear* for at least 10 years. This yawnsome tract is possibly the most over-rated play of all time;
   (5) No Shakespearian production to last more than two hours;
   (6) Booing and throwing of rotten fruit to be permitted;
   (7) Recipients of best actor/actress awards to be intelligible to the audience;
   (8) All Shakespeare clowns must be funny; this instruction to go hand-in-hand with:
   (9) No red noses;
   (10) Fill your own commandment in here.

11 Consider here, Samuel Crowl's statement that 'the weight and influence of critical attention should not be underestimated: G. Wilson Knight, Jan Kott, Peter Brook, and Grigori Kozintsev had stamped *Lear* as the most potent and powerful Shakespeare drama for the twentieth century' (1992: 124).

12 It's symptomatic of current practices, like Marowitz's tirades, that reviewing adopts the descriptor 'scholarly' as a means of dissuading a theatre-going public from seeing a production.

13 This text is published in *Herstory: Vol. I*, eds Gabriele Griffin and Elaine Aston (Sheffield Academic Press, 1991). There is clearly some dispute about authorship. On the cover, *Lear's Daughters* is listed as the co-creation of the Women's Theatre Group and Elaine Feinstein; inside the cover the play is listed as the work of Elaine Feinstein; on the play's title page, it is by the Women's Theatre Group, from an idea by Elaine Feinstein; and, finally, in the opening notes, it states that the play was written by Adjoa Andoh, Janys Chambers, Gwenda Hughes, Polly Irvin, Hazel Maycock, Lizz Poulter and Sandra Yaw. For further

discussion of the Women's Theatre Group and their work, see Catherine Itzin's *Stages in the Revolution: Political Theatre in Britain since 1968* (London: Eyre Methuen, 1980); Michelene Wandor's *Carry On, Understudies* (London: Routledge & Kegan Paul, 1986); and, more recently, Lizbeth Goodman's *Contemporary Feminist Theatres: To Each Her Own* (London: Routledge, 1993).

14 If Howard Barker was aware of the earlier prequel by the Women's Theatre Group, he does not acknowledge it in either the production or text. I'm grateful to Lizbeth Goodman for pointing this out to me. See the previous footnote for discussion of the 'authorship' question around *Lear's Daughters*.

15 I don't mean to suggest here that there is a monolithic audience with a single type of response to the play. Indeed, these proliferations suggest something of the contrary. What I would insist is that audiences have some attachment, essentially nostalgic and necessarily shared (though this latter connection will vary enormously in its significance and intensity), to the production of Shakespeare which is engaged whether they occupy the most expensive seats at a mainstream theatre or drift into a free performance of some manipulated version of one of his texts.

16 What I think is particularly needed (indeed long overdue) in order to understand in more complicated ways the operation of various categories of theatre in Britain is an account of the theory and practice of the arts funding system and its relationship to audience and venue development. Josette Féral's important book, *La culture contre l'art*, on the economics of arts funding in Québec offers a useful model; its application to other countries with strong government funding/ intervention in the arts would provide the necessary framework of elaboration that contemporary dramatic criticism and cultural studies (this text included) has, unfortunately, to preclude.

17 See my discussion of audiences for Theatre Royal, Stratford East in *Theatre Audiences: A Theory of Production and Reception* (London: Routledge, 1990).

18 Giles Gordon (1985), with an enthusiasm that he seems almost ashamed of, praises the innovatory and striking techniques of Footsbarn's production. Not that he can't recuperate this within another traditions – he cites both Marowitz and, interestingly, Mnouchkine.

19 This is how Kershaw opens his article in *Critical Survey* (1991):

> Approach Barrow-in-Furness from any direction and you will be struck by one thing: looming over the town, like a featureless cathedral to an anonymous god, the immense off-white hangar of the Devonshire Dock Hall. The town houses 70,000 people, and about 14,000 of them work for VSEL (Vickers Shipbuilding and Engineering Limited). This company owns the Hall, and inside it they are constructing Armageddon, in the shape of Britain's third Trident-class nuclear submarine, able to deliver in one quick spurt more firepower than the whole of that used in World War II. The town is a remote place, and

often seen by outsiders, such as the *Guardian's* northern arts correspondent Robin Thornber, as a cultural desert.

(249)

20 A professional actor, Marcel Steiner, was used in the lead role. See Kershaw 1992: 215.

21 Kershaw discusses the different spectatorial involvements of live performance and film (1991: 257–258), using notions of intertextuality and contextuality to argue for the existence of a productive reception of both forms of representation. I am extending his argument to suggest the key element of recognition in the capacity for a producerly consumer (Kershaw's citation of John Fiske's term).

22 In Kershaw's many works on Welfare State and their Barrow residency, he cites the description of Barrow by Robin Thornber, the northern arts correspondent for the *Guardian*, as 'a cultural desert' (see, for example, Kershaw 1991: 249).

23 See Kershaw 1992: 220–224.

24 It might be suggested that Robins's citation of a renaissance with which to argue for a global–local nexus does, in its very naming, point to something of his own inevitable nostalgia, located here in the field of economic organization (Robins 1991: 29).

25 Broadmoor has a very specific design and function. Harvey Gordon's description is useful: '[F]rom the outset, Broadmoor, though related to and providing a service for the prison department, was not a prison but an institution of a separate nature. It looked like a prison, built in red brick with bars on the windows. Yet the Head of the institution was a doctor not a Governor. It was staffed by attendants who were the forerunners of nurses and not prison officers. Its purpose and ethos were to provide treatment and not punishment' (in Cox 108).

26 See Cox 179–185.

27 The production had played in Madrid as well as in London.

28 Gow's selection of a name for his schoolteacher is, of course, a wonderfully parodic play on Virginia Woolf's character of the same name in *Between the Acts* and the difficulties of that Miss La Trobe in seeing her outdoor pageant to happy conclusion and, at the same time, on one of Australia's higher education institutions, La Trobe University (no connection to Woolf's character in its naming).

29 An interesting side note is Brisbane's information that Gow wrote *Away* while playing Oswald in a production of *King Lear* (1989: xxii).

30 Full details of the casting are available in Zarrilli (1992: 17–18).

31 See Patrice Pavis's *Theatre at the Crossroads of Culture* (London: Routledge, 1992).

32 This quotation is drawn from Bharucha's critical and controversial reading of Peter Brook's *Mahabharata*. My own sense of these productions is that the *Kathakali King Lear* is not so breathtakingly orientalist but that nonetheless the effects are more or less the same.

33 There is something particularly ironic in Hill's commentary when it is set aside his own involvement in the Lear revision as Edmund. For it is Edmund, as Dollimore explains, who 'embodies the process

whereby, because of the contradictory conditions of its inception, a revolutionary (emergent) insight is folded back into a dominant ideology' (1984: 201).

34 Amy Green deftly notes that the production's 'racial undertones were a sly reminder that the feudal mentality persists today in less obvious, more insidious forms' (1994: 113).

35 For discussion of Robert Wilson's choice of Marianne Hoppe and of Hoppe's conception of the role, see Arthur Holmberg's ' "Lear" Girds for a Remarkable Episode,' *New York Times*, May 20, 1990: 7 and 36.

36 This advertisement is replicated in Smith (1993: 300).

3 NOT-SHAKESPEARE, OUR CONTEMPORARY
Transgression, Dissidence, and Desire

1 The intertextuality of the Jacobean is not restricted to play revivals and citations in critical writings. It is a most pervasive form, appearing in any number of high and low art forms from esoteric dramatic productions to street fashion to popular fiction. Jim Collins, for example, charts the importance of Jacobean revenge tragedy to P.D. James's mainstream detective novel *The Skull Beneath the Skin*. He notes that '[t]he murderer sends letters with quotations drawn from Shakespeare, John Webster, and Christopher Marlowe. In each case the lines concerning death and revenge are perfectly relevant to situations in the 1980s (1989: 47–48).

2 Drawn from reviews in *Film Quarterly* (Winter 1991: 41) by Devin McKinney, *Newsweek* (27 August 1990. 61) by Ansen, and *Sight and Sound* (Autumn 1990: 277) by Jonathan Rosenbaum. Incidentally, Manohla Dargis makes the pertinent observation that *Wild at Heart* produces these qualities in a reactionary way, noting that the submission of women's bodies is stalked by a fear of miscegenation (see '*Thelma and Louise* and the tradition of the male road movie' in *Women and Film*, edited by Pam Cook and Philip Dodd [Philadelphia: Temple University Press, 1993], especially pages 86–88).

3 Jameson argues that 'sadomasochism has become the latest and the last in the long line of taboo forms of content which, beginning with Nabokov's nymphets in the fifties, rise one after the other to the surface of public art in that successive and even progressive widening of transgressions which we once called the counterculture' (1989b: 534). The popularity of the Jacobean aesthetic clearly feeds such a progression well.

4 In the press publicity for *The Cook, The Thief, His Wife and Her Lover*, Greenaway's enthusiasm for the Jacobean is evident – he is quoted as arguing 'Jacobean drama was excited by sheer corporeality. It took high risks with taboo, melodrama, violence and sexual darkness. I wanted to engage in some of the excitements of unrestricted license' (cited in Thomas 1990: 265). Greenaway's comparison of his own film with John Ford's play '*Tis Pity She's A Whore* (a text that compulsively dramatizes taboo) provokes *New York Post* film critic David Edelstein

to comment 'Reading of the comparison, I have to laugh' (1990: 272). Kevin Thomas in the *Los Angeles Times* notes 'Whenever pretentious filmmakers want to defend their excesses on the screen, they invariably cite Shakespeare or – better yet – lurid Jacobean tragedy as a whole. There's where England's Peter Greenaway found his alibi for the lurid, repulsive "The Cook, The Thief, His Wife and Her Lover"' (1990: 265).

5 It is the same sort of impulse which makes possible Ruth Maleczech's and Marianne Hoppe's leads in *King Lear*. Another interesting example is Cath McKinnon's *A Rose by Any Other Name*, a play for six women actors that meshes the sixteenth-century domestic tragedy *Arden of Faversham* with a contemporary Australian court case (in *Around the Edge: Women's Plays*, published by Tantrum Press of South Australia in 1992; the premiere production of McKinnon's play was by the Red Shed Theatre Company in 1989). Yet I've been conscious of how few women are involved in this project of articulating the past, at least through some or other Renaissance counterpart. It is true that the Greek myths have been more powerfully disciplinary for women and it is not surprising that more women's companies have turned their attention to 'vandalizing' the texts of classical Greek theatre. It's also perhaps true that the dizzying power of Shakespeare's place in the literary/dramatic canon as a global phenomenon makes it at once less appealing and more difficult for women to turn to these texts. Certainly the vehemence with which feminist criticism within the field has come under attack is stunning: the salvos in Ivo Kamps's *Shakespeare Left and Right* (1991) are a particularly performative version of this and Linda Woodbridge's essay in that collection is a moving and important account of the prices exacted from the feminist scholar.

6 See, for example, Claire Armistead's review, which concludes: 'The richness of the show to eye and ear, and the skill of the performers in handling a drama which adopts the postures of traditional masque in pursuit of a modern tragedy, did not conceal the suspicion that for once in Red Shift's work, style had overthrown content' (*Financial Times*, 9 February 1989, in *London Theatre Record* 29 January–11 February 1989: 166).

7 Perhaps coincidentally, shortly after the final performances of *Timon* (June 1989) Red Shift learned that their application for revenue funding from the Arts Council had been rejected.

8 For a full account of the vehemence of New York's theatre critics and some responses to it, see Elinor Fuchs and David Leverett's article in the December 1989 issue of *American Theatre*.

9 New York critics have been particularly explicit in their colonialist view of how Shakespeare should be represented. Joseph Papp was regularly lambasted for his cross-cultural casting – for example, John Simon (in 1965) criticized Papp's 'untalented' black actors who were 'ill-equipped to speak the language of Shakespeare' and Martin Gottfried argued that Papp's formation of an exclusively black and Hispanic repertory company would be 'actively offensive as it is based on race not theatrical qualifications' (both in Lee Horn 1992: 276, 294).

NOTES

10 Like some of the 'Jacobean' productions already discussed, *The Ugly Man* also relies on a recognition of a number of filmic intertexts. Those texts are outside the concerns of this particular chapter but should be identified as an equally powerful strategy to access Fraser's specific concerns in/with this play.

11 The stage direction reads: 'Forest takes Acker's head in his hands and turns it sharply. Acker's neck breaks with a sickening crack. Forest drags Acker off into the darkness. Forest is heard breathing heavily. The sound of the storm has receded' (Fraser 1993: 73)

12 The original contemporary version used Angela Rippon – in the revised revised version of *A Mad World, My Masters* this disguise was provocatively changed to Mrs. Thatcher.

13 This description resonates with so many critiques of Jacobean drama – that the characters are typified (often in their names) and that the plays consist of a choreography rather than a fully developed action. Greenaway's lavish design further recalls the heightened artistic reference of early seventeenth-century drama.

14 See Coveney 1990: 169–170.

15 It's interesting that Richard Combs goes on in his review to suggest that *The Cook, The Thief, His Wife and Her Lover* is neither a Jacobean text nor a gangster film (the other code evoked by the performance of Spica and his sidekicks), but instead science fiction 'suggesting that Greenaway rather than David Lynch (though the former is an admirer of the latter) might have adapted Frank Herbert's *Dune*, with its ecological and digestive concerns' (1989: 323).

16 It's interesting and, indeed, suggestive, that William Gaskill was the director of the original productions of both Keeffe's *A Mad World, My Masters* and the Barker/Middleton *Women Beware Women*.

17 See, for example, William Hutchings's suggestion that beyond 'the pervasiveness of "sex and violence" which, in general, conjoins the world-view of the Jacobeans and that of our own time, *Women Beware Women* provides a particularly effective vehicle for Barker's radical commentary on contemporary Britain – which, like Middleton's Florence, has been preoccupied with a profligately celebrated royal wedding in a time of economic problems' (1988: 99). Kathleen McLuskie describes the play's effects somewhat more directly and significantly: 'The stock of romantic matrimony had risen considerably with the media hype surrounding the wedding of Prince Charles to Lady Diana, and Prince Andrew, soon himself to be married, had had his sexual exploits widely discussed in the tabloid press. A sideswipe at the royal family was not central to the play's political focus but it generated a facile, extra-diegetic *frisson* nonetheless' (1989: 21).

18 As the filmmaker terms it in his own screenplay, it is *Edward II* 'improved by' Derek Jarman.

19 It's Shepherd's strategy, in order to displace notions of Shakespeare as a singular and privileged originator of universal truths, that his name is spelled differently each time it is used.

20 Two side notes here: (1) Jarman had already entered the critical fray on the topic of reproducing the Elizabethan past through his version of *The*

174

Tempest, a film that was savaged by the reviewer for the *New York Times*, effectively curtailing its availability in North America. Jarman writes of this experience: 'In such a fragmented culture messing with Will Shakespeare is not allowed. The Anglo-Saxon tradition has to be defended; and putting my scissors in was like an axe-blow to the last redwood' (1984: 206). (2) Given the damage of such a critical attack on his work, Jarman might have gained some satisfaction from the rather grumpy observation in Richard Davenport-Hines's review of *The Sexual Imagination From Acker to Zola: A Feminist Companion*, 'Derek Jarman has a longer entry than Shakespeare' (1993: 32).

21 Section 28 prevents local governments from funding lesbian and gay organizations by making illegal the promotion of homosexuality. This not only entails the disappearance of arts funding but also restricts the use of performing venues. It also prohibits the promotion within schools of positive images of homosexuality and non-traditional living arrangements (what the section refers to as 'pretended families'). Gay Sweatshop, which started in 1974, it is worth noting, lost Arts Council funding and was, unlike most other alternative theatre companies, denied charitable tax status. See Jackie Stacey's "Promoting normality: Section 28 and the regulation of sexuality" in *Off-Centre: Feminism and Cultural Studies*, eds. Sarah Franklin, Celia Lury, and Jackie Stacey (London: HarperCollins, 1992), 284–304.

22 A nostalgia for the vision of a young child recurs in Jarman's work, as in the narration of young Wittgenstein in Jarman's film about the philosopher. This nostalgia seems to value a less complicated performance of queerness that is available to the child.

23 It's worth insisting, as the film still to my book cover reveals, that the 'some sort of puppet' that Young Edward appears to be is an apparent manipulation of the Mother – a signification that once again bespeaks the film's misogyny.

24 An analysis which invites comparison with Jarman's blistering critique of the 'costume drama' cited earlier in this chapter.

4 THE POST-COLONIAL BODY?

Thinking through *The Tempest*

1 'Imperialism without Colonies' is the thesis of Harry Magdoff's 1978 *Imperialism: From the Colonial Age to the Present* (New York and London: Monthly Review Press). Magdoff examines the different structures of imperialism in pre-capitalist and capitalist societies with particular attention to recent global economies of trading and finance which put advanced capitalist nations under the constant challenge of defending their individual positions within an 'inter-imperialist power struggle' (9). It is not always the case that Magdoff's underlying thesis has been unquestioningly adopted, but the mode of identification has proved a useful one.

2 See Meredith Anne Skura's 'Discourse and the Individual: The Case of Colonialism in *The Tempest*,' *Shakespeare Quarterly* 40 (1989), 42–69.

Skura argues that *The Tempest* can perhaps be read as a 'prophetic' text but that New Historicist and Cultural Materialist criticism overstates (and, as such, de-historicizes) the play's power as a text 'descriptive' of the colonial history contemporary to it. Linda Woodbridge also argues '*The Tempest* belongs to a *pre-colonial* discourse: to locate it fully within the discourse of colonialism ... is to miss the power accruing from its position in the interstices of literary history' (Woodbridge and Berry 1992: 292).

3 A particularly insidious version of the answer persists in the Arden edition of Shakespeare's play, edited by Frank Kermode. Kermode argues that there has been 'little memorable criticism' (lxxxi) of Shakespeare's play; his own stance that Caliban is 'an inverted pastoral hero, against whom Civility and the Art which improves Nature may be measured' (xliii) and, worse yet, 'if Aristotle was right [something that the Tradition, of course, has generally imagined him to be] ... then the black mutilated cannibal must be the natural slave of the European gentleman, and, *a fortiori*, the salvage and deformed Caliban of the learned Prospero' (lxii) has been extensively and effectively disseminated. See, for example, Ania Loomba's discussion that '[i]t is no accident that Kermode's text is widely used in India' (1989: 143).

4 It is particularly interesting that Cartelli's assertion (with which I am more or less in agreement) is restricted to 'successive readings and rewritings' (100–101). In other words he reproduces the privilege of the textual body of Shakespeare's play over its realization in performance. It is this absence in an otherwise abundant mapping of the play's bodies that my own discussion seeks to address.

5 As well as thinking of Brown's citation of Sir John Davies's 'A Discovery of the True Causes Why Ireland Was Never Subdued ... Until the Beginning of His Majesty's Happy Reign,' it is worth remembering that England's conquest of Ulster in 1607 and its subsequent and rapid plantation functioned as an exemplar for the efficient possession of other lands desired as colonial properties. See Liz Curtis's *Ain't Nothing But the Same Old Story: The Roots of Anti-Irish Racism* for an account of the expropriation of 85 per cent of Irish territory by the English during the seventeenth-century (1989: 22ff).

6 Violence is, of course, a naturalized component of the civilizing process. As Purchas responds to his own question (the question cited as the opening epigraph to this paper): 'Were bit wee our selves made and not borne civill in our Progenitors dayes? and were not Caesars Britaines as brutish as Virginians? The Romane swords were best teachers of civilitie to this & other Countries neer us.' At the same time as this reveals a recognition that his own ancestors might have had something in common with the native Americans whom Strachey and others were attempting to subject, it more obviously sanctions a seamless history with its natural right to enforce civility on the less powerful.

7 An excerpt from the latter text in Liz Curtis's *Ain't Nothing But the Same Old Story* offers a picture of Lord Kitchener and Rudyard Kipling 'dolls' with a verse caption:

Men of different trades and sizes
Here you see before your eyeses;
Lanky sword and stumpy pen,
Doing useful things for men;
When the Empire wants a stitch in her
Send for Kipling and for Kitchener.

(67)

8   Peter Hulme makes a related point in his insistence that Prospero is not just an archetype of the colonizer, but 'also colonial historian, and such a convincing and ample historian that other histories have to fight their way into the crevices of his official monument' (1986: 125).

9   See Brown 59 for this reading of the playtext. It's interesting to note, too, as described in Derek Jarman's autobiographical collage *Dancing Ledge*, that in his first cut-up of *The Tempest*, Jarman planned to have all the lines spoken by Prospero.

10 The fascinating relationship between Prospero's mastery of the book and Greenaway's mastery of the technological apparatus is discussed in Peggy Phelan's article 'Numbering Prospero's Books,' *Performing Arts Journal* 41.2 (1992), 43–50.

11 Ania Loomba points out that this introduction was written some seventeen years *after* India's independence (1989: 22). Her discussion of the transcendental status of text is useful here (1989: 19–23).

12 For an extended discussion of these representations, see Trevor R. Griffiths's ' "This Island's Mine": Caliban and Colonialism' *The Yearbook of English Studies* 13 (1983), 159–180.

13 Québec, apparently alone, has provided some recourse. Le Théâtre Experimental des Femmes in their 1988 production cast a woman as Caliban. More recently, Robert Lepage's French-language version, *La Tempête*, included Anne-Marie Cadieux's performance as what reviewer Pat Donelly described as a frenetic Caliban 'a punk-rocker on speed' (1993: F6).

14 Plays contemporary with *The Tempest* often, of course, take such an obsession as their focus. *The Duchess of Malfi* (first performed around 1612) is perhaps the best-known example: when the Duchess refuses her brothers' insistence on her chastity and produces three children with her steward, Antonio, a violent revenge and her eventual death are the 'natural' outcome. For an elaboration of this point, see Leonard Tennenhouse's fine discussion of 'Violence Done to Women on the Renaissance Stage' in Armstrong and Tennenhouse (1989: 77–97). It's also worth remembering the critical history of Jacobean drama, which has, until very recently, insisted on its inferiority to the Shakespeare corpus precisely because of its reliance on spectacle and particularly the spectacle of torture inflicted on the female body: 'The reception of the Jacobean text has proceeded in a fashion entirely subjugated to the partitive sign of the *literary* greatness of Shakespeare's verse: the word has found a place of privilege over the image' (Francis Barker 1984: 16).

15 There have been some editorial efforts to reassign these lines to Prospero – see footnote in the Arden edition (32).

16 See also the concluding chapter of Eric Cheyfitz's *The Poetics of Imperialism: Translation and Colonialism from* The Tempest *to* Tarzan (1991), 'Eloquent Cannibals.'

17 The Leininger epilogue is for 'a modern Miranda who refuses to participate in the play's assumptions that Prospero is infallible, that Caliban is a "natural" slave, and that a daughter is a "foot" in a family organism of which the father is the head' (Thompson 53). See also *The Woman's Part*, Carolyn Ruth Swift Lenz *et al.*, eds (Urbana: University of Illinois Press, 1980: 285–294). Miranda has, in fact, been the subject of extended reference and reproduction and particularly in English-Canadian texts (see Chantal Zabus's 'A Calibanic *Tempest* in Anglophone and Francophone New World Writing' *Canadian Literature* 104 (Spring 1985), 35–50 and Diana Brydon's 'Re-writing *The Tempest*' *World Literature in English* 23 (1984), 75–88. These revisions are restricted to texts and there does not seem to be any performance version of Miranda. Zabus's conclusion that 'Miranda *qua* Canada' is beginning to mature is suitably tentative; Brydon's argument that Miranda has been radically redefined is perhaps overstated (77). Gayle Greene's 'Margaret Laurence's *Diviners* and Shakespeare's *Tempest*: The Uses of the Past' is a further example of the Miranda–English Canada connection (in Novy 1990: 165–182).

18 My own favorite incident of such a refusal is an account of *La Tempestada*, an adaptation of *The Tempest* by La Cubana Barcelona for the London International Festival of Theatre (1986), which simply says 'The audience was disconcertingly exposed to real tempest effects, and the production was cancelled after the first night' (*Shakespeare Quarterly* 37).

19 This, briefly, is (as Hulme argues his case) the result of Caliban's function as the axis between Mediterranean and Atlantic geographies and texts, which makes him a 'compromise formation.'

20 These descriptions of shots from *Prospero's Books* are quoted in full (the ellipses are in the original).

21 And, as Prospero recounts their history, he interrupts his historical narrative with constant and further reminders to his daughter to listen: 'Dost thou attend me?' (78); 'Thou attend'st not?' (87); 'Dost thou hear?' (105).

22 Caliban's first line in the play, delivered off-stage, announces 'There's wood enough within' (I, ii, 316) suggesting his completion of a similar and apparently regularly scheduled task.

23 See Nixon's 'Caribbean and African Appropriations of *The Tempest*,' *Critical Inquiry* 13.3 (Spring 1987), 557–578. The same territory is also covered in chapter 6, 'Colonial Metaphors,' of *Shakespeare's Caliban: A Cultural History* (Vaughan and Vaughan 1991: 144–171), Cartelli's 'Prospero in Africa: *The Tempest* as Colonialist Text and Pretext' (Howard and O'Connor 1987: 99–115), Max Dorsinville's *Caliban without Prospero: Essays on Quebec and Black Literature* (Erin, Ontario: Porcepic Press, 1974), Bill Ashcroft *et al.*, *The Empire Writes Back: Theory and Practice in Post-Colonial Literatures* (London: Routledge, 1989: 189–193), and Roberto Fernández Retamar's 'Caliban' (in Fernández Retamar 3–45).

24 And, despite this unmistakable political agenda, it is startling how easy it is for Western criticism to effect its own recuperation of such a text for its own (theatre) history narratives: Ruby Cohn concludes her discussion of the play in the naming of Caliban as a modern and Black Everyman (1976: 308–309).

25 Loomba's reference is to Frantz Fanon's *Black Skins, White Masks*, a book which includes an extended critique of Mannoni's Prospero and Caliban complexes (Fanon 83–108). Loomba comments: 'for women, the split between black skin and white mask is intensified by their gendered alienation from white society, which is perhaps encapsulated in their relationship to the Western canonical text. It is somewhat ironical, then, that its understanding and knowledge is supposed to equip them for their roles as better wives and mothers' (Loomba 1989: 23).

26 Ariel was played by a woman, Monique Mojica, of the Kuna and Rappahannock nation; Caliban by Billy Merasty, a Cree from Northern Manitoba (see Peters 1993: 14).

27 The other concurrent productions paid almost no attention to the colonial mandate of this play: Peter Hall's production at the Royal National Theatre was one of three that marked the end of his artistic reign there – aligned with *The Winter's Tale* and *Cymbeline*, his was a minimalist, choreographed version; Cheek by Jowl did theirs using paring of the text to emphasize the self-conscious, art-as-art interests of the play; and the Royal Shakespeare Company's production concentrated primarily on the thematic reading of forgiveness.

28 It is probably worth reminding ourselves that the first performed Miranda was a man's role and this, if anything, simply confirms what Francis Barker suggests about the body's effect on the internal organization of the cultural experience then recognized as theatre (1984). Of all of History, the body remains a component that we simply cannot accurately reconstruct or even imagine. It is also important to consider that Sycorax's North African identity is also a complex colonial territory.

29 See Nixon 574, footnote 28.

30 Brydon in fact notes one Caliban-centered novel by a Canadian author but points out that this is set outside Canada. Admittedly her interest is with the novel, but there are at least three contemporary volumes of Canadian poetry which take Caliban as part or all of their title. It would be interesting, too, to consider the effect of the performance of Caliban in the 1988 production by Montreal's Le Théâtre Experimental des Femmes (already cited in a previous footnote).

31 Despite Greenwald's undoubtedly deserved criticism, it is worth measuring the intent of this production against the distaste of the New York critics in the 1960s and 1970s for Joseph Papp's cross-racial casting for Shakespeare. See note 9 in the previous chapter.

32 See note 17 in the previous chapter for an outline of Britain's notorious Section 28.

33 This is, perhaps only incidentally, a wonderfully ironic commentary on traditional Shakespearean criticism which ignored the colonial impulse of the text to claim *The Tempest* as the Bard's great play of reconciliation.

34 '[L]e "post" de "postmoderne" ne signifie pas un mouvement de *come-back*, de *flashback*, de *feedback*, c'est-à-dire de répétition, mais un procès d'analyse, d'anamnèse, d'anagogie, et d'anamorphose, qui élabore un "oubli initial"' (*La Postmoderne expliquée aux enfants* Paris: Editions Galilée, 1986: 126)

35 II, ii, 59. Editor Kermode notes that *The Tempest* is the only play in which Shakespeare used this particular spelling.

5 ASIDES

1 Knowles is also, in this quoted passage, discussing productions of two other Canadian plays that were transplanted from constituency audience bases to mainstream Toronto theatres.

2 See, too, Michael Bristol's most instructive *Shakespeare's America, America's Shakespeare* (1990).

BIBLIOGRAPHY

Abu-Lughod, Janet (1989). 'On the Remaking of History: How to Reinvent the Past,' in Kruger and Mariani (1989) 111–129.

Aers, Lesley and Wheale, Nigel (1991). *Shakespeare in the Changing Curriculum*. London: Routledge.

Allen, David (1985). *Cheapside*. Sydney: Currency Press.

Appiah, Kwame Anthony (1990). 'Race,' in Frank Lentricchia and Thomas McLaughlin (eds) *Critical Terms for Literary Study*. Chicago: University of Chicago Press.

Armistead, Claire (1988). Review of Barrie Keeffe's *King of England* at Theatre Royal, London. *Financial Times*. 3 February. In *London Theatre Record* 29 January–11 February 1988: 124.

—— (1994). 'LIFTing the Theatre: The London International Festival of Theatre,' in Shank (1994) 152–165.

Armstrong, Isobel (1989). 'Thatcher's Shakespeare.' *Textual Practice* 3.1 (Spring): 1–14.

Armstrong, Nancy and Tennenhouse, Leonard (1989). *The Violence of Representation*. London: Routledge.

Atkins, Harold (1981). Review of *King Lear* at the Young Vic. *Daily Telegraph*. In *London Theatre Record* 8–21 October: 534.

Awasthi, Suresh (1993). 'The Intercultural Experience and the Kathakali *King Lear*.' *New Theatre Quarterly* 9/34 (May): 172–178.

Baker, Houston A., Jr. (1986). 'Caliban's Triple Play.' *Critical Inquiry* 13 (Autumn): 182–196.

Barker, Francis (1984). *The Tremulous Private Body: Essays on Subjection*. London: Methuen.

Barker, Francis and Hulme, Peter (1985). 'Nymphs and Reapers Heavily Vanish: the Discursive Con-texts of *The Tempest*,' in Drakakis 191–205.

Barker, Howard (1986). 'The Redemptive Power of Desire.' *The Times*. 6 February: 15a.

—— (1990). *Seven Lears/Golgo*. London: John Calder.

Barker, Howard and Middleton, Thomas (1986). *Women Beware Women*. London: John Calder.

Barker, Simon (1984). 'Images of the Sixteenth and Seventeenth Centuries as a History of the Present,' in Francis Barker (ed.) *Confronting the Crisis:*

War, Politics & Culture in the Eighties. Colchester, England: University of Essex, 15–26.

Barnes, Philip (1986). *A Companion to Post-War British Theatre*. London: Croom Helm.

Bartlett, Neil (1988). Review of Barrie Keeffe's *King of England* at Theatre Royal, London. *Time Out*. 10 February. In *London Theatre Record* 29 January–11 February 1988: 122.

Baudrillard, Jean (1983). *Simulations*. Trans. Paul Foss, Paul Patton, and Philip Beitchman. New York: Semiotext(e).

Beer, Gillian (1989a). *Arguing with the Past: Essays in Narrative from Woolf to Sidney*. London: Routledge.

—— (1989b) 'Representing Women: Re-presenting the Past,' in Catherine Belsey and Jane Moore (eds) *The Feminist Reader: Essays in Gender and the Politics of Literary Criticism*. New York: Basil Blackwell. 63–80.

Belhassen, S. (1972) 'Aimé Césaire's *A Tempest*, in Lee Baxandall (ed.) *Radical Perspectives in the Arts*. Harmondsworth: Pelican. 175–177.

'Best Wishes, Bill' (1991) *Independent*. April 22: 17.

Bhabha, Homi (1990). 'DissemiNation: Time, Narrative, and the Margins of Modern Nation,' in Homi Bhabha (ed.) *Nation and Narration*. London: Routledge. 291–322.

Bharucha, Rustom (1993). *Theatre and the World: Performance and the Politics of Culture*. London: Routledge.

Billington, Michael (1988). Review of Barrie Keeffe's *King of England* at Theatre Royal, London. *Guardian*. 3 February. In *London Theatre Record* 29 January–11 February: 125.

—— (1990). Review of *Kathakali King Lear* at Royal Lyceum Theatre, Edinburgh. *Guardian*. 17 August. In *London Theatre Record* 13–26 August: 1,083.

—— (1992). Review of *A Midsummer's Night's Dream* at the Royal National Theatre. 11 July. In *London Theatre Record* 1–14 July: 822.

Bogdanov, Michael and Pennington, Michael (1990). *The English Stage Company: The Story of 'The Wars of the Roses' 1986–1989*. London: Nick Hern Books.

Bond, Edward (1971). *Lear*, in *Plays: Two* (1978). London: Methuen. 1–102.

Brantlinger, Patrick (1990). *Crusoe's Footprints: Cultural Studies in Britain and America*. New York: Routledge.

Brisbane, Katherine (1989). *Australia Plays: New Australian Drama*. London: Nick Hern Books.

Bristol, Michael (1990). *Shakespeare's America, America's Shakespeare*. London: Routledge.

—— (1991). 'Where Does Ideology Hang Out?,' in Kamps (1991) 31–44.

Bromley, Roger (1988). *Lost Narratives: Popular Fictions, Politics and Recent History*. London: Routledge.

Brooke, Nicholas (1979). *Horrid Laughter in Jacobean Tragedy*. London: Macmillan.

Brown, Paul (1985). '"This thing of darkness I acknowledge mine": *The Tempest* and the Discourse of Colonialism,' in Dollimore and Sinfield (1985) 48–71.

Brustein, Robert (1992). *Reimagining American Theatre*. Chicago: Ivan Dee.

Brydon, Diana (1984). 'Re-writing *The Tempest.*' *World Literature Written in English* 23.1: 75–88.

Butler, Judith (1990). *Gender Trouble.* London: Routledge.

—— (1993). *Bodies That Matter: On the Discursive Limits of Sex.* London: Routledge.

Callahan, Dympna (1991). 'Buzz Goodbody: Directing for Change,' in Marsden (1991) 163–182.

Carne, Rosalind (1981). Review of *Maid's Tragedy* at the Warehouse. In *London Theatre Record* 8–21 October: 556.

—— (1983). Review of *Lear* at the Pit. In *London Theatre Record* 7–20 May: 390.

Cartelli, Thomas (1987). 'Prospero in Africa,' in Howard and O'Connor, 99–115.

Carter, Angela (1986). 'Overture and Incidental Music,' in *Black Venus.* London: Picador.

Césaire, Aimé (1985). *A Tempest.* Trans. Richard Miller. New York: Ubu Repertory Theater Publications.

Chase, Malcolm and Shaw, Christopher (1989a). 'The Dimensions of Nostalgia,' in Chase and Shaw (1989b) 1–17.

—— (1989b) *The Imagined Past: History and Nostalgia.* Manchester: Manchester University Press.

Cheyfitz, Eric (1991). *The Poetics of Imperialism: Translation and Colonization from The Tempest to Tarzan.* New York: Oxford University Press.

Chow, Rey (1992). 'Postmodern Automatons,' in Judith Butler and Joan Scott (eds) *Feminists Theorize the Political.* London: Routledge. 101–120.

Church, Michael (1988). Review of Barrie Keeffe's *King of England* at Theatre Royal, London. *Daily Telegraph.* 3 February. In *London Theatre Record* 29 January-11 February 1988: 124.

Cobham, Rhonda (1992). 'Misgendering the Nation: African Nationalist Fictions and Nuruddin Farah's *Maps,*' in Andrew Parker, Mary Russo, Doris Sommer and Patricia Yaeger (eds) *Nationalisms and Sexualities.* London: Routledge. 42–59.

Cohen, Walter (1987). 'Political Criticism of Shakespeare,' in Howard and O'Connor (1987) 18–46.

Cohn, Ruby (1976). *Modern Shakespearean Offshoots.* Princeton: Princeton University Press.

—— (1991). *Retreats from Realism in Recent English Drama.* Cambridge: Cambridge University Press.

Collick, John (1989). *Shakespeare, Cinema and Society.* Manchester: Manchester University Press.

Collins, Jim (1989). *Uncommon Cultures: Popular Culture and Post-Modernism.* London: Routledge.

Combs, Richard (1989). Review of Peter Greenaway's *The Cook, The Thief, His Wife and Her Lover. Monthly Film Bulletin.* November: 323. In *Film Review Annual* 1991: 266–268.

Connerton, Paul (1989). *How Societies Remember.* Cambridge: Cambridge University Press.

Corner, John and Harvey, Sylvia (1991a). *Enterprise and Heritage: Crosscurrents of National Culture.* London: Routledge.

—— (1991b). 'Introduction: Great Britain Limited,' in Corner and Harvey (1991a) 1–20.

—— (1991c). 'Mediating Tradition and Modernity: the Heritage/enterprise Couplet,' in Corner and Harvey (1991a) 45–75.

Coult, Tony and Kershaw, Baz (1990). *Engineers of the Imagination: The Welfare State Handbook*. Revised and expanded edition. London: Methuen.

Cousin, Geraldine (1985). 'Shakespeare from Scratch: the Footsbarn *Hamlet* and *King Lear*.' *New Theatre Quarterly* 1.1 (February): 105–127.

Coveney, Michael (1988). Review of *The Changeling* at the Royal National Theatre, London. *Financial Times*. 24 June. In *London Theatre Record* 17–30 June: 860.

—— (1990). *The Citz: 25 Years of the Glasgow Citizens Theatre*. London: Nick Hern Books.

Cox, Murray (1992). *Shakespeare Comes to Broadmoor – the Actors are Come Hither: the Performance of Tragedy in a Secure Psychiatric Hospital*. London: Jessica Kingsley.

Crowl, Samuel (1992). *Shakespeare Observed: Studies in Performance on Stage and Screen*. Athens, OH: Ohio University Press.

Curtis, Liz (1989). *Ain't Nothing But the Same Old Story: The Roots of Anti-Irish Racism*. London: Information on Ireland.

Cushman, Robert (1983). Review in *Observer*. In *London Theatre Record* 21 May–3 June: 422.

Davenport-Hines, Richard (1993). Review of Harriet Gilbert (ed.) *The Sexual Imagination From Acker to Zola: A Feminist Companion*. In *Times Literary Supplement*. 29 October: 32.

Davis, Fred (1979). *Yearning for Yesterday: A Sociology of Nostalgia*. New York: The Free Press.

Dawson, Anthony B. (1987). '*Women Beware Women* and the Economy of Rape.' *Studies in English Literature* 27: 314–320.

—— (1988). '*Tempest* in a Teapot: Critics, Evaluation, Ideology,' in Maurice Charney (ed.) *'Bad' Shakespeare: Re-evaluations of the Shakespeare Canon*. Rutherford: Fairleigh Dickinson University Press. 61–73.

de Certeau, Michel (1984). *The Practice of Everyday Life*. Trans. Steven F. Rendell. Berkeley, CA: University of California Press.

—— (1988). *The Writing of History*. Trans. Tom Conley. New York: Columbia University Press.

Doane, Janice and Hodges, Devon (1987). *Nostalgia and Sexual Difference: The Resistance to Contemporary Feminism*. London: Methuen.

Doane, Mary Ann (1990). 'Technophilia: Technology, Representation and the Feminine,' in Jacobus, Fox Keller and Shuttleworth (1990) 163–176.

Dollimore, Jonathan (1984). *Radical Tragedy: Religion, Ideology and Power in the Drama of Shakespeare and his Contemporaries*. Chicago: University of Chicago Press.

—— (1985). 'Shakespeare, Cultural Materialism and the New Historicism.' Introduction to Dollimore and Sinfield (1985) 2–17.

—— (1991). *Sexual Dissidence: Augustine to Wilde, Freud to Foucault*. Oxford: Clarendon.

Dollimore, Jonathan and Sinfield, Alan (1985). *Political Shakespeare: New Essays in Cultural Materialism*. Manchester: Manchester University Press.

BIBLIOGRAPHY

Donaldson, Laura E. (1992). *Decolonizing Feminisms: Race, Gender & Empire-Building*. Chapel Hill: University of North Carolina Press.

Donaldson, Peter S. (1990). *Shakespearean Films/Shakespearean Directors*. London: Unwin Hyman.

Donnelly, Pat (1993). Review of *La Tempête* at the Festival of the Americas. In *Montreal Gazette* June 7: F6.

Drakakis, John (1985). *Alternative Shakespeares*. London: Methuen.

Durgnat, Raymond (1988). Review of Jean-Luc Godard's *King Lear*. *Monthly Film Bulletin*. February. In *Film Review Annual* 1989: 798.

Edelstein, David (1990). Review of Peter Greenaway's *The Cook, The Thief, His Wife and Her Lover*. *New York Post*. 6 April 1990. In *Film Review Annual* 1991: 271–272.

Edwards, Christopher (1990). Review of *King Lear* at the Royal National Theatre. *Spectator*. 11 August. In *London Theatre Record* 16–29 July: 952.

Elsom, John, ed. (1989). *Is Shakespeare Still Our Contemporary?* London: Routledge.

Erickson, Peter (1991). *Rewriting Shakespeare, Rewriting Ourselves*. Berkeley, CA: University of California Press.

—— (1993). 'Afterword: "Trying Not to Forget"' in Novy (1993) 251–264.

Fanon, Frantz (1967). *Black Skins, White Masks*. New York: Grove.

Feingold, Michael (1992). 'Leaps of Faith.' Review of Ariane Mnouchkine's *Les Atrides* at Brooklyn Academy of Music. In *Village Voice* 13 October: 107, 110.

Felperin, Howard (1990). *The Uses of Canon: Elizabethan Literature and Contemporary Theory*. Oxford: Clarendon.

Féral, Josette (1990). *La culture contre l'art: essai d'economique politique du théâtre*. Sillery: Presses de l'Université du Québec.

Ferguson, Margaret W., Quilligan, Maureen and Vickers, Nancy J. (1986). *Rewriting the Renaissance: The Discourses of Sexual Difference in Early Modern Europe*. Chicago: University of Chicago Press.

Fernández Retamar, Roberto (1989). *Caliban and Other Essays*. Trans. Edward Baker. Minneapolis: University of Minnesota Press.

Folena, Lucia (1989). 'Figures of Violence: Philogists, Witches and Stalinistas,' in Armstrong and Tennenhouse (1989) 219–238.

Foucault, Michel (1972). *The Archaeology of Knowledge & The Discourse of Language*. Trans. A.M. Sheridan Smith. New York: Pantheon.

—— (1977). *Language, Counter-memory, Practice: Selected Essays and Interviews*, ed. Donald F. Bouchard. Ithaca: Cornell University Press.

—— (1978). *The History of Sexuality*, Vol. I. Trans. Robert Hurley. New York: Pantheon.

—— (1979). *Discipline and Punish: The Birth of the Prison*. Trans. Alan Sheridan. New York: Vintage.

Francke, Lizzie (1992). Review of Gus Van Sant's *My Own Private Idaho*. In *Sight & Sound* 12 (January): 55.

Fraser, Brad (1993). *The Ugly Man: A Play*. Edmonton: NeWest Publishers.

Frost, Christine Mangala (1992). '30 Rupees for Shakespeare: a Consideration of Imperial Theatre in India.' *Modern Drama* 35 (May): 90–100.

Frow, John (1991). 'Tourism and the Semiotics of Nostalgia.' *October* 57 (Summer): 123–151.

Fuchs, Elinor and Leverett, James (1989). ' "Cymbeline" and its Critics.' *American Theatre* 9 (December): 24–31.

Garber, Marjorie (1993). 'Character Assassination: Shakespeare, Anita Hill, and *JFK*,' in Garber, Marjorie, Matlock, Jann and Walkowitz, Rebecca L. (eds) *Media Spectacles*. London: Routledge, 23–39.

Gargi, Balwant (1991). 'Staging *King Lear* as the Indian Maharaja.' *TDR: The Drama Review* 35.3 (Fall): 93–100.

George, David (1989-90). 'Casebook: *The Tempest in Bali* – a director's log.' *Australasian Drama Studies* 15–16: 21–46.

Goldberg, Jonathan (1991). 'Sodomy and Society: The Case of Christopher Marlowe,' in Kastan and Stallybrass (1991) 75-82.

Goodman, Lizbeth (1993). 'Women's Alternative Shakespeares and Women's Alternatives to Shakespeare in Contemporary British Theater,' in Novy (1993) 206–226.

Gordon, Giles (1985). Review of Footsbarn's *King Lear* at the Shaw Theatre. *Punch* 23 January. In *London Theatre Record* 1–15 January: 27.

Gordon, Harvey (1992). 'The Setting – Broadmoor Hospital,' in Cox (1992) 107–114.

Gow, Michael (1989). *Away in Brisbane* [first performed in 1986]. Brisbane: 279–337.

Green, Amy S. (1994). *The Revisionist Stage: American Directors Reinvent the Classics*. Cambridge: Cambridge University Press.

Greenaway, Peter (1991). *Prospero's Books*. London: Chatto & Windus.

Greenblatt, Stephen J. (1990). *Learning to Curse: Essays in Early Modern Culture*. London: Routledge.

Greenwald, Michael L. (1992). Review of *The Tempest* (Shakespeare Festival of Dallas, 9–21 July 1991). *Theatre Journal* 44.1 (March): 113–116.

Griffin, Gabriele and Aston, Elaine (1991). *Herstory: Volume I, Plays by Women for Women*. Sheffield: Sheffield Academic Press.

Griswold, Wendy (1986). *Renaissance Revivals: City Comedy and Revenge Tragedy in the London Theatre 1576–1980*. Chicago: University of Chicago Press.

Gunew, Sneja (1991). 'Feminism/Theory/Postcolonialism: Agency Without Identity.' Paper given at Canada/Australia Women's Writing Conference, Calgary, Canada, February.

Handler, Richard and Linnekin, Jocelyn (1984). 'Tradition, Genuine or Spurious.' *Journal of American Folklore* (97): 273–290.

Harron, Mary (1985). Review of *King Lear* at the Almeida Theatre, London. *Observer*. 24 November. In *London Theatre Record* 20 November–3 December: 1,169.

Hawkes, Terence (1992). *Meaning by Shakespeare*. London: Routledge.

Heinemann, Margot (1985). 'How Brecht read Shakespeare,' in Dollimore and Sinfield (1985) 202–230.

Henning, Standish (1965). Introduction to Thomas Middleton's *A Mad World, My Masters*. Lincoln, NB: University of Nebraska Press.

Hewison, Robert (1987). *The Heritage Industry: Britain in a Climate of Decline*. London: Methuen.

—— (1991). 'Commerce and Culture,' in Corner and Harvey (1991a) 162–177.

Hiley, Jim (1988). Review of *The Tempest* at the Old Vic, London. *The Listener.* 20 October. In *London Theatre Record* 7–20 October: 1,426.

—— (1990). Review of *King Lear* at the Royal National Theatre, London. *The Listener.* 9 July. In *London Theatre Record* 16–29 July: 951.

Hill, Eric (1988). 'Where's Kent?' in Holmberg (1988) 18–19.

Holderness, Graham (1988a). 'Bardolatry: or, The Cultural Materialist's Guide to Stratford-upon-Avon,' in Holderness (1988b) 2–15.

——, ed. (1988b). *The Shakespeare Myth.* Manchester: Manchester University Press.

—— (1992a). 'Shakespeare and Heritage.' *Textual Practice* 6.2 (Summer): 247–263.

—— (1992b). *Shakespeare Recycled: The Making of Historical Drama.* Hemel Hempstead: Harvester Wheatsheaf.

Holloway, Jonathan (no date). Unpublished manuscript on the history of Red Shift Theatre Company.

Holmberg, Arthur (1988). 'The Liberation of Lear.' *American Theatre* July/August: 12–19.

—— (1990). '"Lear" Girds for a Remarkable Episode.' *New York Times* 20 May: 7 and 36.

Howard, Jean E. and O'Connor, Marion (1987). *Shakespeare Reproduced: The Text in History and Ideology.* London: Routledge.

Hoyau, Philippe (1988). 'Heritage and "the conserver society": the French Case,' trans. Chris Turner, in Robert Lumley (ed.) *The Museum Time-Machine.* London: Routledge.

Hoyle, Martin (1989). Review of *King Lear* at the Almeida Theatre, London. *Financial Times.* 18 September. In *London Theatre Record* 10–23 September: 1,249.

—— (1990). Review of *King Lear* at the Royal National Theatre, London. *Financial Times.* 28 July. In *London Theatre Record* 16–29 July: 955.

Hulme, Peter (1986). *Colonial Encounters: Europe and the Native Caribbean 1492–1797.* London: Routledge.

—— (1981). 'Hurricanes in the Caribbees: The Constitution of the Discourse of English Colonialism,' in Francis Barker, Jay Bernstein, John Coombes, Peter Hulme, Jennifer Stone and Jon Stratton (eds) *1642: Literature and Power in the Seventeenth Century.* Colchester: University of Essex, 1981: 55–83.

Hurren, Kenneth (1992). Review of *A Midsummer's Night's Dream* at Royal National Theatre, London. *Mail on Sunday.* 12 July. In *London Theatre Record* 1–14 July: 822.

Hutchings, William (1988). '"Creative Vandalism" Or, A Tragedy Transformed: Howard Barker's "Collaboration" with Thomas Middleton on the 1986 Version of *Women Beware Women*,' in Karelisa Hartigan (ed.) *Text and Presentation: The University of Florida Department of Classics Comparative Drama Conference Papers,* Volume VIII. Lanham, MD: University Press of America.

Itzin, Catherine (1980). *Stages in the Revolution: Political Theatre in Britain since 1968.* London: Eyre Methuen.

Jacobus, Mary, Fox Keller, Evelyn and Shuttleworth, Sally (1990). *Body/Politics: Women and the Discourses of Science.* London: Routledge.

Jameson, Fredric (1989a). Foreword in Fernández Retamar (1989).
—— (1989b). 'Nostalgia for the Present.' *South Atlantic Quarterly* 88.2 (Spring): 517–537.
Jarman, Derek (1984). *Dancing Ledge*. London: Quartet.
—— (1991). *Queer Edward II*. London: British Film Institute.
Jeffreys, Stephen (1990). *The Clink*. London: Nick Hern Books.
Jones, Eldred D. (1986). 'Shakespeare in Africa.' *Fourah Bay Studies In Language and Literature: Journal of the English Department* 3: 3–6.
Kamps, Ivo, ed. (1991). *Shakespeare Left and Right*. New York: Routledge.
Kastan, David Scott and Stallybrass, Peter, eds (1991). *Staging The Renaissance: Reinterpretations of Elizabethan and Jacobean Drama*. London: Routledge.
Kavanagh, James H. (1985). 'Shakespeare in Ideology,' in Drakakis (1985) 144–165.
Kaye, Harvey J. (1991). *The Powers of the Past: Reflections on the Crisis and Promise of History*. New York: Harvester Wheatsheaf.
Keeffe, Barrie (1977). *A Mad World, My Masters*. London: Eyre Methuen.
Kennedy, Dennis (1993a). *Foreign Shakespeares*. Cambridge: Cambridge University Press.
—— (1993b). *Looking at Shakespeare: A Visual History of Twentieth-Century Performance*. Cambridge: Cambridge University Press.
Kerrigan, John (1994). 'A Complete History of Comic Noses,' in Michael Cordner, Peter Holland and John Kerrigan (eds) *English Comedy*. Cambridge: Cambridge University Press.
Kershaw, Baz (1991). 'King Real's King Lear: Radical Shakespeare for the Nuclear Age.' *Critical Survey* 3.3: 249–259.
—— (1992). *The Politics of Performance: Radical Theatre as Cultural Intervention*. London: Routledge.
King, T.J. (1992). *Casting Shakespeare's Plays: London Actors and their Roles, 1590–1642*. New York and Cambridge, UK: Cambridge University Press.
Knowles, Richard Paul (1993–94). 'Reading Material: Transfers, Remounts, and the Production of Meaning in Contemporary Toronto Drama and Theatre.' *Essays on Canadian Writing* 51–2 (Winter-Spring): 258–295.
—— (1994). 'Shakespeare, 1993, and the Discourses of the Stratford Festival, Ontario.' *Shakespeare Quarterly* 45.2 (Summer): 211–225.
Kott, Jan (1966) *Shakespeare Our Contemporary*. Trans. Boleslaw Taborski. New York: Norton.
Krauss, Rosalind (1991). ' "Nostalgie de la Boue" ' *October* 56 (Spring): 111–120.
Kruger, Barbara and Mariani, Phil, eds (1989). *Remaking History*. Seattle: Bay Press.
Kruger, Loren (1992). *The National Stage: Theatre and Cultural Legitimation in England, France and America*. Chicago: University of Chicago Press.
—— (1993). Review of Baz Kershaw's *The Politics of Performance* in *Theatre Journal* 45.4 (December): 129.
Lee Horn, Barbara (1992). *Joseph Papp: A Bio-Bibliography*. New York: Greenwood Press.
Leggatt, Alexander (1991). *Shakespeare in Performance: King Lear*. Manchester: Manchester University Press.

Levine, Lawrence W. (1988). *Highbrow/Lowbrow: The Emergence of Cultural Hierarchy in America*. Cambridge, MA: Harvard University Press.

Linklater, Kristin (1992). *Freeing Shakespeare's Voice: The Actor's Guide to Talking the Text*. New York: Theatre Communications Group.

Loomba, Ania (1989). *Race, Gender, Renaissance Drama*. Manchester: Manchester University Press.

—— (1993). 'Hamlet in Mizoram,' in Novy (1993) 226–250.

Loughrey, Bryan and Holderness, Graham (1991). 'Shakespearean Features,' in Marsden (1991) 183–202.

Lowe, Stephen, ed. (1985). *Peace Plays*. London: Methuen.

Lowenthal, David (1985). *The Past is a Foreign Country*. Cambridge: Cambridge University Press.

—— (1989). 'Nostalgia Tells It Like It Wasn't,' in Chase and Shaw (1989b) 18–32.

McCabe, Colin (1991). 'Throne of Blood.' *Sight & Sound* 1.6 (January): 12–14.

MacDonald, Ann-Marie (1990). *Goodnight Desdemona, Good Morning Juliet*. Toronto: Coach House Press.

McDonald, Marianne (1992). *Ancient Sun, Modern Light: Greek Drama on the Modern Stage*. New York: Columbia University Press.

McKinney, Devin (1991). Review of David Lynch's *Wild at Heart. Film Quarterly* (Winter 1991: 41). In *Film Review Annual* 1991: 1,583.

McLuskie, Kathleen (1989). *Renaissance Dramatists*. Atlantic Highlands, NJ: Humanities Press International.

McLuskie, Kathleen and Uglow, Jennifer, eds (1989). *The Duchess of Malfi* by John Webster. Bristol, UK: Bristol Classical Press.

Malouf, David (1988). *Blood Relations*. Sydney: Currency Press.

Mannoni, Octave (1964). *Prospero & Caliban: The Psychology of Colonization*. New York: Frederick A. Praeger.

Marowitz, Charles (1991). *Recycling Shakespeare*. London: Macmillan.

Marsden, Jean I. (1991). *The Appropriation of Shakespeare: Post-Renaissance Reconstructions of the Work and the Myth*. New York: St. Martin's.

Merquior, J.G. (1986). *From Prague to Paris: A Critique of Structuralist and Post-Structuralist Thought*. London: Verso.

Miller, Jonathan (1986). *Subsequent Performances*. London: Faber and Faber.

Moisan, Thomas (1991). '"Knock me here soundly": Comic Misprision and Class Consciousness in Shakespeare.' *Shakespeare Quarterly* 42.3 (Fall): 276–290.

Montrose, Louis A. (1989). 'Professing the Renaissance: The Poetics and Politics of Culture,' in H. Aram Veeser (ed.) *The New Historicism*. London: Routledge, 15–36.

Narasimhaiah, C.D. (1964). *Shakespeare Came to India*. Bombay: Popular Prakashan.

Nathan, David (1988). Review of Barrie Keeffe's *King of England* at Theatre Royal, London. *Jewish Chronicle*. 5 February. In *London Theatre Record* 29 January–11 February: 122.

Neely, Carol Thomas (1991). '"Documents in Madness": Reading Madness and Gender in Shakespeare's Tragedies and Early Modern Culture.' *Shakespeare Quarterly* 42.3 (Fall): 315–338.

Nightingale, Benedict (1983). Review of *Lear* at the Pit, London. *New Statesman*. In *London Theatre Record*. 7–20 May: 391.

—— (1990). Review of *The Old Law* at the Lyric Theatre, London. *The Times*. 6 October. In *London Theatre Record* 24 September–7 October: 1,334.

Nixon, Rob (1987). 'Caribbean and African Appropriations of *The Tempest*.' *Critical Inquiry* 13.3: 557–578.

Nouryeh, Andrea J. (1991). 'JoAnne Akalaitis: Post Modern Director or Socio-Sexual Critic.' In *Theatre Topics* 1.2 (September): 177–191.

Novy, Marianne (1990). *Women's Re-Visions of Shakespeare*. Urbana: University of Illinois Press.

—— (1993). *Cross-Cultural Performances: Differences in Women's Re-Visions of Shakespeare*. Urbana: University of Illinois Press.

O'Pray, Mike (1991). 'Edward II: Damning Desire.' *Sight & Sound* 1.6 (January): 8–11.

Orgel, Stephen (1986). 'Prospero's Wife,' in Margaret W. Ferguson, Maureen Quilligan and Nancy J. Vickers: 33–49.

Orkin, Martin (1991). *Drama and the South African State*. Manchester: Manchester University Press.

Osment, Philip (1988). *This Island's Mine*, in *Gay Sweatshop: Four Plays and a Company*. London: Methuen. 81–120.

Pavis, Patrice (1992). *Theatre at the Crossroads of Culture*. London: Routledge.

—— (1993). 'Wilson, Brook, Zadek: an Intercultural Encounter?,' in Kennedy (1993a): 270–289.

Percival, John (1990). Review of *Kathakali King Lear* at the Royal Lyceum Theatre, Edinburgh. *The Times*. 17 August. In *London Theatre Record* 13–26 August: 1,084.

Peters, Helen (1993). 'Lewis Baumander Directs *The Tempest* (1987, 1989): Towards Canadian Postmodernism.' *Canadian Theatre Review* Fall (76): 13-17.

Porter Benson, Susan, Brier, Stephen and Rosenzweig, Roy, eds (1986). *Presenting the Past: Essays on History and the Public*. Philadelphia: Temple University Press.

Potter, Gerry (1993). Afterword in Fraser (1993) 151–55.

Purchas, Samuel (1965). *Hakluytus Posthumus or Purchas His Pilgrimes*, Vol. XIX. New York: AMS Press Inc.

Quart, Leonard (1990). Review of Peter Greenaway's *The Cook, The Thief, His Wife & Her Lover. Cinéaste* 18.1: 45. In *Film Review Annual* 1991: 255–257.

Ratcliffe, Michael (1985). Review of Footsbarn's *King Lear* at the Shaw Theatre, London. *Observer*. 13 January. In *London Theatre Record* 1–15 January: 26.

Reade, Simon (1991). *Cheek by Jowl: Ten Years of Celebration*. Bath, UK: Absolute Classics.

Roach, Joseph R. and Reinelt, Janelle G. (1992). *Critical Theory and Performance*. Ann Arbor: University of Michigan Press.

Robins, Kevin (1991). 'Tradition and Translation: National Culture in its Global Context,' in Corner and Harvey (1991a): 21–44.

Rose, Mary Beth (1991). 'Where Are the Mothers in Shakespeare? Options for Gender Representation in the English Renaissance.' *Shakespeare Quarterly* 42.3 (Fall): 291–310.

Rosler, Martha (1983). 'Notes on Quotes.' *Open Letter* 5:5-6 (Summer): 194–205.

Rubens, Robert (1981). 'The Backward Glance: A Contemporary Taste for Nostalgia.' *Contemporary Review* 238 (September): 149–150.

Russo, Mary (1986). 'Female Grotesques: Carnival and Theory,' in Teresa de Lauretis (ed.) *Feminist Studies/Critical Studies*. London: Macmillan.

Rutherford, Malcolm (1991). Review of *The Changeling* at the Finborough Arms, London. *Financial Times*. 19 January. In *London Theatre Record*. 15–28 January: 66.

Said, Edward (1993). *Culture and Imperialism*. New York: Alfred A. Knopf.

Satuloff, Bob (1992). 'I Just Called to Say I Hate You.' Review of Derek Jarman's *Edward II*. In *Christopher Street* 14/15 (174): 3–5.

Schudson, Michael (1992). *Watergate in American Memory: How We Remember, Forget, and Reconstruct the Past*. New York: Basic Books.

Scott, Michael (1989). *Shakespeare and the Modern Dramatist*. New York: St. Martin's.

Sedgwick, Eve Kosofsky (1993). *Tendencies*. Raleigh, NC: Duke University Press.

Shakespeare, William (1979). *King Lear*, ed. Kenneth Muir. Arden Edition. London: Methuen.

—— (1985). *The Tempest*, ed. Frank Kermode. Arden Edition. London: Methuen.

Shank, Theodore, ed. (1994). *Contemporary British Theatre*. London: Macmillan.

Shepherd, Simon (1988). 'Shakespeare's Private Drawer: Shakespeare and Homosexuality,' in Holderness (1988b) 96–110.

Shorter, Eric (1983). Review of *Lear* at the Pit, London. *Daily Telegraph*. In *London Theatre Record*. 7–20 May: 390.

Sinfield, Alan (1985a). 'Give an Account of Shakespeare and Education, Showing Why you Think they are Effective and What you have Appreciated about them. Support your Comments with Precise References,' in Dollimore and Sinfield (1985) 124–157.

—— (1985b). 'Introduction: Reproductions, Interventions,' in Dollimore and Sinfield (1985) 130–133.

—— (1985c). 'Royal Shakespeare: Theatre and the Making of Ideology,' in Dollimore and Sinfield (1985) 158–181.

—— (1989). *Literature, Politics and Culture in Postwar Britain*. Berkeley: University of California Press.

Singh, Jyostna (1989). 'Different Shakespeares: the Bard in Colonial/Postcolonial India.' *Theatre Journal* 41.4 (December): 445–458.

Slemon, Stephen (1990). 'Modernism's Last Post,' in Ian Adam and Helen Tiffin (eds) *Past the Last Post*. Calgary: University of Calgary Press. 1–12.

Smith, Iris (1993). 'Mabou Mines's *Lear*: A Narrative of Collective Authorship.' *Theatre Journal* (45.3): 279–302.

Spencer, Charles (1983). Review of *Lear* at the Pit. *London Standard*. In *London Theatre Review* 7-20 May: 391.

—— (1990). Review in *Daily Telegraph*. 17 August. In *London Theatre Record* 17. 13–26 August: 1,084.

Spargo, Tamsin and Botting, Fred (1993). 'Re-iterating desire.' *Textual Practice* 7.3 (Winter): 379–383.

Sprung, Guy (1993). 'Born-again Berlin Reaches a New Stage.' *Globe and Mail* January 12: C1, C3.

Stallybrass, Peter (1986). 'Patriarchal Territories: The Body Enclosed,' in Margaret W. Ferguson, Maureen Quilligan and Nancy J. Vickers (1986) 123–144.

—— (1991). 'Reading the Body and the Jacobean Theater of Consumption: *The Revenger's Tragedy* (1606),' in Kastan and Stallybrass (1991) 210-220.

Stallybrass, Peter and White, Allon (1986). *The Poetics and Politics of Transgression*. London: Routledge.

Sterritt, David (1988). Review of Jean-Luc Godard's *King Lear*. *Christian Science Monitor*. 22 January. In *Film Review Annual* 1989: 795.

Stevenson, Randall (1990). Review of *Kathakali King Lear* at Royal Lyceum Theatre, Edinburgh. *Independent*. 18 August. In *London Theatre Record* 13–26 August: 1,083.

Stewart, Susan (1984). *On Longing: Narratives of the Miniature, the Gigantic, the Souvenir, the Collection*. Baltimore: Johns Hopkins University Press.

Taylor, Gary (1989). *Reinventing Shakespeare: A Cultural History from the Restoration to the Present*. New York and Oxford: Oxford University Press.

Taylor, Paul (1988). Review of Barrie Keeffe's *King of England* at Theatre Royal, London. *Independent*. 4 February. In *London Theatre Record* 29 January–11 February: 123.

—— (1992). Review of *A Midsummer's Night's Dream* at Royal National Theatre, London. *Independent*. 11 July. In *London Theatre Record* 1–14 July: 823.

Tennenhouse, Leonard (1989). 'Violence Done to Women on the Renaissance Stage,' in Armstrong and Tennenhouse (1989) 77–92.

Thomas, Kevin (1988). Review of Jean-Luc Godard's *King Lear*. *Los Angeles Times*. 19 February. In *Film Review Annual* 1989: 797.

—— (1990). Review of Peter Greenaway's *The Cook, The Thief, His Wife and Her Lover*. *Los Angeles Times*. 13 April. In *Film Review Annual* 1991: 265–266.

Thompson, Ann (1991). '"Miranda, Where's Your Sister?": Reading Shakespeare's *The Tempest*,' in Susan Sellers (ed.) *Feminist Criticism: Theory and Practice*. Toronto: University of Toronto Press, 45–55.

Tiffin, Helen (1988). 'Post-Colonialism, Post-Modernism and the Rehabilitation of Post-Colonial History.' *Journal of Commonwealth Literature* 23.1: 169–181.

Treves, Simon (1992). 'Old Bill in the High Street.' *Observer Magazine* 28 June.

Trinh, T. Minh-Ha (1989). *Woman Native Other*. London: Indiana University Press.

Trotter, David (1986). 'An End to Pageantry.' Review of Howard Barker and Thomas Middleton's *Women Beware Women*. *Times Literary Supplement*. 21 February: 194c.

BIBLIOGRAPHY

Vanden Heuvel, Michael (1991). *Performing Drama/Dramatizing Performance: Alternative Theatre and the Dramatic Text*. Ann Arbor: University of Michigan Press.

Van Wert, William F. (1990–91). Review of Peter Greenaway's *The Cook, The Thief, His Wife and Her Lover*. *Film Quarterly*. Winter: 42. In *Film Review Annual* 1991: 257–265.

Vaughan, Alden T. and Vaughan, Virginia Mason (1991). *Shakespeare's Caliban: A Cultural History*. Cambridge: Cambridge University Press.

Viswanathan, Gauri (1989). *Masks of Conquest: Literary Study and British Rule in India*. New York: Columbia University Press.

Walvin, James (1987). *Victorian Values*. Athens, GA: University of Georgia Press.

Wayne, Don E. (1987). 'Power, Politics, and the Shakespearean Text: Recent Criticism in England and the United States,' in Howard and O'Connor (1987) 47–67.

Wetzsteon, Ross (1990). 'Queen Lear: Ruth Maleczech Gender Bends Shakespeare.' *Village Voice* 30 January: 39–42.

Whigham, Frank (1991). 'Incest and Ideology: *The Duchess of Malfi* (1614),' in Kastan and Stallybrass (1991) 263–274.

Wiles, David (1992). Review of Marianne McDonald's *Ancient Sun, Modern Light: Greek Drama on the Modern Stage*. *New Theatre Quarterly* 8.3 (November): 394.

Williamson, Judith (1988). Review of Jean-Luc Godard's *King Lear*. 5 February. In *New Statesman* 1989: 800.

Willis, Susan (1991). *The B.B.C. Shakespeare Plays: Making the Televised Canon*. Chapel Hill, NC: University of North Carolina Press.

Wilson, Elizabeth (1988). *Hallucinations: Life in the Post-Modern City*. London: Radius.

Woddis, Carole (1983). Review of *Lear* at the Pit, London. *City Limits*. In *London Theatre Record* 7–20 May: 390.

Wolf, Matt (1992). Review of *A Midsummer's Night's Dream* at Royal National Theatre, London. *Globe and Mail*. August 12: A10.

Wolff, Janet (1990). *Feminine Sentences: Essays on Women & Culture*. Cambridge: Polity.

Women's Theatre Group and Feinstein, Elaine (1991). *Lear's Daughters*, in Griffin and Aston (1991) 19–70.

Woodbridge, Linda (1992). 'Palisading the Body Politic,' in Linda Woodbridge and Edward Berry (eds) *True Rites and Maimed Rites: Ritual and Anti-Ritual in Shakespeare and His Age*. Champaign, IL: University of Illinois Press.

Wright, Nicholas (1983). *The Custom of the Country*. London: Methuen.

Wright, Patrick (1985). *On Living in an Old Country*. London: Verso.

Zabus, Chantal (1985). 'A Calibanic Tempest in Anglophone and Francophone New World Writing.' *Canadian Literature* 104: 35–50.

Zarilli, Phillip B. (1992). 'For Whom Is the King a King? Issues of Intercultural Production, Perception, and Reception in a *Kathakali King Lear*,' in Roach and Reinelt (1992) 16–40.

INDEX